PUBLIC REASON AND DIVERSITY

Gerald Gaus was one of the leading liberal theorists of the late twentieth and early twenty-first centuries. He developed a pioneering defense of the liberal order based on its unique capacity to handle diversity and disagreement, and he presses the liberal tradition towards a principled openness to pluralism and diversity. This book brings together Gaus's most seminal and creative essays in a single volume for the first time. It also covers a broad span of his career, including essays published shortly before his death, and topics including reasonable pluralism, moral rights, public reason, and the redistributive state. The volume makes accessible the work of one of the most important recent liberal theorists. Many readers will find it of value, especially those in political philosophy, political science, and economics.

GERALD GAUS was James E. Rogers Professor of Philosophy, and Head of the Department of Political Economy and Moral Science, at the University of Arizona. His books include *The Order of Public Reason* (Cambridge, 2011), *The Tyranny of the Ideal* (2016), and *The Open Society and Its Complexities* (2021).

KEVIN VALLIER is Associate Professor of Philosophy at Bowling Green State University. His books include *Liberal Politics and Public Faith* (2014), *Must Politics Be War?* (2019), and *Trust in a Polarized Age* (2020).

T0384626

PUBLIC REASON AND DIVERSITY

Reinterpretations of Liberalism

GERALD GAUS

EDITED BY

KEVIN VALLIER

CAMBRIDGE
UNIVERSITY PRESS

Shaftesbury Road, Cambridge CB2 8EA, United Kingdom

One Liberty Plaza, 20th Floor, New York, NY 10006, USA

477 Williamstown Road, Port Melbourne, VIC 3207, Australia

314–321, 3rd Floor, Plot 3, Splendor Forum, Jasola District Centre, New Delhi – 110025, India

103 Penang Road, #05–06/07, Visioncrest Commercial, Singapore 238467

Cambridge University Press is part of Cambridge University Press & Assessment, a department of the University of Cambridge.

We share the University's mission to contribute to society through the pursuit of education, learning and research at the highest international levels of excellence.

www.cambridge.org
Information on this title: www.cambridge.org/9781009068307

DOI: 10.1017/9781009067867

First published 2022
First paperback edition 2024

A catalogue record for this publication is available from the British Library

Library of Congress Cataloging-in-Publication data
NAMES: Gaus, Gerald F., author. | Vallier, Kevin, editor.
TITLE: Public reason and diversity: reinterpretations of liberalism / Gerald Gaus; Edited by Kevin Vallier.
DESCRIPTION: Cambridge, United Kingdom; New York, NY: Cambridge University Press, 2022. | Includes bibliographical references and index.
IDENTIFIERS: LCCN 2022010291 (print) | LCCN 2022010292 (ebook) | ISBN 9781316512593 (hardback) | ISBN 9781009068307 (paperback) | ISBN 9781009067867 (epub)
SUBJECTS: LCSH: Liberalism. | Political science–Philosophy. | Pluralism. | Political ethics.
CLASSIFICATION: LCC JC574 .G387 2022 (print) | LCC JC574 (ebook) | DDC 320.51–dc23/eng/
20220401
LC record available at https://lccn.loc.gov/2022010291
LC ebook record available at https://lccn.loc.gov/2022010292

ISBN   978-1-316-51259-3   Hardback
ISBN   978-1-009-06830-7   Paperback

Contents

v

Figures

Tables

A Note on the Essays

These essays were published in the following venues.

"Reasonable Pluralism and the Domain of the Political: How the Weaknesses of John Rawls's Political Liberalism Can be Overcome by a Justificatory Liberalism." *Inquiry*, 42 (June 1999): 229–58. Reprinted in *Liberalism: Critical Assessments*, vol. III: *The Limits of Liberalism*, ed. Geoffrey Smith (London: Routledge, 2002).

"On Justifying the Liberties of the Moderns: A Case of Old Wine in New Bottles." *Social Philosophy & Policy*, 25 (2007): 84–119. Republished in *Liberalism: Old and New*, ed. Ellen Frankel Paul, Fred D. Miller, and Jeffrey Paul (Cambridge University Press, 2007).

"Recognized Rights as Devices of Public Reason." *Philosophical Perspectives: Ethics*, 23 (2009): 111–36.

"The Moral Foundations of Liberal Neutrality." In *Debates in Contemporary Political Philosophy*, ed. Thomas Christiano and John Christman)Oxford: Blackwell, 2009), 81–98.

"Coercion, Ownership, and the Redistributive State: Justificatory Liberalism's Classical Tilt." *Social Philosophy & Policy*, 27 (Winter 2010): 233–75. Reprinted in *Ownership and Justice*, ed. Ellen Frankel Paul, Fred D. Miller, and Jeffrey Paul (Cambridge University Press, 2010), 233–75.

"A Tale of Two Sets: Public Reason in Equilibrium." *Public Affairs Quarterly*, 25 (October 2011): 305–25.

"Self-Organizing Moral Systems: Beyond Social Contract Theory." *Politics, Philosophy & Economics*, 17 (May 2018): 119–47.

"Political Philosophy as the Study of Complex Normative Systems." *Cosmos + Taxis*, 5/2 (2018): 62–78.

Introduction

Gerald ("Jerry") Gaus was a distinguished political philosopher who died unexpectedly in August of 2020. Indeed, he died within days of finishing his final book, *The Open Society and Its Complexities*. The book adds further depth to Gaus's corpus, which has received increasing attention over the last twenty years. Awareness grew quickly after Gaus published his magnum opus, *The Order of Public Reason*, in 2011.

However, Gaus's five monographs – *Value and Justification* (Cambridge University Press, 1990), *Justificatory Liberalism* (Oxford University Press, 1996), *The Order of Public Reason* (Cambridge University Press, 2011), *The Tyranny of the Ideal* (Princeton University Press, 2016), and *The Open Society and Its Complexities* (Oxford University Press, 2021) — can be demanding reads. First, they are thoroughly interdisciplinary. Readers cannot fully appreciate these works without familiarity with other fields, such as epistemology, moral psychology, social choice theory, game theory, evolutionary theory, and complexity theory. Second, Gaus makes sustained arguments across each volume. Unlike many works of philosophy, one cannot fully appreciate the chapters separately.

Hence the need for this volume. Tackling a Gaus essay is easier than engaging an entire treatise, as one can read the essays independently. We also need the book because Gaus published generously, writing for any venue that invited him. His pieces are often locked away in old edited volumes and paywalled journals, but now people can find the best of them in one place. Further, the book should aid younger philosophers and social theorists who value Gaus's work. Gaus invested enormous time and energy in his students, both at the graduate and undergraduate levels. He also developed new curricula and academic degrees and wrote several textbooks. These investments paid dividends, influencing young scholars with long and fruitful careers ahead of them.

In this introduction, I explain Gaus's philosophical project. I then review the content of each essay, organized around Gausian themes.

1. Gaus's Project

We can understand Gaus's philosophical project with a passage that he may have intended to place in his final essay, "Philosophical Fables."

> For much of my career I have developed an account of how people who deeply disagree about the basis of normativity and have serious disagreements about what is right and wrong, can nevertheless converge on common social-moral rules for cooperative living. The core idea is "convergent normativity": while we disagree on many of the grand issues of morality we can, in the interests of achieving a cooperative order based on relations of mutual moral accountability, reconcile on common rules that each of us, for her own reasons, endorses. This tale draws on empirical literature concerning moral psychology, norms, social cooperation, punishment and practice(s) of accountability.

For Gaus, political philosophy is a *reconciliation project* focused on resolving conflict between diverse persons without minimizing their differences.

Gaus hoped that diverse people could maintain cooperative relationships despite forceful challenges: Large and powerful states threaten us with coercion, harm, and death. Members of free societies disagree ever more frequently. And our institutions are now so complex that we barely understand them. How can we preserve our relationships with others when we live under coercive threat, when we share few common values, and when we cannot grasp how we are governed?

What's more, we often give in to the natural temptation to reason only from our own point of view and impose our values and commitments on others. We thereby imbue our lives with stunted relationships, browbeating, coercion, moral dogmatism, authoritarianism, ignorance and tyranny, and failed reconciliation and self-governance.

Human beings can only address these institutional and psychological threats if we can all accept the moral and legal rules we use to direct one another's behavior. If our social rules are justified to each person's reason, we will limit the state's power in order to protect our freedom and equality. We will overcome the challenge of pluralism because we have common rules to govern our behavior, even though our values differ. And we can manage complex institutions more effectively when we mutually accept their terms.

We neutralize the psychological threats to moral relations if we abide by mutually acceptable rules and hold others to them. A jointly chosen social morality ensures that our moral demands are neither brow-beating nor authoritarian. Such a public moral code spurs free ethical inquiry because we may pursue our own experiments in living.

Gaus calls "convergent normativity" *public justification*. But, unlike most philosophers working in this field, Gaus does not equate public justification with public deliberation or an actual public agreement. Gaus uses models of deliberation and agreement as heuristics to uncover moral rules and laws that each of us has reason to endorse, even if she does not actually endorse them. Gaus thinks that if we have reasons to abide by these laws and moral rules, even diverse and conflicting reasons, the rules can reconcile us. Indeed, the rules can reconcile us even if they are not ideal from our perspectives.

Gaus grew more impressed by diverse reasoning in free societies throughout his career. He self-consciously developed his account of public justification to accommodate diversity. His approach thus contrasted with the political liberalism of John Rawls. Rawls thought public justifications consist of reasons derived from shared values. Gaus thought that Rawls misrepresented the reasoning of real persons. Homogenizing models of public reasoning cannot reconcile people with diverse values and beliefs.

In *Value and Justification*, Gaus argued that idealized agents would accept liberal institutions, and they would even agree for shared reasons. (Though he allowed that their reasons could differ.) Yet Gaus begins *Justificatory Liberalism* by noting that he realized that public justification could not vindicate particular institutional arrangements in the six years between the two books. Gaus abandons a shared reasons model of public justification. Fifteen years later, in *The Order of Public Reason*, Gaus embraced diverse thought as a resource for reconciliation. His later works expanded on this theme. Gaus argued that we could reconcile under more and more varied social conditions.

Gaus defended a liberal social order that treats all as naturally free and equal because he believed that only liberal arrangements sustain moral relations between diverse persons. State power, in particular, must be publicly justified, and free and equal peoples should restrict the state to enforcing mutually acceptable rules. But since we have diverse beliefs and values, our reasons are diverse as well. These diverse reasons undermine the justification of sectarian regimes – political orders that govern people according to some reasonably contestable conception of the good or justice. Diverse reasons defeat the rationale for these regimes.

Yet even non-liberals can endorse a liberal constitution as acceptable, if not optimal, from their point of view. A liberal order protects non-liberals from the hegemony of competing groups. Liberal societies are thus uniquely publicly justified to a diverse public. Liberal order alone can reconcile diverse persons and sustain moral relations between them.

Hence the title of this volume. Gaus provided an original and rigorous 21st-century liberalism based on a doctrine of diverse public reasoning. It is well-suited to address recent challenges to liberal orders like the United States.

2.   Gaus's Essays

Gaus's most essential essays have several common themes, which I have organized into two groups: liberalism and diverse public reason.

Liberalism. The first essay in the volume, "Reasonable Pluralism and the Domain of the Political," is Gaus's central statement of the difference between his "justificatory" liberalism and Rawls's political liberalism. Gaus argues that reasonable pluralism – informed, sincere disagreement about what morality requires – extends "over most of what we call the political." So reasonable pluralism must be broader than Rawls thought. The essay, published in 1999, illustrates Gaus's wavering attitude towards shared reasons requirements in public justification, which he would permanently abandon ten years later.

In the second essay, "On Justifying the Moral Rights of the Moderns," Gaus argues that individual rights are essential to the process of public justification because they disperse moral authority to individuals to make their own choices. Rights mitigate the difficulties in making collective decisions in the face of pluralism. The third essay, "Recognized Rights as Devices of Public Reason," extends these arguments. A publicly justified social morality must recognize "jurisdictional rights," rights that assign individuals and small groups the authority to decide how to organize their partition of social space. Therefore, most moral claims in a diverse order will appeal to jurisdictional moral rights.

The fourth essay, "The Moral Foundations of Liberal Neutrality," defends the traditional liberal commitment to state neutrality on matters where people reasonably disagree. If we draw on a plausible conception of persons as both rational and moral, we will find morally neutral institutions attractive. This form of neutrality sharply limits what government may do.

The final essay claims that public reason liberalism must embrace markets and limited government, a stark contrast with the Rawlsian liberalism of the extensive state. In "Coercion, Ownership, and the Redistributive State: Justificatory Liberalism's Classical Tilt," Gaus argues that justifying extensive state coercion is difficult due to enormous diversity and disagreement. While the public reason project is friendly to a range of liberal views, the family must tilt towards market-based, limited government forms.

Diverse Public Reason. The last three essays outline the growing role of diversity and complexity in Gaus's political thought. The first essay, "A Tale of Two Sets: Public Reason in Equilibrium," is Gaus's most developed defense of his "convergence" conception of social normativity. Public reason liberalism involves idealizing persons to determine their justifying reasons, but they do not bracket their conceptions of justice or other diverse considerations in deciding what is justified. The Rawlsian attempt to insulate public justification from these forms of diversity does not succeed. We must allow diverse reasons into public justification.

The second essay, "Self-Organizing Moral Systems: Beyond Social Contract Theory," attempts a radical reconstruction of public reason liberalism to grapple with real-world diversity. The social contract tradition tends to devise a "centrally planned" social contract that sets our most important disagreements aside. But because we disagree in our judgments of justice and the degree of reconciliation we value, social contract reasoning will not always lead to reconciliation.

To resolve a disagreement about the relative value of reconciliation, we must appeal to the idea of a self-organizing moral system. Each individual, acting on their own views of justice, responds to the decisions of others, forming systems of shared justice. Here Gaus formulates a model to show how diverse persons can converge on common rules without central direction. Surprisingly, his model implies that disagreement about the relative value of reconciliation can sometimes increase the likelihood of achieving it.

The final essay in the volume, "Political Philosophy as the Study of Complex Normative Systems," initiates what was likely to become the next significant period of Gaus's research. Here Gaus introduces the New Diversity Theory, which analyses moral diversity, not as moral reasoning gone awry or even a threat to free societies, but as a fundamental moral phenomenon. According to the New Diversity Theory, moral diversity is not simply a challenge to reasonably stable moral order but a critical resource for free societies to discover better ways of living together.

The New Diversity Theory led Gaus to synthesize the themes of liberalism, public reason, and diversity to defend a new philosophical method as essential to progress in political philosophy. For Gaus, political philosophy is not a distinct field that we integrate with politics and economics and the moral sciences like moral psychology. Political philosophy is the attempt to grapple with real-world morality and diversity. Political philosophers should attempt to uncover the possibilities for social order under diverse conditions. They should develop models of our social world to determine whether diverse moral reasoning can help us cooperate better. The New Diversity Theory thereby unites Gaus's political philosophy with his work as a methodologist of political thought.

PART I

Liberalism

CHAPTER I

Reasonable Pluralism and the Domain of the Political
How the Weaknesses of John Rawls's Political Liberalism Can Be Overcome by a Justificatory Liberalism

Introduction

John Rawls's political liberalism is best understood as a response to the fact that the free exercise of human reason in modern democratic societies leads us to embrace a 'diversity of reasonable comprehensive doctrines'.[1] Because of this, Rawls insists, any (successful) attempt to unite society on a shared comprehensive doctrine requires the oppressive use of state power to suppress competing, reasonable, comprehensive doctrines. If we are to achieve unity without oppression we must 'all affirm' a public political conception (PL: 38) that is supported by, or at least does not conflict with, the diverse reasonable comprehensive doctrines that characterize our democratic societies. This political conception is a 'module' that fits into our many reasonable, irreconcilable, comprehensive views. And because this political conception can be affirmed by all reasonable comprehensive doctrines, oppressive state power is not required to uphold it.

In the first part of this essay I argue that Rawls's conception of the political is an inadequate response to the threat of state oppression under conditions of reasonable pluralism. I argue that the free use of human reason leads to reasonable pluralism over most of what we call the political; the political issues not characterized by reasonable pluralism are, as Rawls admits, few and highly abstract. So narrow and thin is this consensus that Rawls is driven to accept a conception of the political that allows citizens to appeal to their comprehensive doctrines when justifying the employment of state power against their fellows. Thus, I shall argue, political liberalism does not avoid state oppression based on comprehensive views. In the second part of the essay I try to show how justificatory liberalism provides a conception of the political that both (1) takes seriously the fact that the

---

[1] John Rawls, *Political Liberalism* (New York: Columbia University Press, 1993), p. 36. (Henceforth referred to as PL.)

free use of human reason leads us to sharply disagree in the domain of the political and (2) articulates a conception of the political according to which the coercive intervention of the state must be justified by public reasons.

I. Political Liberalism

1. The Basic Argument

1.1. Rawls tells us that his motivation for writing *Political Liberalism* was the realization that, as presented in *A Theory of Justice*, justice as fairness was a 'comprehensive, or partially comprehensive' doctrine (PL: xvi).

> The serious problem is this. A modern democratic society is characterized not simply by a plurality of comprehensive religious, philosophical and moral doctrines, but by a pluralism of incompatible yet reasonable comprehensive doctrines. No one of these doctrines is affirmed by citizens generally. Nor should one expect that in the foreseeable future one of them, or some other reasonable doctrine, will ever be affirmed by all, or nearly all, citizens. Political liberalism assumes that, for political purposes, a plurality of reasonable yet incompatible comprehensive doctrines is the normal result of the exercise of human reason within the framework of free institutions of a constitutional regime. (PL: xvi)

Elsewhere Rawls goes so far as to claim that there exists a plurality of 'perfectly reasonable' comprehensive doctrines (PL: 24n). This reasonable pluralism of comprehensive views renders them unacceptable as bases for the justification of political power. '[P]olitical power is always coercive power backed by the government's use of sanctions' (PL: 136). Now, says Rawls, according to the 'liberal principle of legitimacy': 'our exercise of political power is fully proper only when it is exercised in accordance with a constitution the essentials of which all citizens as free and equal may reasonably be expected to endorse in the light of principles and ideals acceptable to their common human reason' (PL: 137). Thus, it would seem that because there exists a reasonable plurality of comprehensive doctrines, basing the justification of political power on any single doctrine – or subset of comprehensive doctrines – would violate the liberal principle of legitimacy.

This leads Rawls to seek a political conception that 'all affirm' (PL: 38) and is 'shared by everyone' (PL: xix). Such a conception would be supported by, or at least not conflict with, the diverse reasonable comprehensive doctrines that characterize our democratic societies. This political conception is a 'module' (PL: 12–13, 144–5)[2] that fits into our many reasonable, yet irreconcilable, comprehensive views. And because this political conception can be affirmed by all reasonable comprehensive doctrines, oppressive state power is not required to uphold it (PL: 37). Justice as fairness is offered as such a political conception: 'If justice as fairness were not expressly designed to gain the reasoned support of citizens who affirm reasonable although conflicting comprehensive doctrines . . . it would not be liberal' (PL: 143).

1.2. Let us make this argument more precise. Rawls argues:

(1)   The Principle of Liberal Legitimacy (LL): The exercise of political power is legitimate only if it accords with a constitution the essentials of which all free and equal citizens may reasonably be expected to endorse.

(2)   In our democratic societies, there exists a reasonable pluralism of comprehensive religious, philosophical and moral views.

(3)   If (i) free and equal citizen Alpha holds a reasonable comprehensive view C_α, and (ii) if citizen Beta's reasonable comprehensive view C_β is 'irreconcilable' with C_α, then (iii) Alpha cannot reasonably be expected to endorse C_β.

(4)   If Alpha cannot reasonably be expected to endorse C_β, he cannot reasonably be expected to endorse a constitution whose justification requires endorsing C_β.

(5)   Therefore, a constitution relying on C_β as in step 4 violates LL (step 1).

(6)   Given step 2, for every reasonable comprehensive view C_x there exists another reasonable comprehensive view held by some free and equal citizen that is irreconcilable with it.

(7)   Therefore, there exists no constitution satisfying LL that requires the endorsement of any specific comprehensive view.

(8)   However there exists a political conception P such that there exists no reasonable comprehensive view C_x, where it is the case that C_x is irreconcilable with P.

(9)   Given step 8, a constitution relying on P for the justification of political power does not violate **LL**.

[2] See also Rawls's 'Reply to Habermas', *Journal of Philosophy*, vol. 92 (March 1995), pp. 132–80, p. 143 (hereafter referred to as RH).

Step (3) is necessary. Fundamental to Rawls's political liberalism is the (uncontentious) claim that it is unreasonable to expect a person to endorse an otherwise reasonable comprehensive view that is irreconcilable with his own reasonable view. Step (8) also seems necessary; unless (8) holds, a constitution depending on P is open to the same objection as a constitution depending on a comprehensive view. Interestingly, Rawls sometimes qualifies the claim in (8). He tells us, for example, that consensus on the political conception should include 'all the reasonable opposing religious, philosophical, and moral doctrines *likely to persist over generations and to gain a sizable body of adherents*' (PL: 15).[3] This suggests an alternative to step 8:

(8*)   However there exists a political conception P such that there exist few reasonable comprehensive views C_x, where it is the case that C_x is irreconcilable with P.

As we will see, whether we adopt (8) or (8*) has important implications for Rawls's political liberalism.

2.   *Comprehensive Views and the Political Conception*

2.1. Rawls's core argument – and so his entire political liberalism – apparently depends on the contrast between comprehensive views and the political conception. Rawls repeatedly describes as 'comprehensive', 'philosophical', 'moral', and 'religious' 'doctrines' (PL: xxv, 4, 36, 38, 160) or 'beliefs' (PL: 63). Indeed, so often does Rawls characterize comprehensiveness in terms of moral, religious and philosophical doctrines or beliefs that a reader may be tempted to conclude:

> C is comprehensive if and only if it is a moral, religious or philosophical doctrine or belief.

This would make sense of Rawls's insistence that 'political liberalism applies the principle of toleration to philosophy itself' (PL: 10). Just as a traditional liberal political order tolerates a variety of religious views and does not invoke any in the justification of laws and policies, Rawls apparently seeks to tolerate all reasonable philosophical and moral doctrines while abjuring appeal to any in the justification of constitutional essentials. But though tempting, this would be wrong. Rawls is clear that:

---

[3] My emphasis.

the distinction between the political conception and other moral conceptions is a matter of scope; that is, the range of subjects, to which a
conception applies and the content a wider range requires. A moral conception is general if it applies to a wide range of subjects, and in the limit to
all subjects universally. It is comprehensive when it includes conceptions of
what is of value in human life, and ideals of personal character, as well as
ideals of familial and associational relationships, and much else that is to
inform our conduct, and in the limit to our life as a whole. A conception is
fully comprehensive if it covers all recognized values and virtues within one
rather precisely articulated system; whereas a conception is only partially
comprehensive when it comprises a number of, but by no means all,
nonpolitical values and virtues and is rather loosely articulated. Many
religious and philosophical doctrines aspire to be both general and comprehensive. (PL: 13)

Comprehensive and general doctrines cover a wide range of topics, values
and ideals applicable to various areas of life while, in contrast, the scope of
the political is narrow.

However, Rawls tells us later on that '[m]ost people's religious, philosophical, and moral doctrines are not seen by them as fully general and
comprehensive, and these aspects admit of variations and of degree' (PL:
160). It is not certain whether Rawls believes that most people are correct
in this self-conception, but it seems clear that they must be. Few people
have all-embracing philosophies of life that provide a single, coherent
perspective on questions of value, human character and social life.[4] So
most people do not actually possess, and so cannot rely on, (fully)
comprehensive moral, religious and philosophical doctrines.

2.2. Once we recognize that Rawls's argument is against comprehensive
views qua systems of thought that are wide in scope and rich in content,
ranging over many areas of life, we see that the argument does not exclude
moral, religious or philosophical beliefs – as opposed to comprehensive
views or general theories – from serving as the basis for an exercise of
political power that passes the test of Liberal Legitimacy. That a belief is
moral, religious or philosophical does not itself show that it is comprehensive or general. Indeed, Rawls himself indicates that the political
conception has moral, epistemological and metaphysical elements

---

[4] I do not mean to bemoan this fact. It is difficult not to be a bit frightened by those who embrace fully
comprehensive and general views of life. They remind one of Isaiah Berlin's 'hedgehog' who sees
only one truth, as opposed to the 'fox' who grasps the plurality of considerations. Isaiah Berlin, *The
Hedgehog and the Fox* (London: Weidenfeld & Nicolson, 1953).

(PL: 10, 11, 13, 62). Moral, religious and philosophical beliefs need not be, and very often are not, comprehensive or general. They may cover a limited topic and stand alone. Consider, for example, the beliefs that: (A) God exists; (B) the external world is real, and a proposition is true if it describes the world accurately; (C) children should respect their parents; (D) stealing is wrong; (E) people who work hard deserve more than those who do not.

For each of these beliefs, it could be argued that: (1) it is narrow in scope, and is embraced by a wide variety of people with different comprehensive views and (2) it is the object of a wide, though certainly not complete, consensus in the United States. (A), for example, meets the test of (8*). Belief (B) is interesting; it is philosophical, and is debated by philosophers, but there is probably much more consensus on it than on any political claim that Rawls makes. Beliefs (C)–(E) are all very widely shared moral beliefs, though it seems that Rawls is one of the few who denies (E).[5]

It might be objected that, although (A)–(E) are simply beliefs and not comprehensive doctrines, they are inevitably embedded in some comprehensive doctrine; thus appeal to them necessarily brings some comprehensive doctrine into play. In reply, though, we can first query whether this is so. Many people have abstract and isolated intuitions that there is a deity, that true statements in some way correspond to a real external world or that certain actions simply are morally right or wrong. But second, Rawls's doctrine of an overlapping consensus (see §3.1) relies on comprehensive doctrines supporting a shared political conception. So that a belief such as (A) is endorsed by a wide variety of religious and philosophical views hardly constitutes an objection to advancing it in the justification of constitutional essentials: it shows that it is an object of an overlapping consensus.

This may seem to be making too much of a small point: all Rawls has to do is be clear that the test of Liberal Legitimacy requires the rigorous step (8) rather than the looser (8*). For while (A)–(E) may be endorsed by the huge majority of reasonable citizens, each is rejected by some reasonable citizen. However, we still see from all this that it is not comprehensive doctrines that Rawls must object to, but simply appeal (in the justification of constitutional essentials) to any reasonable belief b when it is the case that some citizen entertains a reasonable belief that is irreconcilable with b. The relevant distinction is not between the comprehensive and the

---

[5] For a discussion, see my *Social Philosophy* (Armonk, NY: M. E. Sharpe, 1999), chs. 6, 9.

political, but the reasonably disputed and the not reasonably disputed. Thus, it would appear that we should reformulate step (3) as:

> If (i) free and equal citizen Alpha holds a reasonable comprehensive view C_α, and (ii) if Beta's reasonable belief b is 'irreconcilable' with C_α, then (iii) Alpha cannot be reasonably expected to endorse b.

But this is still not quite correct. As we have seen, Rawls himself apparently admits that most people do not possess fully comprehensive doctrines. Suppose Alpha is one of these citizens whose views do not hang together into a highly coherent scheme; but suppose that, while he does not obtain the integration of a fully comprehensive view, he still has various reasonable beliefs, and b is inconsistent with them. His system of beliefs is 'partially comprehensive' insofar as it does form some sort of system, but it has no single or few leading idea(s), and a number of issues are not covered. It still would seem unreasonable to expect him to endorse b. Thus, we have:

(3*) If (i) free and equal citizen Alpha holds a reasonable belief b_α and (ii) if reasonable belief b is 'irreconcilable' with b_α, then (iii) Alpha cannot be reasonably expected to endorse b.

Some might object that downgrading the source of Alpha's objection to b from that premised on a comprehensive view of life to a mere reasonable belief undermines the conviction that it is wrong to expect Alpha to endorse b. But it is hard to see why this should be so. Alpha is not a schizoid personality without an integrated belief structure; he has obtained sufficient integration such that, having considered his other beliefs and values, he has come to a reasonable belief that b_α. To disregard this still seems to ignore his status as a free and equal person. Recall, moreover, that Rawls does not think that most people possess fully comprehensive doctrines (§2.2): to insist that only fully comprehensive doctrines are the grounds for genuine complaints based on LL implies that most citizens are precluded from appealing to LL. Surely this would be an unwelcome result for a political liberal.

2.3. Having freed ourselves of the confusing and distracting reference to comprehensive doctrines, Rawls's claim must be that only political beliefs pass the implied test of (3*), and so can satisfy LL. But now it is hard to see how this can be explained simply as a difference in scope; although the political may well have a more limited scope than a religious, philosophical or moral fully comprehensive doctrine, it is implausible to suppose that, inherently, any religious or moral belief is of greater scope than any political belief. Why should we believe that?

We have seen that sometimes Rawls indicates (1) that the political conception is a 'module' that fits into many comprehensive views (PL: 12–13, 144–5); the implied contrast might be to (2) a religious or moral belief that is inherently non-modular, necessarily presupposing an entire comprehensive doctrine. However, we already rejected the second claim (§2.2). Regarding (1) I have argued elsewhere that conceptions of the political can themselves be deeply influenced by one's moral, religious and philosophical beliefs and so are themselves open to dispute.[6] Employing the familiar distinction between a concept and a conception,[7] it seems that the concept of the political perspective is characterized by competing conceptions. A Marxist has very different ideas about the nature of politics from that of a political liberal, or a libertarian or a Fundamentalist. It is important to stress that this is not the banal point that the Marxist, political liberal, libertarian, and Fundamentalist all have different political proposals - it is the more interesting point that they entertain different conceptions of the political. As Habermas notes, 'the boundaries between public and private' [by which he means the political and non-political] are 'historically shifting' and 'in flux'[8] – indeed, they have been one of the main sources of dispute between different 'compre-hensive' theories of theories of self and society – i.e. what we often call 'political theories'. The concept of politics, it has been argued, is 'essen-tially contested', being composed of a number of dimensions that can be ordered differently, producing different conceptions, each of which is a reasonable interpretation of the concept.[9]

Perhaps I have misunderstood Rawls. Like Habermas, I have read Rawls as positing a logically basic (in Habermas's words, an 'a priori') distinction

---

[6] See my 'Reason, Justification and Consensus: Why Democracy Can't Have It All', in James Bohman and William Rehg (eds.), *Deliberative Democracy* (Cambridge, MA: MIT Press, 1997), pp. 207–42. The comments in this paragraph sketch the conclusions of a much longer argument present there.

[7] For helpful discussions of this distinction, see Christine Swanton, *Freedom: A Coherence Theory* (Indianapolis: Hackett, 1992), ch. 1; Fred D'Agostino, *Free Public Reason* (New York: Oxford University Press, 1996), ch. 2. See also Rawls, *A Theory of Justice* (Cambridge, MA: Harvard University Press, 1971), p. 5; Ronald Dworkin, *Law's Empire* (Cambridge, MA: Harvard University Press, 1986), p. 71.

[8] See Jürgen Habermas, 'Reconciliation through Public Reason: Remarks on John Rawls's Political Liberalism', *The Journal of Philosophy* 92 (March 1995), pp. 109–31, p. 129. See also S. I. Benn and G. F. Gaus, 'The Liberal Conception of the Public and Private', in Benn and Gaus (eds), *Public and Private in Social Life* (New York: St Martin's Press, 1983), pp. 31–65.

[9] See William E. Connolly, *The Terms of Political Discourse*, 2nd edn (Princeton, NJ: Princeton University Press, 1983), ch. 1. See also W. B. Gallie, 'Essentially Contested Concepts', in his *Philosophy and the Historical Understanding* (New York: Schocken, 1968), ch. 8.

between the political and non-political spheres.[10] And at times Rawls certainly suggests this. For example, in the above quotation (§2.1) Rawls explains the difference in scope between comprehensive doctrines and the political conception by pointing out that '[a] conception is fully comprehensive if it covers all recognized values and virtues within one rather precisely articulated system; whereas a conception is only partially comprehensive when it comprises a number of, but by no means all, *nonpolitical values* and virtues and is rather loosely articulated'. The italicized phrase suggests that the distinction between the political and the nonpolitical is logically prior to the distinction between the comprehensive and the political: Rawls explicates a comprehensive doctrine as one that appeals to nonpolitical values. Elsewhere Rawls seems to posit a basic distinction between the 'political' and the 'social', the latter being the realm of 'comprehensive doctrines of all kinds – religious, philosophical, moral' (PL: 14). It would seem that on this view we need to know what are the boundaries of the political before we can know whether a doctrine is comprehensive. Habermas would thus seem correct that Rawls's political liberalism relies on a logically basic contrast between the concepts of the political and non-political (or social), one that on reflection seems dubious and contentious. That the political is focused on the justice of the basic structure (PL: Lecture VIII) is a reasonable – perhaps the correct – view, but it is by no means an uncontentious conception of the political endorsed by all reasonable citizens.

An alternative, however, is to understand the political conception as constructed out of that which we share. On this reading the nonpolitical is, by definition, those matters on which our use of reason leads us to different, reasonable conclusions. It is, by its very nature, the realm of reasonable pluralism. In contrast, we can define the political as those matters on which human reason converges, and so necessarily generates constitutional principles that satisfy the Principle of Liberal Legitimacy.[11]

This approach to identifying the political avoids the problems I have thus far been canvassing. It does not rely on the ideas of a 'comprehensive doctrine', or a priori or uncontroversial (within the limits of reasonability) notions of what is inherently political, moral, philosophical or religious. To be sure, it implies that what prima facie appears to be a moral belief can

---

[10] Habermas, 'Reconciliation through Public Reason', op. cit., p. 129.
[11] Rawls's notion of 'political constructivism' (PL: Lecture III) suggests this interpretation, but even there Rawls supposes a prior understanding of what is political. Only by assuming a prior conception of the political can we make sense of the claim that 'political constructivism is limited to the political' (PL: 89).

end up part of the political, but Rawls expressly allows this: the political conception, he tells us, 'is a moral conception worked out for a specific kind of subject, namely, for political, social, and economic institutions' (PL: 11).[12] Let us explore, then, this constructed understanding of the domain of the political.

3. The Political: Where Human Reason Agrees?

3.1. Fred D'Agostino has identified two ways in which human reason can agree: consensus and convergence.[13] A consensus argument seeks to show that everyone has reason R to accept b. Such an argument seeks to show that we share a reason for endorsing b. In contrast, a convergence argument seeks to show that we have different reasons for endorsing b, though we all have some reason for endorsing it. Rawls employs both types of arguments in his case for agreement on the political.

Rawls argues that the political conception can be justified as free-standing (PL: 10): it is based on a conception of persons as reasonable and rational, free and equal – a conception that is said to be implicit in our democratic society, and so shared by all. Justice as fairness thus expresses a 'shared reason' (PL: 9). Rawls thus argues that justice as fairness is a justified political conception as it articulates the requirements of the concepts of the person and society that all reasonable citizens in our democratic societies share. However, Rawls does not believe that this exhausts justification. In later stages of justification – what he refers to as 'full' and 'public' justification' – citizens draw on their full range of beliefs and values and find further reasons for endorsing the political conception (RH: 142–3). Thus 'overlapping consensus' constitutes a convergent public justification, drawing on our various 'comprehensive doctrines'.

3.2. The key idea, then, is that the political conception exemplifies a consensus and convergence of the powers of our reasoning. The content of this political conception is 'broadly liberal in character':

> By this I mean three things: first, it specifies certain basic rights, liberties, and opportunities (of the kind familiar from constitutional democratic regimes); second, it assigns a special priority to these rights, liberties and opportunities, especially with respect to claims of the general good and of

---

[12] Once again, Rawls suggest here that some topics are inherently (and within the bounds of reasonability) uncontroversially political.

[13] D'Agostino, *Free Public Reason*, op. cit., pp. 30–1.

perfectionist values; and third, it affirms measures assuring all citizens adequate all-purpose means to make effective use of their basic liberties and opportunities. (PL: 223)

Justice as fairness, we are told, is simply one such liberal conception; because 'each of these elements can be seen in many different ways, so there are many liberalisms' (PL: 223). This is significant: Rawls believes that there are diverse interpretations of the basic concept of a liberal political order. Indeed, he insists that '*it is inevitable and often desirable that citizens have different views as to the most appropriate political conception*; for the public culture is bound to contain different fundamental ideas that can be developed in different ways' (PL: 227).[14] Rawls also accepts that citizens arguing in good faith and employing public reason will not accept 'the very same principles of justice' (PL: 214).

Now in many ways this is puzzling. If citizens entertain 'different views as to the most appropriate political conception' a society cannot be well-ordered. In a well-ordered society 'everyone accepts, and knows everyone accepts, the very same principles of justice' (PL: 35). It thus seems that reason will not itself lead us to a well-ordered society; the reasoning of free and equal citizens may lead them to all accept the liberal concept of justice, but will not lead them to all embrace justice as fairness, the 'very same principles of justice' or the same views of constitutional essentials. And no evidence indicates that Rawls believes disputes about the favored political conception and the principles of justice are a sign that some citizens are either irrational or unreasonable. Indeed, it seems an instance of the 'burdens of judgment', which was originally introduced to show why we disagree about moral, philosophical and religious matters. In his account of the burdens of judgment, Rawls stresses the complexity of value disputes, and the different way of ordering and weighing values (PL: 54–8). It seems that it is precisely this complexity in ordering and weighing 'political values,' and the complexity of developing democratic ideals, that leads to competing reasonable political conceptions. Reasonable pluralism does, after all, apply to political conceptions. At only the most abstract level – the level of the very concept of a liberal order – does Rawls indicate that the exercise of the powers of human reason produces agreement. At more specific levels – and by 'specific' here I mean something as abstract as justice as fairness – our use of reason leads to reasonable disagreement.[15]

---

[14] My emphasis.
[15] John Gray long ago insisted that as soon as we move beyond abstract Rawlsian principles to their application in specific cases, 'indeterminacy' arises. We see here that such 'indeterminacy' arises at a

3.3. Now it may be thought that Rawls's claim is that: (1) justice as fairness is a reasonable liberal political conception of justice and (2) citizens living under it will tend to develop allegiance to it, and thus (3) a society ruled by justice as fairness will move toward being well-ordered as citizens come to see that it coheres with their moral, religious and philosophical views. Thus, we might interpret Rawls as saying that, while reason alone does not now produce consensus on his favored liberal political conception of justice, the long-run tendency of a society living under justice as fairness is to converge on it. As Rawls stresses, there is a path to an overlapping consensus on justice as fairness that, through a series of steps, leads to a well-ordered society (PL: 158–68).

However, before a society converges on justice as fairness, there will be some period in which free and equal citizens exercising their reason will disagree whether justice as fairness is the favored political conception. Indeed, it is very difficult to believe that this period will not extend indefinitely. That the reasoning of free and equal people will someday lead everyone to accept justice as fairness seems, at best, a controversial prediction. During this period – however long it lasts – the exercise of political power on the basis of a constitution justified by appeal to justice as fairness violates the criterion of Liberal Legitimacy. Recall (from §§1.2, 2.2):

LL: The exercise of political power is legitimate only if it accords with a constitution the essentials of which all free and equal citizens may reasonably be expected to endorse.

(3*) If (i) free and equal citizen Alpha holds a reasonable belief b_α, and (ii) if reasonable belief b is 'irreconcilable' with b_α, then (iii) Alpha cannot be reasonably expected to endorse b.

Now suppose citizen Alpha believes that the most reasonable liberal political conception of justice enshrines private property, allows for a social provision of a minimum income (with no further provision of equality), and seeks to award people differentially on the grounds of economic desert. We can assume that this reasonable articulation of the liberal concept of justice – which is in fact a popular one[16] – departs in important ways from justice as fairness. Assume further that the majority accepts justice as fairness as the favored political conception; on that basis, they adopt a constitution that allows socialism, and the legislature proceeds to institute

---

far more abstract level. John Gray, 'Contractarian Method, Private Property and the Market Economy' in his *Liberalisms* (London: Routledge, 1989), pp. 161–98 at pp. 169ff., 186ff.

[16] For a basic exposition, see my Social Philosophy, op. cit., ch. 9.

a market socialist regime. Citizen Alpha, however, has a reasonable belief that private property ought to be protected by a just constitution; it is thus unreasonable to expect him to endorse a constitution that allows socialism. Consequently, if we demand allegiance to the Principle of Liberal Legitimacy, a society cannot start on the path to being well-ordered under justice as fairness.

3.4. It might be replied in Rawls's defense that, while there may be reasonable disagreement as to whether justice as fairness is the favored political conception, rational and reasonable citizens can reach consensus on constitutional essentials. As Rawls notes, Kurt Baier suggests that Americans already have broad consensus on these matters (PL: 149).[17] The Principle of Liberal Legitimacy does not require consensus on a conception of justice, but only on constitutional essentials. Moreover, in Rawls's steps to a well-ordered society based on justice as fairness, a constitutional consensus is prior to an overlapping consensus based on justice as fairness. So, as long as rational and reasonable free and equal citizens endorse the same constitutional essentials, the Principle of Liberal Legitimacy is satisfied.

Rawls, however, explicitly tells us that reasonable and rational free and equal citizens disagree about constitutional essentials. 'A vote can be held on a fundamental [constitutional] question as on any other; and if the question is debated by appeal to political values and citizens vote their sincere opinion, the ideal is sustained' (PL: 241). Public reason, Rawls tells us, rarely leads to close agreement, even on matters of constitutional essentials and basic justice (PL: 241). And, again, this is essentially because of what we might call the 'burdens of political judgment' (see §3.2). The political values relevant to constitutional essentials are multiple and complex, and so free and equal citizens exercising their powers of practical rationality and reasonability come to good-faith different answers about their proper weighing, leading to diverging views of justified constitutional essentials. Even in the political – in this case, constitutional – sphere reasonable pluralism manifests itself. If citizen Alpha has a reasonable belief that clause x is essential to a just constitution, then employing political power under a constitution that contains y, where y is irreconcilable with x, violates the Principle of Liberal Legitimacy. And, as a matter of fact, such debates occur in constitutional deliberations in the United

[17] See Kurt Baier, 'Justice as the Aims of Political Philosophy', *Ethics* 99 (July 1989), pp. 771–90, esp. pp. 775ff.

States. Some American liberals insist that constitutional clauses upholding freedom of contract and preventing the taking of private property are constitutional essentials (that have been ignored); others follow Rawls in insisting that the protection of extensive private property rights is not a constitutional essential.[18]

To be sure, here too Rawls believes that a series of steps can lead to a constitutional consensus (PL: 158–64). But, as we saw above, it must be true that before there is such a consensus the exercise of political power is illegitimate. As long as the Principle of Liberal Legitimacy is honored, the process cannot get under way. If we view LL as a side-constraint on the exercise of political power, it not only blocks a constitution premised on 'comprehensive' doctrines, it blocks justice as fairness – and indeed any specific liberal conception – as well.

3.5. Rawls is aware of these problems; his response is to implicitly weaken the Principle of Liberal Legitimacy to allow for such reasonable political pluralism. Two alterations are important.

(1) Rawls seems to exploit an ambiguity between strong and weak senses of what it is 'reasonable' to endorse. Rawls often tells us that the 'political conception is a reasonable expression of the political values of public reason and justice between citizens seen as free and equal' (PL: 247; see also xx, 243, 246, 253) or gives 'reasonable' answers to questions about how to weigh political values and constitutional essentials (PL: 225). We are also told that citizens may 'reasonably accept' the terms of cooperation specified by the political conception (PL: 16). Now this is much less than Rawls required of 'comprehensive doctrines.' Recall our initial step (3):

If (i) free and equal citizen Alpha holds a reasonable comprehensive view C_α, and (ii) if citizen Beta's reasonable comprehensive view C_β is 'irreconcilable' with C_α, then (iii) Alpha cannot reasonably be expected to endorse C_β.

The political parallel would be:

If (i) free and equal citizen Alpha holds a reasonable political view of constitutional essentials, P, and (ii) if citizen Beta's reasonable political view P_β is 'irreconcilable' with P_α, then (iii) Alpha cannot reasonably be expected to endorse P_β.

[18] The now classic work on this matter is, of course, Richard A. Epstein, *Takings: Private Property and the Power of Eminent Domain* (Cambridge, MA: Harvard University Press, 1985). Cf. Bruce Ackerman, *We The People*, vol. 1: *The Foundations* (Cambridge, MA: Harvard University Press, 1991), ch. 5 and PL: 262–5.

If we accept this, the claim that P_β is 'reasonable' or gives 'reasonable answers' is in no way sufficient to show that it passes the test of Liberal Legitimacy; simply put, on this stronger criterion, it is not reasonable to expect a citizen to endorse a doctrine just because it is a reasonable doctrine. Indeed the whole problem of reasonable pluralism is that there are numerous reasonable views that are irreconcilable with other reasonable views; political liberalism's search for consensus in the domain of the political was intended as a response to this very problem: to 'resolve the impasse in our recent political history ... that there is no agreement on the way basic social institutions should be arranged if they are to conform to the freedom and equality of citizens as persons' (PL: 300). Yet Rawls often seems content to rely on the claim that his favored political conception is simply a reasonable political view. But that would imply the following Principle of Weak Liberal Legitimacy:

> WLL: The exercise of political power is legitimate if it accords with a constitution the essentials of which all free and equal citizens can see as reasonable.

Weak Liberal Legitimacy suggests that it is reasonable to expect a citizen to endorse a political view just because it is a reasonable political view. This, though, would allow various reasonable comprehensive views – such as Mill's liberalism – as bases for the legitimate exercise of political power.
(2) More formally, Rawls tells us:

> Let us say that we honor public reason and its principle of legitimacy when three conditions are satisfied: (a) we give very great and normally overriding weight to the idea it prescribes; (b) we believe public reason is suitably complete, that is, for at least the great majority of fundamental questions, possibly for all, some combination and balance of political values *alone* reasonably shows the best answer; and finally, (c) we believe that the particular view we propose, and the law or policy based thereon, expresses a reasonable combination and balance of those values. (PL: 241)[19]

Clause (b) is more demanding than the test implied in WLL. It requires us to assume that there is a uniquely reasonable best answer to the political question. Surprisingly, however, clause (c) does not require a person to believe that the answer she is proposing is the best answer supposed in (b), only that it is a reasonable answer (thus reverting to the view I considered in 1 above). It is not clear that this is simply an oversight. Rawls tells us

---

[19] My emphasis.

that the answer provided by public reason 'must at least be reasonable, if not the most reasonable' (PL: 246). Again, this suggests that any reasonable answer is sufficient. However, even supposing that one interprets (c) to require a good-faith belief that one's reasonable answer is the uniquely most reasonable answer, if we apply this criterion to 'comprehensive doctrines', it would allow, say, a Millian to advocate a perfectionist constitution. For the Millian could claim: (1) that he believes that there is a uniquely best answer to this question (the Millian one), though of course there are other reasonable views too, and (2) he is advocating the doctrine which, in good faith, he believes is the uniquely most reasonable one. If we reduce the demands of Liberal Legitimacy to requiring simply a good faith belief that one's reasonable view is the best or most reasonable one, constitutions relying on 'comprehensive' doctrines are legitimate.

Rawls, however, insists that the answer provided by public reason 'must at least be reasonable, if not the most reasonable, *as judged by public reason alone*' (PL: 246).[20] Thus Rawls can insist that in the case of a Millian constitution, its reasonability is not judged by public reason alone, but in reference to the Millian comprehensive view. This reply brings us full circle, for it supposes a basic (what Habermas called an 'a priori') contrast between the political and the non-political (§2.3). If we could distinguish in a reasonably uncontentious manner the properly political from the non-political or social, then we would be in a position to distinguish what is inconclusive on political grounds from what is non-politically inconclusive. However, having given up that attempt, we have been seeking to construct the notion of the political out of the reasons we can share. If both Millian liberalism and justice as fairness are reasonable views, that their adherents believe to be correct but which cannot be shown to be uniquely reasonable to others, we do not have the conceptual resources to say that one appeals to the properly political while the other does not.

3.6. We now can see the dilemma of political liberalism. If Rawls could identify a uniquely reasonable political point of view – one which manifestly excluded Millian and other 'comprehensive' liberalisms as reasonable political doctrines – he could identify a realm of reasonable though conflicting political opinions that was restricted to a small family of political conceptions, one of which would be justice as fairness. Thus, the idea of a basic contrast between 'comprehensive' and 'political'

---

[20] My emphasis. Note that I omitted the italicized phrase when I quoted this sentence in the previous paragraph.

doctrines. We have seen, though, that this basic contrast cannot be maintained. We have reasonable differences about what is properly political, while many beliefs associated with comprehensive doctrines are widely shared. The alternative, then, is to abandon any logically basic contrast between the political and the social, and to instead construct the notion of the political out of the reasons we share. But since the use of human reason leads us to reasonable disagreement about conceptions of justice and constitutional essentials, the political qua shared is limited to the abstract concept of a liberal political order.

3.7. I have been stressing here the way in which reasonable pluralism characterizes the thinking of free and equal citizens on matters of basic justice and constitutional essentials in Rawls's political liberalism. As such, I have argued, political liberalism fails to satisfy its own principle of legitimacy, and so is self-defeating. It should be stressed that LL is itself a weak – and in my view much too weak – principle of legitimacy. As long as an exercise of political power is consistent with a constitution the essentials of which all reasonable citizens can be expected to endorse, this power is justified. As Rawls sees it, this allows 'citizens and legislators' to 'properly vote their more comprehensive views when constitutional essentials and basic justice are not at stake' (PL: 235, but cf. 252).[21] Suppose, then, a matter is before us that does not involve a constitutional essential, say, whether we should have a government-provided education system or one which is government funded but which is provided by private schools (e.g. through vouchers). Now suppose that the main argument given by those supporting government provision is that a single, government-run system will be better able to ensure that citizens are raised to endorse certain controversial views: overall, the system will be more favorable to, say, multiculturalism and environmentalism. It will not go so far as to repress competing views, for it will be careful to remain within the bounds of the basic liberal constitution; but within those bounds the majority explicitly advocates the use of state power to uphold its own comprehensive views.

It is hard not to see this as an illiberal and oppressive policy. Some citizens are to be subjected to coercive state enactments that are designed to further (reasonable) doctrines that are irreconcilable with their own reasonable views. It is hard to see why any citizen should reasonably be

---

[21] This 'dualist' conception of democracy has been more fully articulated by Ackerman, *We the People*, op. cit.

expected to accept a coercively-imposed law when this law has been justified by appeal to comprehensive doctrines that the citizen reasonably opposes. To be sure, a Rawlsian state will not be grossly oppressive, as it must respect the publicly justified essentials; it does, though, allow many small coercive impositions that are explicitly justified on what seem manifestly non-public grounds. In its day-to-day operations, political liberalism sanctions the majority's use of state power to advance its 'comprehensive doctrines'.

We can see why Rawls is driven to this conception of politics. If the political is the realm of the respect for the freedom and equality of our fellow citizens because it manifests our agreement, the political obviously cannot be instantiated in day-to-day politics, which is, first and foremost, about the ways in which we differ. Hence Rawls must accept a radical dualistic conception of politics, sharply distinguishing the constitutional, which (at least at times) Rawls depicts as a matter of shared reasoning, and the normal business of politics, which is about the ways in which we differ and which constitutes a hostile arena for the use of public reason.

II. Justificatory Liberalism

4.   Five Compelling Ideas

I have thus far been critical of Rawls's political liberalism. It is important to stress, though, that its problems are important, as they stem from five compelling ideas.

(1)   Respect for the freedom and equality of our fellow citizens requires that the state's exercise of coercive authority must be justified to each and every citizen. This, of course, is the core idea of the Principle of Liberal Legitimacy (LL). Difficulties arise when we add the second compelling idea:

(2)   The free exercise of human reason leads us to disagree on a wide variety of issues concerning value, goods, ideals of the good life and so on. One citizen's reasonable views are often reasonably rejected by others. Consequently:

(3)   Many of the beliefs we hold most dear are not available to us in our efforts to meet LL, as they are the subject of reasonable disagreement.

(4)   If we are to meet LL, we must thus restrict the beliefs or considerations to which we appeal, restricting ourselves somehow to those reasons which we all share.

(5)   However, as we have seen, even in politics our reason leads us to disagree. We cannot go very far by understanding the political as characterized by the absence of reasonable disagreement.

5.   Reasonable Disagreement Reexamined

5.1. To accommodate all five of these ideas, while still showing how a liberal regime can meet LL, we need to better grasp the idea of reasonable disagreement, and how it leads to problems in satisfying the Principle of Liberal Legitimacy. Rawls always assumes a close link between (1) being a reasonable person and (2) entertaining reasonable beliefs or doctrines (PL: 59). Rawls supposes that reasonable people have reasonable beliefs. If we grant this, and also accept that the Principle of Liberal Legitimacy requires that a sound justification of coercive state power must not be irreconcilable with any citizen's reasonable beliefs (see (3*), §3.3), it is not hard to see why LL appears to require a consensus of reasonable people on constitutional essentials. Any reasonable person's veto apparently demonstrates that she has a reasonable belief that is irreconcilable with the justification, hence the justification does not meet LL.

I have tried to show elsewhere that reasonable people often have unreasonable beliefs.[22] A number of empirical studies indicate that intelligent, normal reasoners who manifestly qualify as reasonable people – they are, in general, disposed to reasonable beliefs – can entertain strikingly unreasonable (indeed, irrational) beliefs in specific cases. Reasonable people, for example, very often refuse to believe what is manifestly highly credible, instead persevering in irrational beliefs. P. C. Wason and P. N. Johnson-Laird report an experiment in which subjects were given three numbers, and were told that the experimenter had in a mind a rule for the generation of a series of numbers, and that these three numbers fit the rule. The task of the subjects was to 'test hypotheses' about what the rule might be by asking the experimenter questions of the form 'Do numbers n, m, o fit the series?' where the subjects themselves supplied various candidates. The aim was to test hypotheses about what the rule might be; when the subjects felt sure they knew what the rule was, they were to announce it to

[22] See 'The Rational, the Reasonable and Justification', *The Journal of Political Philosophy* 3 (September 1995), pp. 234–58; *Justificatory Liberalism: An Essay on Epistemology and Political Theory* (New York: Oxford University Press, 1996), ch. 9; 'Reason, Justification and Consensus: Why Democracy Can't Have It All', op cit.

the experimenters. Wason and Johnson-Laird found many subjects poor at such hypothesis testing, but of immediate interest are some of the responses of subjects once they discovered that their confident announcements about the rule regulating the series were wrong.

> EXPERIMENTER: 'If you were wrong, how could you find out?'
> SUBJECT A: 'I can't be wrong since my rule was correct for those numbers.'
> SUBJECT B: 'Rules are relative. If you were the subject, and I were the experimenter, then I would be right.'[23]

In some cases, subjects simply remained immune to the fact they were wrong, even to the point of simply insisting that they must be right: they refused to accept the manifestly credible statement that they had guessed wrong. As Wason and Johnson-Laird point out, the evidence showing they were wrong was clearly before them and indeed they obviously had good reason to accept it. And this is by no means an unusual reaction: the research of Deanna Kuhn and her colleagues found that at least half her subjects share an epistemic attitude, central to which is a personal certainty that their own beliefs are correct, even when they are not based on extensive knowledge.[24] Not only is it the case that reflection often fails to induce reasonable people to abandon irrational beliefs, but reflection can induce them to abandon perfectly rational ones. For example, Stephen Stich and Richard Nisbett report that it is not difficult to teach people the gambler's fallacy and induce them to jettison sound views about the probability of independent events.[25]

5.2. Once we appreciate that the notions of reasonable people and reasonable beliefs diverge in this way, we can see that satisfying the Principle of Liberal Legitimacy should not lead us to seek the consensus of reasonable people, but to seek arguments that are not irreconcilable with reasonable beliefs. We seek a justification for the exercise of political power that is not

---

[23] P. C. Wason and P. N. Johnson-Laird, *The Psychology of Reasoning: Structure and Content* (London: B. T. Batsford, 1972), p. 237.

[24] In Kuhn's study, ordinary reasoners were asked to formulate theories explaining crime, unemployment and children failing in school. Deanna Kuhn, *The Skills of Argument* (Cambridge: Cambridge University Press, 1991), pp. 174–5.

[25] Stephen P. Stich and Richard E. Nisbett, 'Justification and the Psychology of Human Reasoning', *Philosophy of Science* 47 (June 1980), pp. 188–202. Research also shows that people employing faulty inferential rules can be taught the correct approach. See Richard E. Nisbett, Geoffrey T. Fong, Darrin R. Lehman, and Patricia W. Cheng, 'Teaching Reasoning', *Science* 238 (October 1987), pp. 625–31; Darrin R. Lehman and Richard E, Nisbett, 'A Longitudinal Study of Undergraduate Training on Reasoning', *Developmental Psychology* 26 (1990), pp. 952–60.

open to reasonable objections, although it may be rejected by many reasonable people. Constitutional politics, then, is not the realm of consensus, but of conclusive justifications – those not open to reasonable doubt. The domain of constitutional politics is not to be grasped in terms of the quasi-sociological notion of a possible consensus, but in terms of an epistemology that reveals to us the conditions that render it unreasonable to reject a justification. A liberalism appreciating this is justificatory rather than political – it rests on a theory of justified, reasonable, belief and argument. This is crucial: the application of LL presupposes a criterion of reasonable belief. Moreover, this criterion cannot itself be defined as the conception of reasonable belief that all reasonable people would accept, or which can itself be the object of reasonable consensus; all these ideas are logically derivative of the epistemic criterion of reasonability.[26]

5.3. For a justificatory liberalism, then, satisfying LL requires a justification of coercive authority that is not open to reasonable doubt. This leads us to Rawls's third compelling idea: few of the beliefs around which we construct our lives achieve this level of justification. For the most part, our guiding beliefs are credible but not conclusively justified. Given the relevant evidence, adopting them is typically reasonable. However, our judgments on these matters are almost always inconclusive; many of our most cherished and important beliefs involve complex matters involving a number of values and considerations, and the evidence on which we make decisions is almost always incomplete; and even if it is not, our cognitive ability to process all the evidence and weigh the various considerations is inadequate to the task. Moreover, people's belief systems differ: considerations that are salient and important in one person's system may have little relevance in another's: thus, even if I am sure that I have made the correct choice for me, it is dubious whether it is surely the correct choice for others. Consequently, because most of our beliefs are reasonably held, but can be reasonably rejected by others, arguments that require others to accept these beliefs are inadequate from the perspective of LL.

5.4. Note that this analysis does not suppose any basic distinction between comprehensive doctrines and the political, or between, on the one hand, the moral, the religious, the philosophical and, on the other, the political. The basic contrast is between justifications that are open to reasonable

---

[26] Cf. David Estlund, 'The Insularity of the Reasonable: Why Political Liberalism Must Admit the Truth', *Ethics* 108 (January 1998), pp. 252–75.

objections (because they are irreconcilable with a reasonable, justified, belief) and those that are not. Any of one's beliefs that are not open to reasonable doubt by others – they do not entertain justified beliefs incompatible with them – can be legitimate parts of a justification meeting the demands of LL. Although there is no a priori reason why such beliefs cannot be religious, it is certainly a modern liberal conviction that the history of religious political debate has shown that all candidates proposed – all the religious beliefs that have been advanced as beyond reasonable doubt – have been shown to be lacking. This has led liberals to conceive of religion as inherently personal and based on faith rather than public reason; in this way it has been eliminated as a basis for public justification. Pace Rawls, moral and philosophical beliefs are different from the religious.[27] We cannot say in advance that a justification which necessarily relies on a philosophic doctrine is, just for that reason, inconsistent with LL. Insofar as philosophers seek to present public 'knock-down' arguments, they are endeavoring to live up to the ideal of public justification and LL. To be sure, philosophers and moral theorists may typically fail, but they are engaged in public reasoning, not articulating articles of faith or personal preferences, and as such are not to be equated with those seeking to justify the use of political power on their view of God and his commands.

6.   Conclusive and Inconclusive Political Justification: The Moderate Dualism of Public Reason

6.1. Are there any justifications of political authority that do not essentially depend on claims that are irreconcilable with reasonable beliefs held by some? Our problem, it will be recalled, has been set by the Principle of Liberal Legitimacy – LL is a supposition of the liberal analysis. Now although Rawls applies LL only to political institutions, there is no reason why its scope should be so restricted: just as a governmental use of power that cannot be justified to some citizens manifests disrespect for their freedom and equality, a coercive imposition by one person against another manifests the same disrespect. LL is a constraint on individuals as well as

---

[27] In passing, it might be noted how remarkable it is that philosophers have quickly accepted Rawls's claim that philosophy and morality have the same public status as religion. American bookstores often have a section entitled 'Religion, the Occult and Philosophy'. In my experience this categorization has typically driven philosophers to distraction: oddly enough, Rawls seems to have made it official liberal policy.

states. Liberals are thus committed to what we might call the Principle of Individualized Liberal Legitimacy:

> ILL: Alpha's coercion against Beta is legitimate only if there exists a justification for it that Beta may reasonably be expected to endorse.

Given, then, that all liberal individuals are committed to ILL, they have but two options: (1) to abjure coercive imposition on others or (2) arrive at public justified principles that sanction such imposition. The first is not a real option. To opt for (1) would be to unilaterally renounce what Hobbes called 'the right of nature' – to defend ourselves.[28] Rational liberal citizens are thus committed to option (2): arriving at justified principles that sanction interference. It is because we all have a moral interest in arriving at such a justification that, as Rawls puts it, we all have reason to seek a mutual accommodation (PL: 253) and meeting others half-way is a virtue of civility. Given this, liberals have insisted, it would be unreasonable to reject coercion required to support a regime of extensive equal liberty that protects the person of each from invasion, and provides a structure for property rights.

6.2. We seem to have arrived at exactly Rawls's position. He too, it will be remembered, argued that reasonable citizens will concur on the basic concept of a liberal regime (§3.2). It was 'only' on more specific political questions that reasonable pluralism asserts itself. And it is certainly correct that citizens will disagree about the interpretation and application of basic liberal principles. If each relies on his own (private) judgment about the best interpretation of liberal principles – What are the bounds of our rights and freedoms? What coercive interferences do these principles justify? – reasonable pluralism produces deep disagreement. Indeed, for Kant, relying on one's individual judgment in this way characterizes the state of nature:

> Although experience teaches us that men live in violence and are prone to fight one another before the advent of external compulsive legislation, it is not experience that makes public lawful coercion necessary. The necessity of public lawful coercion does not rest on a fact, but on an a priori Idea of reason, for, even if men to be ever so good natured and righteous before a public lawful state of society is established, individual men, nations and states can never be certain they are secure against violence from one another because each will have the right to do what *seems just and good to him*, entirely independently of the opinion of others.[29]

---

[28] Thomas Hobbes, *Leviathan*, ed. Michael Oakeshott (Oxford: Basil Blackwell, 1946), p. 85 (ch. 14).

[29] Immanuel Kant, *Metaphysical Elements of Justice*, trans. John Ladd (Indianapolis: Bobbs-Merrill, 1965), p. 76 (§44).

Kant goes on to insist that justice is absent in the state of nature because each relies on his own judgment, and thus 'when there is a controversy concerning rights (jus controversum), no competent judge can be found to render a decision having the force of law'.[30] Indeed, Hobbes, Locke, and Kant all maintain that the chief inconveniences of the state of nature arise from individuals relying on their individual, controversial, judgments about natural rights and natural law.[31] The chief inconveniences are two, one moral and one practical.

The moral flaw of the state of nature ruled by individual judgment is that we act without justification. If Alpha believes that b_α is the best interpretation of liberal principles while Beta believes that b_β is, where b_α is irreconcilable with a reasonable belief b_β, Alpha's acting on b_α violates our Principle of Individualized Liberal Legitimacy: he coercively imposes on Beta even though she has a reasonable belief that leads her to reject his justification. Leaving aside its moral shortcomings, a state of nature (i.e. a regime in which people all relied on their rationally contentious judgments about the demands of liberal justice) would be characterized by uncertainty and conflict, undermining the basis for cooperation. Inconsistent interpretations of each other's rights and responsibilities would lead to conflict and thwart the development of settled expectations. This, of course, is a familiar theme in liberal, and especially contractualist, political philosophy: Hobbes's, Locke's and Kant's accounts of the state of nature all aim to establish variations of it. Although on some matters we can agree to differ, disputes engendered by competing judgments about our rights and duties will block common action.[32]

6.3. Relying on our reasonable but by no means conclusive judgments thus would lead to injustice and conflict. For Kant, if one 'does not wish to renounce all concepts of justice', one must 'quit the state of nature, in which everyone follows his own judgments' and subject oneself to 'public lawful external coercion'.[33] Hobbes, Locke, and Kant concur that an

---

[30] Ibid.
[31] For Hobbes, see R. E. Ewin, *Virtues and Rights: The Moral Philosophy of Thomas Hobbes* (Boulder, CO: Westview Press, 1991), pp. 27, 43–4, 67, 125–6, 196–205; for Locke, see *The Second Treatise of Government* in *Two Treatises of Government*, ed. Peter Laslett (Cambridge: Cambridge University Press, 1960), §§13, 87–9, 123–31.
[32] Ewin, *Virtues and Rights*, op. cit., p. 32. The main theme of Ewin's work is the necessity of abandoning reliance on 'private' judgment to achieve cooperation.
[33] Kant, *Metaphysical Elements of Justice*, op. cit., p. 76 (§44).

umpire or judge is required to make public determinations of our rights and duties. Says Hobbes:

> And because, though men be never so willing to observe these laws [of nature], there may nevertheless arise questions concerning a man's actions; first, whether it were done, or not done; secondly, if done, whether against the law or not against the law; the former whereof, is called a question of fact; the latter a question of right, therefore unless the parties to the question, covenant mutually to stand to the sentence of another, they are as far from peace as ever. This other to whose sentence they submit is called an ARBITRATOR. And therefore, it is of the law of nature, that they that are at controversy, submit their right to the judgment of an arbitrator.[34]

The social contract theories of Hobbes, Locke, and Kant, first and foremost, are justifications of an 'arbitrator' (Hobbes), 'umpire' (Locke) or 'judge' (Kant) whose task is to provide public, definitive, resolutions of conflicting, reasonable judgments about the demands of justice.

6.4. According to Hobbes, Locke, and Kant, then, citizens committed to respecting each other and gaining the fruits of social cooperation require government just because of reasonable pluralism about the political. For Hobbes, Locke, and Kant our common human reason produces some conclusions that are beyond reasonable doubt; for Kant we all have reason to see that a regime of equal liberty is justified while for Locke it is beyond reasonable doubt that a just regime must respect and protect the rights to life, liberty and property. And, as I have said, they concur that reason instructs us to submit to an impartial judge to resolve our disputes about justice. Writes Kant:

> The postulate of public Law comes out of private Law in the state of nature. It says: If you are so situated as to be unavoidably side by side with others, you ought to abandon the state of nature and enter, with others, a juridical state of affairs, that is, a state of distributive legal justice.[35]

Conclusive reasoning, I have tried to show elsewhere, can take us somewhat further, specifying the broad procedures identified with the rule of law and constitutional democracy.[36] However, it will not take us much further. The realm of political is characterized by reasonable dispute because our judgments differ about the demands of justice and the interpretation of liberal principles and constitutional provisions.

[34] Hobbes, *Leviathan*, op. cit., p. 102 (ch. 15.) See Ewin, *Virtues and Rights*, op. cit., p. 34.
[35] Kant, *Metaphysical Elements of Justice*, op. cit., p. 71 (§42).
[36] See *Justificatory Liberalism*, op. cit., part II.

The crucial task of government, then, is to serve as an umpire, judge or arbitrator, providing a practical resolution of our reasonable disputes about justice. Umpiring is based on the suppositions that (1) there is intractable difference of opinion that calls for different courses of action; (2) to proceed with practice, there must be a practical resolution of the dispute about what to do; (3) this practical resolution about what to do need not be accepted by all the parties as being based on the correct or most reasonable judgment; however, (4) the authority of the umpire's practical decision requires that it does its best to arrive at the most reasonable answer. Citizens committed to ILL in a world of pluralism require precisely this sort of umpiring of their disputes. It honors their commitment to Individualized Liberal Legitimacy because they do not act coercively against another simply on the basis of their own controversial reasoning: all have conclusive reason to submit their dispute to the umpire, who provides an impartial practical resolution of the dispute.

The umpire's legitimate decision is, then, simply a reasonable judgment. Umpires are not sages who we suppose always give the best answer. It is not at all inconsistent with accepting the authority of an umpire to insist that your opinion is more reasonable than his. Rather, umpires are unique in that they alone have the authority to use coercion to support a reasonable, though contentious, interpretation of liberal principles. Note, then, that justificatory liberalism provides a coherent account supporting Rawls's observation that the judgment of public reason 'must at least be reasonable, if not the most reasonable' (PL: 246). Because of their intractable disputes about what is the most reasonable interpretation of publicly justified liberal principles, free and equal individuals would embrace an umpire who is empowered to act on its reasonable, but by no means conclusively correct, judgment about these matters.

This is important. Liberal legitimacy, Rawls and I have agreed, requires that coercion must be justified in a way that is not subject to reasonable objection; because of that the justification must be strongly reasonable – not subject to reasonable dissent or objection. But because of political pluralism, normal politics can, at its best, only claim to result in weakly reasonable conclusions; in Rawls's words, they are 'reasonable, if not the most reasonable' (§3.5). As we have seen, citizens can reasonably dissent from weakly reasonable laws and policies. The idea of liberal adjudication explains why the government can satisfy ILL, even though its results are only weakly reasonable. Because (1) we require a common answer on questions of justice, (2) we have conclusive reason to embrace an umpire, (3) we thus have conclusive reason to follow the directives of the umpire even though they are only weakly reasonable. In short, there is a strongly reasonable justification to follow the weakly reasonable decisions of the umpire.

6.5. Democracy, I have argued, can itself be understood as an umpiring mechanism.[37] In his or her deliberations each citizen presents what he or she believes is the best public justification; the voting mechanism constitutes a publicly justified way to adjudicate our deep disagreements about what is publicly justified. It does not seek political consensus, but reasoned debate about what is best justified, and procedures that do a tolerable job in tracking justification. Adjudicative democracy recognizes that the political is required just because even rough consensus is not a plausible political ideal.

Under an adjudicative conception of democracy, however, citizens are not free to draw willy-nilly on their reasonable beliefs so long as they do not violate constitutional constraints and the rights of others. In contrast to Rawls, who restricts public reason to constitutional essentials and matters of basic justice, all legitimate political deliberation must be an exercise of public reasoning. When proposing coercive laws citizens must advance arguments that they believe are the best interpretation of basic liberal principles. The telos of politics is not to allow citizens the opportunity to impose their contentious ideals of life on each other, but to adjudicate our inconclusive reasoning about the demands of justice. Liberal citizens accept an umpire because they need to impartially resolve their disputes about justice if they are to honor their commitment to the Principle of Individualized Liberal Legitimacy; they have, as Kant stressed, conclusive reason to submit these disputes to an umpire. However, they have no reason to submit their disputes about religion, ways of having sex, the good life or good beers to adjudication: on these matters it is entirely reasonable to object that no public judgment is required, and so the use of state power – even in the service of reasonable views – is illegitimate.

We must distinguish limiting and empowering conceptions of constitutionalism.[38] On the limiting conception of constitutional essentials, a constitution spells out limits to the government's rightful authority (the

---

[37] See ibid., chs. 13–15, and my 'Public Justification and Democratic Adjudication', *Constitutional Political Economy* 2 (1991), pp. 251–81.
[38] See further *Justificatory Liberalism*, op. cit., pp. 204–7.

model here is the United States Bill of Rights). A government is unjust if it enacts legislation that oversteps these bounds by, say, seeking to establish a religion or severely curtailing freedom of speech. On the limiting conception, however, as long as the government respects these constraints, its legislation is just: within the limits of the constitution, government (or, say, the majority) may do as it wishes. Justificatory liberalism and its allied notion of adjudicative democracy reject this conception of limited government. Instead, they advocate an empowering conception of constitutionalism: the constitution empowers government to act to interpret abstract, conclusively justified, principles of justice that we reasonably interpret differently. Unless these matters are adjudicated, we cannot live moralized lives meeting the requirement of Individualized Liberal Legitimacy. If an issue is not one on which the state is empowered to act, it is outside the bounds of political dispute.

7. Conclusion: Liberal Legitimacy, Reasonable Pluralism and the Domain of the Political

I have tried to show how, under Rawls's political liberalism, the domain of the political is a response to the reasonable pluralism of comprehensive doctrines: Rawls wishes it to provide a common point of view that allows the Principle of Liberal Legitimacy to be satisfied. However, I have insisted that (1) the domain of the political is itself characterized by reasonable pluralism and (2) Rawls does not, and I believe cannot, show how this reasonable pluralism is a distinctive political sort of pluralism that does not run afoul of LL, and so is not a worry for political liberalism.

Rawls, I believe, is correct in that there is conclusive rational consensus on the basic concept of a liberal regime, and the broad outlines of liberal principles. But consensus only characterizes liberal politics at the most abstract level. As in many other complex matters, the use of human reason under free institutions leads us to disagree. The political cannot be insulated from this, nor can the realm of public reason be convincingly constricted so as not to be affected by it. The contract theories of Hobbes, Locke and Kant are not tempted to understand the political as essentially the realm of shared judgment. For them the state's rationale is the reasonable pluralism of political judgment, and the need to provide practical resolution of our political differences. Because the pluralism of the political manifests our different interpretations of the demands of liberal justice, the political is constituted by a plurality of articulations of public reason, of citizens seeking to construct arguments to convince each other about the best interpretation of the demands of justice. As such, political pluralism is distinct from our wider pluralism of personal beliefs and values, which we have no compelling reason to submit to the authoritative judgment of the umpire.[39]

---

[39] This paper was originally presented at a conference on multiculturalism and moral objectivity, sponsored by the Ethics Priority Area, University of Oslo. I would like to thank the conference organizers, and in particular Professor Jon Wetlesen, for the opportunity to discuss these matters, and the conference participants for their helpful comments.

CHAPTER 2

On Justifying the Moral Rights of the Moderns
A Case of Old Wine in New Bottles*

1. Something Old, Something New

We are familiar with one divide between "old" and "new" liberalism – that between classical liberalism and social justice liberalism.[1] Although this divide between the old and the new is multifaceted, the crux is a debate about the place of the market, private property, and democracy in a liberal polity.[2] According to common wisdom, classical liberals insist on rights of the person against others and against a limited government, freedom of association, freedom of conscience, and a free market within a framework of laws against fraud and violence, laws enforcing contracts, and strong rights of private property, including robust rights of investment, exchange, and inheritance. Limited democracy is endorsed as a way to control government, but not as a source of fundamental norms. Social justice liberals, while endorsing traditional civil rights – for example, the freedoms of speech, press, and religion, rights against search and seizure, the right to a fair trial, privacy rights, equal protection of the laws, and, generally, liberties of the person – argue that justice fundamentally concerns the distribution of resources or that one's basic claims of justice are to

---

* Earlier versions of this essay were presented at the University of North Carolina, Chapel Hill, Philosophy Department workshop on the morality of capitalism, and at the conference on rights theory at the Murphy Institute, Tulane University. I am grateful for the comments of the participants; my special thanks to David Schmidtz, Julian Lamont, and Andrea Houchard for their useful written comments and suggestions.

[1] "Social justice liberalism" is more appropriate than either "welfare state liberalism" or "egalitarian liberalism." "Welfare state liberalism" is a misnomer since obvious members of this group – such as John Rawls – believe that the welfare state is inadequate. "Egalitarian liberalism" is inappropriate since "new liberals" such as L. T. Hobhouse were not egalitarians. All "new liberals," however, have been concerned with the idea of social justice. Hobhouse's *Elements of Social Justice* (London: Allen & Unwin, 1922) was one of the first books on the subject. On the division between the old and the new liberalism, see Michael Freeden, *The New Liberalism: An Ideology of Social Reform* (Oxford: Clarendon Press, 1978), and Freeden, *Liberalism Divided: A Study in British Political Thought, 1914–1939* (Oxford: Oxford University Press, 1986).

[2] See my essay "Liberalism at the End of the Century," *Journal of Political Ideologies* 5 (2000): 179–99.

resources that one needs or deserves. Thus, such liberals lay great stress on policies to alter the distribution of property, or to enforce social rights to assistance. Moreover, such liberals emphasize the role of democratic institutions in a liberal polity. Indeed, in recent years, social justice liberals such as John Rawls and his followers have declared themselves to be "deliberative democrats," who value political participation rights equally with civil liberties.[3] While of course inadequate, this familiar stylized contrast between classical liberalism and social justice liberalism captures a good deal of the truth.[4]

Michael Freeden, a contemporary political theorist, has drawn our attention to another interesting contrast between old and new conceptions of liberalism.[5] Freeden plausibly argues that liberal thinking – especially in the United States – has become increasingly the domain of abstract and technical philosophy since, say, the publication of Rawls's *A Theory of Justice* in 1971. Freeden unfavorably compares this new philosophical liberalism to older conceptions of liberalism that were widely accessible and firmly grounded in actual political practice. An upshot of the shift to the terrain of abstract philosophy is, I think, that many theories explicate the requirements of liberalism in an increasingly idealized, indeed often utopian, way. Liberalism is said to require implementation of a fully egalitarian society, or a society with the highest possible minimum income for all, or perhaps some version of market socialism. Although most of the interesting work in this new, highly philosophic approach to liberalism has been by advocates of social justice liberalism,[6] the approach has also been employed by classical liberals and libertarians, offering highly philosophical and abstract arguments based on intuitions about Lockean property rights,

[3] See John Rawls, *Political Liberalism*, paperback ed. (New York: Columbia University Press, 1996), 413. This is often put in terms of the contrast between the "liberty of the ancients and of the moderns": I consider this contrast further in Section VII.D. Originally, Rawls insisted that civil rights were more important than political participation rights, but he came to revise his views. On Rawls's changing views, see note 105. Rawls declares himself to be a "deliberative democrat" in Rawls, "The Idea of Public Reason Revisited," *University of Chicago Law Review* 64 (Summer 1997): 764–807, at 772; reprinted in John Rawls, *The Law of Peoples* (Cambridge, MA: Harvard University Press, 1999), and in Samuel Freeman, ed., *John Rawls: Collected Papers* (Cambridge, MA: Harvard University Press, 1999), chap. 26.

[4] I have considered the differences between the old and the new liberalism in a more nuanced way in my essay "Public and Private Interests in Liberal Political Economy, Old and New," in S. I. Benn and G. F. Gaus, eds., *Public and Private in Social Life* (New York: St. Martin's Press, 1983), 183–222.

[5] See Michael Freeden, *Ideologies and Political Theory: A Conceptual Approach* (Oxford: Clarendon Press, 1996), chap. 6.

[6] See, for example, Ronald Dworkin, *Sovereign Virtue* (Cambridge, MA: Harvard University Press, 2000); and Philippe Van Parijs, *Real Freedom for All* (Oxford: Oxford University Press, 1995).

unlimited rights of self-ownership, and hypothetical histories.[7] This new variety of liberal theory can be contrasted to the older and more accessible accounts of liberalism presented by public intellectuals such as Herbert Spencer, Liberal Party intellectuals such as L. T. Hobhouse (in his famous little book *Liberalism*, published in 1911), or even philosophers such as John Stuart Mill (in *On Liberty*, 1859). All of these were British, but even earlier Americans such as John Dewey in his *Liberalism and Social Action* (1935) presented fairly simple and concise statements of liberal principles that were accessible to most educated members of the public.[8] In the hands of these political theorists, liberalism still looked to be a practical political program rather than a technical and highly idealized philosophic construction.

I believe that there is something right and enlightening about Freeden's version of the "old" and "new" divide, although of course it must be highly qualified. Liberalism has traditionally been a radical doctrine; criticizing the current order and presenting idealized proposals is part and parcel of the liberal tradition. Liberals are often radicals. And, of course, liberal theories were sometimes abstract and technical long before Rawls and the rise of academic liberalism in the United States. The nineteenth-century British philosopher T. H. Green, whose liberalism inspired Hobhouse and others, based his political theory on a version of absolute idealism drawn from G. W. F. Hegel, as abstruse a philosophical doctrine as one is apt to encounter.[9] Still, Freeden has an important insight. If one reads Hobhouse's *Liberalism*, or Dewey's *Liberalism and Social Action* (or, I should add, Isaiah Berlin's "Two Concepts of Liberty"),[10] one encounters a very different genre of liberal theorizing from that found in current philosophy journals and books. While there have always been both genres, I think it is fair to say that today liberalism's center of gravity is in the academy and, especially, in philosophy departments.

---

[7] I have in mind, of course, Robert Nozick, *Anarchy, State, and Utopia* (New York: Basic Books, 1974).

[8] See Herbert Spencer, "From Freedom to Bondage," in Spencer, *The Man Versus the State, with Six Essays on Government, Society, and Freedom* (Indianapolis: Liberty Fund, 1982), 487–518; L. T. Hobhouse, *Liberalism* (London: Oxford University Press, 1911); J. S. Mill, *On Liberty* (1859), in John Gray, ed., *On Liberty and Other Essays* (New York: Oxford University Press, 1991); and John Dewey, *Liberalism and Social Action* (1935; New York: G. P. Putnam's Sons, 1980).

[9] I should note that, in the hands of British philosophers such as Green, this theory was certainly more intelligible than in its original German version.

[10] Isaiah Berlin, "Two Concepts of Liberty" (1958), in Berlin, *Four Essays on Liberty* (Oxford: Oxford University Press, 1969).

The movement from the older, more practical and accessible approach, to the newer, more academic and philosophical approach to liberal theorizing has been a mixed good. In my view, a clear deficit is the plethora of opposed moral blueprints for social institutions, each insisting that departures from its ideal scheme render existing institutions unjust and illegitimate. We now have before us libertarian theories based on self-ownership and rights to initial acquisition (telling us that nearly any redistribution of market outcomes is illegitimate);[11] left-libertarian theories also supportive of a conception of self-ownership but often upholding intuitions about the common ownership of the earth (telling us that extensive redistribution of market outcomes is mandatory for justice);[12] desert-based theories of various types (some insisting on the necessity of strong private ownership rights, and others upholding strongly redistributive policies);[13] neo-Kantian theories (some supporting welfare-state rights to well-being, others leaning toward libertarianism);[14] theories upholding an equal distribution of resources (or welfare, or basic capabilities) which challenge strong ownership rights while embracing some version of the market;[15] and neo-Hobbesian accounts (some defending robust private property rights, others upholding a right to welfare).[16] As a rule, these theories worry very little about connecting up with actual social practices except insofar as the author supposes that his moral intuitions are widespread. It is a caricature – but not an entirely unfair one – to depict all this as the activity of philosophers, ensconced in their ivory towers, instructing everyone as to the system of morality and politics that is clearly demanded by rational reflection, yet talking in a babble of conflicting voices. Yet the movement to rigorous philosophical analysis has had great payoffs. A contemporary reader cannot help but be struck by the vagueness and,

---

[11] See, for example, Nozick, *Anarchy, State, and Utopia*; and Eric Mack, "Self-Ownership and the Right of Property," *The Monist* 73 (October 1990): 519–43. For an overview, see Eric Mack and Gerald F. Gaus, "Classical Liberalism and Libertarianism," in Gerald F. Gaus and Chandran Kukathas, eds., *Handbook of Political Theory* (London: Sage, 2004): 115–30.

[12] See Hillel Steiner and Peter Vallentyne, eds., *Left-Libertarianism and Its Critics* (Basingstoke: Palgrave, 2000).

[13] For the former, see my *Social Philosophy* (Armonk, NY: M. E. Sharpe, 1999), chap. 9; for the latter, see Julian Lamont, "Incentive Income, Deserved Income, and Economic Rents," *Journal of Political Philosophy* 5 (1997): 26–46.

[14] For the former, see Alan Gewirth, *Reason and Morality* (Chicago: University of Chicago Press, 1981); for the latter, see Marcus Verhaegh, "Kant and Property Rights," *Journal of Libertarian Studies* 18 (Summer 2004): 11–32.

[15] See esp. Dworkin, *Sovereign Virtue*, but there are a host of others who take this view.

[16] For the former, see David Gauthier, *Morals by Agreement* (Oxford: Clarendon Press, 1986); for the latter, see Gregory Kavka, *Hobbesian Moral and Political Theory* (Princeton, NJ: Princeton University Press, 1986).

one can only say, sloppiness of the analyses of Hobhouse's *Liberalism*, Dewey's *Liberalism and Social Action*, or the works of Spencer. Even John Locke's *Second Treatise of Government* does not fare well by the standards of current argument. Our understandings of liberty, justice, equality, and the nature of public reasoning in a diverse society have improved immensely.

As I said, it is tempting to lay both the praise and the blame – if blame is appropriate – for the development of this more philosophical brand of liberal theorizing at Rawls's feet. Rawls's thinking, though, is always more complex than it first appears, and almost always more subtle than those whom he inspired. Rawls, we must remember, developed his philosophical liberalism into a political one where the overriding concern was meshing philosophical analysis with social facts. According to Rawls:

> [E]ven if by some convincing philosophical argument – at least convincing to us and a few like-minded others – we could trace the right to private or social property back to first principles or to basic rights, there is a good reason for working out a conception of justice which does not do this. For . . . the aim of justice as fairness as a political conception is to resolve the impasse in the democratic tradition as to the way in which social institutions are to be arranged if they are to conform to the freedom and equality of citizens as moral persons. Philosophical argument alone is most unlikely to convince either side that the other is correct on a question like that of private or social property in the means of production. It is more fruitful to look for bases of agreement implicit in the public culture of a democratic society and therefore in its underlying conceptions of the person and of social cooperation.[17]

Rawls presents us with a paradox. His work was a major impetus to developing abstract theories of distributive justice, and he himself insists that his own rather abstract philosophical theory demonstrates that both laissez-faire and welfare-state capitalism are unjustifiable.[18] However, he insists that "convincing philosophical argument" grounding a justification of capitalism on basic rights is not the right way to go about developing a conception of justice. If we accept this latter idea, much recent liberal political philosophy – whether endorsing classical or social justice liberalism – rests on a mistake: even if its abstract arguments are sound, they cannot achieve their ends.

---

[17] Rawls, *Political Liberalism*, 338–39.
[18] John Rawls, *Justice as Fairness: A Restatement*, ed. Erin Kelly (Cambridge, MA: Belknap Press of Harvard University Press, 2001), 136ff.

In this essay, I sketch a philosophical conception of liberal morality that stays true to Rawls's complex insight: although abstract philosophical argument alone cannot resolve our moral differences, careful philosophical reasoning is necessary to see our way to a resolution. Thus, I shall argue, we can develop a "new" (qua philosophical) liberalism that takes existing social facts and mores seriously while, at the same time, retaining the critical edge characteristic of the liberal tradition. However, pace Rawls, I shall argue that once we develop such an account, we are led toward a vindication of "old" (qua classical) liberal morality. Hence the old (vintage) wine in the new, more Rawlsian bottles.

Section II begins by sketching the basis for the claim that liberal principles must be "publicly justified" – justified to everyone. Section III argues that our deep disagreements about the proper standards of evaluation pose a challenge to all attempts at public justification. Sections IV through VI analyze methods for publicly justifying a morality under these conditions of disagreement on evaluative standards. Section VII then argues that the morality that is justified under these conditions is not the social justice/deliberative democratic liberalism of Rawls, but closer to what Benjamin Constant called the "liberty of the moderns."[19]

2. Public Justification among Free and Equal Moral Persons

2.1 Free and Equal Moral Persons

I take as my starting point the supposition that we conceive of ourselves and others as (1) moral persons who are (2) free and equal. Although these features are assumed in this essay, we should not suppose that these assumptions cannot themselves be defended. Rawls rightly argues that this general conception of moral persons is implicit in our public culture.[20] In much the same vein, I have argued that our commitment to the public justification of our moral demands on each other follows from our conception of ourselves and others as such persons.[21] Let me briefly explain each of these fundamental ideas: (i) moral personality, (ii) free moral persons, and (iii) equal moral persons.

---

[19] See Benjamin Constant, "The Liberty of the Ancients Compared with That of the Moderns," in Constant, *Political Writings*, ed. Biancamaria Fontana (Cambridge: Cambridge University Press, 1988), 308–28.

[20] See John Rawls, "Kantian Constructivism in Moral Theory," in Freeman, ed., *John Rawls: Collected Papers*, 303–58, esp. 305ff. This is not to say that Rawls and I advance precisely the same conception of free and equal moral persons, as will become clear in what follows.

[21] See my *Value and Justification* (Cambridge: Cambridge University Press, 1990), 278ff.

(i)　A moral person is one who makes, and can act upon, moral demands. Moral persons thus conceive of themselves as advancing moral claims on others and being subject to such claims. Alternatively, we can say that moral persons understand themselves as owed, and owing, certain restraints and acts.[22] Not all humans – not even all functioning adult humans – are moral persons: psychopaths do not appear to understand themselves as pressing moral claims on others that demand respect, nor do they see others as moral persons.[23] As well as advancing moral claims, moral persons have the capability to act on justified moral claims made on them. In this sense, moral persons are not solely devoted to their own ends; they have a capacity to put aside their personal ends and goals to act on justified moral claims. Moral persons, then, are not simply instrumentally rational agents;[24] they possess a capacity for moral autonomy. Insofar as moral autonomy presupposes the ability to distinguish one's own ends from the moral claims of others, the idea of a moral person presupposes some cognitive skills.[25]

(ii)　In the Second Treatise, Locke held that "[t]he natural liberty of man is to be free from any superior power on earth, and not to be under the will or legislative authority of man, but to have only the law of Nature for his rule."[26] To conceive of oneself as morally free is to understand oneself as free from any natural moral authority that would accord others status to dictate one's moral obligations. This is not at all to say that one sees oneself as unbound by any external morality. Locke thought we have the law of nature as our rule. Although we are by no means committed to a natural-law conception of morality, the crucial point, again one in the spirit of Locke, is that free moral persons call on their own reason when determining the dictates of moral law. A free person employs her own standards of evaluation when presented with claims about her moral liberties

---

[22] See J. R. Lucas, *On Justice* (Oxford: Clarendon Press, 1980), 7. For a development of this conception of morality, see Thomas Scanlon, *What We Owe Each Other* (Cambridge, MA: Belknap Press of Harvard University Press, 1998), esp. 177ff. On this view, interpersonal claims are the crux of morality, though, of course, such claims need not be explicitly advanced: a moral person "makes claims on herself" in the sense that she accepts as reasons for actions the rights of others, and she acts on these reasons without prompting.

[23] I argue this in *Value and Justification*, 281ff.　　　[24] See Rawls, *Political Liberalism*, 51.

[25] I argue for this claim in "The Place of Autonomy in Liberalism," in John Christman and Joel Rogers, eds., *Autonomy and the Challenges to Liberalism* (Cambridge: Cambridge University Press, 2005), 272–306.

[26] John Locke, *Second Treatise of Government*, in Locke, *Two Treatises of Government*, ed. Peter Laslett (Cambridge: Cambridge University Press, 1960), sec. 21.

and obligations. A free person, we can say, has an interest in living in ways that accord with her own standards of value and goodness. At a minimum, to conceive of oneself as a morally free person is to see oneself as bound only by moral requirements that can be validated from one's own point of view; it is not necessarily to view morality as one's creation or the result of one's will or choice.[27]

(iii) To say that moral persons are equal is to claim, first, that qua moral persons they possess the minimum requisite moral personality so that they are equal participants in the moral enterprise and, second, that each is equally morally free insofar as no one is subjected to the moral authority of others. The equality of moral persons is their equality qua free moral persons: it is not a substantive principle of moral equality but a presupposition of the practice of moral justification insofar as it defines the status of the participants in moral justification. While this is a modest conception of moral equality, it rules out some conceptions of moral justification. Rawls not only conceives of moral persons as advancing claims against each other, but stresses that they view themselves as "self-authenticating sources of valid claims."[28] It would seem, and apparently Rawls agrees, that those who understand themselves as authenticating their own claims would not see themselves as bound to justify their claims against others to those others – they would not suppose that only claims justified to others are valid.[29] To advance a self-authenticating claim against others, however, is not to respect their moral freedom, for others are bound only by moral claims that they can validate through their own reason. The supposition of equal moral freedom thus requires that one's moral claims be validated by those to whom they are addressed.

Many have advanced stronger conceptions of moral equality. Some have claimed, for example, that the very practice of morality presupposes an

---

[27] It also provides the basis for understanding morality as self-legislated. I develop this idea further in "The Place of Autonomy in Liberalism."

[28] Rawls, *Justice as Fairness*, 23. The importance of the idea of self-authentication is easily overlooked in Rawls's thinking. It first appeared in his 1951 paper "Outline of a Decision Procedure for Ethics," which conceived of ethics as adjudicating the claims of individuals, which he clearly saw as self-authenticating. See section 5 of that paper, in Freeman, ed., *John Rawls: Collected Papers*, chap. 1.

[29] Hence, because of this, parties to Rawls's original position are not required to advance justifications for their claims. Rawls argues this in "Kantian Constructivism," 334.

"equal right of each to be treated only with justification."[30] In a similar vein, S. I. Benn and R. S. Peters, in their classic political theory text, defended the principle that "[t]he onus of justification rests on whoever would make distinctions ... Presume equality until there is a reason to presume otherwise."[31] Benn and Peters' principle does not simply require us to justify our moral claims to others: it requires us to justify all our actions that disadvantage some others. Leaving aside whether some such presumptive egalitarian principle could be morally justified,[32] this conception of moral equality is not presupposed by the very idea of a justified morality among free and equal moral persons. If I accept this principle, I claim that others act wrongly if they disadvantage me without good justification. But unless this nondiscriminatory principle itself can be validated by others, I disrespect their moral freedom, as I am making a moral claim on them to non-discriminatory action that is not validated by their own reason.

Validation from the rational and reflective perspective of another, however, is not the same as her actual consent. To treat another as a free and equal moral person is to accept that moral claims must be validated from her perspective when she rationally reflects upon them. Now, although, as Mill noted, there is a strong presumption that each knows her own perspective best, this is not necessarily so.[33] Just as others can make sound judgments about a person's beliefs and principles, and can be correct even when the person disagrees, so can others be correct, and the moral agent wrong, about what is validated from her perspective. Knowledge of oneself is generally superior to others' knowledge of one, but it is not indefeasible. People may withhold assent for a variety of reasons, including strategic objectives, pigheadedness, confusion, manifestly false beliefs, neurosis, and so on. Nevertheless, respect for the equal moral freedom of another requires that the presumption in favor of

[30] Hadley Arkes, *First Things: An Inquiry into the First Principles of Morals and Justice* (Princeton, NJ: Princeton University Press, 1986), 70; italics omitted. Compare Ted Honderich: "To have a liberty in the relevant sense, whatever else it comes to be, is to act in a way that has recommendation or justification. You have to have a right." On this view, one may only act if one has a justified claim on others to allow one to act. Ted Honderich, *After the Terror* (Edinburgh: Edinburgh University Press, 2002), 45.

[31] S. I. Benn and R. S. Peters, *Social Principles and the Democratic State* (London: George Allen & Unwin, 1959), 110.

[32] I argue that it cannot in *Justificatory Liberalism* (New York: Oxford University Press, 1996), 162ff.

[33] Mill, *On Liberty*, 84–85 (chap. IV, para. 4). Mill also was aware that this assumption does not always hold true. See his *Principles of Political Economy*, in J. M. Robson, ed., *The Collected Works of John Stuart Mill* (Toronto: University of Toronto Press, 1963), vols. II and III, 947 (bk. V, chap. xi, sec. 9).

self-knowledge only be overridden given strong reasons supporting the conclusion that she has misunderstood what is validated from her own point of view. Suppose that Alf and Betty reasonably disagree about whether some moral principle P is validated from Betty's rational perspective. Say that Alf has good reasons to conclude that Betty has misunderstood what is validated from her point of view: P, he says, really is validated from her point of view. Betty, we suppose, has reason to insist it isn't. For Alf to insist that his merely reasonable view of Betty's commitments overrides her own reasonable understanding of her moral perspective constitutes a violation of her moral freedom, since Alf is claiming authority to override Betty's own reasonable understanding of her moral commitments with his merely reasonable view.[34] Of course, just where to draw the line between a person's reasonable and unreasonable understandings of her commitments is difficult (I have spent more than a few pages trying to do so).[35] The core idea though, is not obscure. As Jeffrey Reiman argues in his account of justice, when one person's judgment prevails over another's, there is always the suspicion of "subjugation," which Reiman defines as "any case in which the judgment of one person prevails over the contrary judgment of another simply because it can and thus without adequate justification." To "dispel" this suspicion, we must be able to show that our judgment is valid "beyond reasonable doubt."[36]

2.2 *The Principle of Public Justification*

Given the requirements for treating others as free and equal moral persons, the task of publicly justifying a moral principle P requires that P be validated from the perspective of each (sufficiently) reasonable free and equal moral person. To publicly justify a moral principle is to justify it to all reasonable free and equal moral persons within some public, who confront each other as strangers.[37] I shall assume that the relevant public here is something like a society; we could also define the public in terms of all persons (a universalistic cosmopolitan morality) or a smaller community. As our main concern is with morality insofar as it relates to political justice, focusing on the notion of a society's morality is appropriate.

---

[34] I deal with this complex question more formally in *Justificatory Liberalism*, parts I and II.
[35] See ibid. and *Value and Justification*, 399–404.
[36] Jeffrey Reiman, *Justice and Modern Moral Philosophy* (New Haven, CT: Yale University Press, 1990), 1–2.
[37] On the concept of the public, see S. I. Benn and G. F. Gaus, "The Liberal Conception of the Public and Private," in Benn and Gaus, eds., *Public and Private in Social Life*, 31–66.

(Moreover, as we shall see, there is some reason to think that societies, broadly conceived, may possess justified moral codes in a way that mankind does not. Should it be the case, however, that cosmopolitan morality is similar to the morality I defend in the later sections of this essay, the restriction may not be significant.)

I have employed the unfamiliar idea of "validating" a principle. Validating is, I think, especially appropriate in this context. To validate a moral principle P is to exercise one's authority to inspect P and confirm that it meets the relevant requirements (as when a visa is validated). Validation is not voluntaristic in the way that consent is, or "acceptance" or "rejection" might be taken to be. Validation first involves substantive requirements: to be valid, P must meet the test of respecting others' rational natures – there must be a conclusive reason justifying P. (What else could respecting others' rational natures require, other than providing them with reasons?) But validation is not simply a matter of in fact meeting the requirements – of there being a reason for P. It requires that this fact be confirmed by one who has the authority to do so. Surely, to respect the free moral and rational natures of others is to provide them with conclusive considerations for P that can be seen as such by them insofar as they are reasonable; given that we are free and equal, each of us alone has the moral authority to confirm principles binding him- or herself. If Alf appeals to P, and Betty, a free and equal rational moral person, cannot see how she has adequate reason to accept P, then Alf is not respecting her as a free and equal rational moral person if he nonetheless insists that she does have good reason to accept P and thus is morally required to abide by P. Alf's understanding of the demands of reason cannot trump Betty's reasonable understanding if he is to respect her as a free and equal rational moral person. To be more precise, let us work with the following understanding of public justification:

> P is a bona fide moral principle only if each reasonable free and equal moral person would, upon presentation of P, validate it.

According to this understanding of public justification, to possess a bona fide moral claim does not require that everyone has already validated it, and this is the case for two reasons. (i) A bona fide moral claim only requires the validation of reasonable, not actual, moral persons. (ii) Public justification conceives of moral claims as carrying the guarantee that they can be justified to reasonable others, even if these justifications have not yet actually been presented. This, I think, points the way to a plausible version of what Rawls calls "the proviso."[38] Principles that meet the test of public justification are publicly justified principles.

3. The Problem of Evaluative Diversity

An obvious point of departure in publicly justifying moral principles would be to identify some "conception of the good" – involving a systematic relation of the various goods – that is shared by each free and equal moral person in the relevant public.[39] However, it seems most unlikely that free and equal moral persons share any such "comprehensive" understandings of the good or of value.[40] Contemporary liberal theory has stressed the reasonable pluralism that obtains about such comprehensive understandings of value or of the good. Pluralism about the good poses obvious problems for public justification, such as when my comprehensive understanding of value leads me to endorse P on the grounds that P promotes V1, and you deny that V1 is a value; V2, you say, is correct, and it does not validate P. This may not entirely preclude public justification, as we might still converge on P' because it promotes both V1 and V2.[41] Still, the difficulties in appealing to such comprehensive systems of value in the justification of moral claims is formidable in a society characterized by deep-seated reasonable differences about what makes life worth living. In any event, I shall put aside this well-discussed problem of clear value disagreement, and consider the problems raised by the case in which we all concur on the normative considerations that justify moral claims. This is not to say that I deny that sometimes our evaluative standards simply clash; however, I wish to stress that even if we share evaluative standards, the problem of evaluative diversity remains.

Suppose we disaggregate conceptions of the good, or systems of value, into their component goods, values, and other normative principles. Even though we do not share full-blown systems of values, we do share many specific values, such as the good of bodily integrity, the good of personal resources, and the good of health; we also share moral "intuitions," such as the wrongness of inflicting gratuitous pain on others. Abstracting from the

---

[38] John Rawls, "The Idea of Public Reason Revisited," *University of Chicago Law Review* 64 (Summer 1997): 764–807, pp. 783–84.
[39] Henceforth, the clause "in the relevant public" will be assumed.
[40] I focus on this problem in *Contemporary Theories of Liberalism: Public Reason as a Post-Enlightenment Project* (London: Sage, 2003). See also my *Social Philosophy*, chap. 3.
[41] On convergence as a mode of justification, see Fred D'Agostino, *Free Public Reason: Making It Up As We Go* (New York: Oxford University Press, 1996), 30–31.

notions of goods, values, moral "intuitions," and so on, let us provisionally say that S is an evaluative standard for moral person Alf if and only if holding S is relevant to the validation of a candidate moral principle given Alf's rational point of view.[42] Evaluative standards, then, are to be distinguished from publicly justified moral principles. Now assume that everyone in the relevant public holds S1 and the relevant beliefs about the world such that P1 is validated in the perspective of everyone.

Thus, P1 is publicly justified. Assume further that the same holds for S2 and P2: everyone shares S2 as a normative standard, and everyone shares the relevant beliefs that validate P2. It would seem that the project of public justification is well under way. However, as Fred D'Agostino, a philosopher of social sciences, recently has shown, so long as individuals order S1 and S2 differently, the real problems for public justification remain unresolved.[43] If Alf's ranking is S1 > S2 (read as "S1 is ranked above S2"), while Betty maintains that S2 > S1, then if the degree of justification of the moral claims is monotonic with the ranking of normative standards,[44] Alf will hold P1 > P2, while Betty will maintain P2 > P1. Thus, in an N-person society in which everyone holds all the same normative standards and relevant beliefs, we can still get N rankings of moral principles.

Many believe that a morality requires priority rules.[45] If so, this problem of plurality of rankings is indeed an obstacle to the public justification of a morality. To some extent, perhaps, the necessity of priority rules has been exaggerated. As the great moral theorist W. D. Ross argued, our moral knowledge is about moral principles; the correct way to order the principles in cases where more than one is applicable is, for Ross, a matter of practical judgment about which people will often disagree.[46] Perhaps in many matters of private life it would be enough to agree on moral

---

[42] I leave aside here whether S is itself a belief about the world, as ethical naturalists would have it. It is important to stress that nothing in my account precludes moral realism as a metaethical or metaphysical thesis; the epistemic constraint on moral reasons is the crucial principle on which the analysis rests.

[43] See Fred D'Agostino, *Incommensurability and Commensuration: The Common Denominator* (Aldershot, Hampshire: Ashgate, 2003). I draw upon D'Agostino's insightful analysis throughout Sections III–V and in Section VII. I consider these issues in a different way in "Liberal Neutrality: A Radical and Compelling Principle," in Steven Wall and George Klosko, eds., *Perfectionism and Neutrality: Essays in Liberal Theory* (Lanham, MD: Rowman & Littlefield, 2003), 136–65, 156ff.

[44] This is to say that the normative standard passes on a degree of justification commensurate with its ranking within a perspective.

[45] See Kurt Baier, "The Point of View of Morality," *Australasian Journal of Philosophy* 32 (1954): 104–35.

[46] W. D. Ross, *The Right and the Good* (Oxford: Clarendon Press, 1930), 27ff.

principles, accepting that priority judgments will vary from person to person. Even this, though, is a cause for some concern, as our account indicates not simply that we disagree about the proper weighting of the principles in specific cases, but that there simply is no publicly justified weighting.

Because so many issues of public morality require not only the justification of a set of moral claims, but some priority rules, we require some way to publicly commensurate individual evaluative standards to arrive at a public ordering of moral claims. The problem, then, is this: A public ranking of moral principle P1 over P2 is obviously justified only if the evaluative standards (and sound beliefs) of each rational and reflective moral person give her good reason to rank P1 over P2.[47] Given reasonable evaluative diversity, this, I conjecture, will seldom occur (which is not to say it will never occur; see Sections V and VI). Indeed, empirical research indicates that the main source of value conflicts among Americans lies in their rankings. According to Milton Rokeach, a psychologist, Americans agree in affirming a set of thirty-six values; what they differ on is "the way they organize them to form value hierarchies or priorities."[48] Our disputes are not generally about what is good, but what is better. And given that all action has opportunity costs – doing one thing means forgoing others – disputes about what is more important result in endemic disagreement about what to do.

The problem of disagreement about public morality arising out of an agreement in evaluative standards is even more daunting than I have depicted it. I assumed above that each claim is to be validated by a single evaluative standard (along with relevant beliefs). More realistically, we must allow that, in each individual's perspective, a number of evaluative standards contribute to the validation of a moral principle. Thus, even if we all agree on the same set of evaluative standards and relevant beliefs, and all agree what standards are relevant to the validation of a specific moral claim, we may not all validate any specific moral claim. To see this, suppose that both S1 and S2 are relevant to the justification of P-type

---

[47] This is too simple. A consistent system of trade-off rates between P1 and P2 need not, and most plausibly will not, be a simple priority according to which the satisfaction of P1, in any circumstance, is ranked above the satisfaction of P2. I focus on this idea in "Why All Welfare States (Including Laissez-Faire Ones) Are Unreasonable," *Social Philosophy and Policy* 15, no. 2 (1998): 1–33. However, the more complicated analysis would only reinforce the point of the text: different sets of rational evaluative criteria will endorse different trade-off rates.

[48] See Milton Rokeach, *The Nature of Human Values* (New York: The Free Press, 1973), 110; Milton Rokeach, "From Individual to Institutional Values," in Rokeach, *Understanding Values* (London: Collier Macmillan, 1979), 208.

Table 2.1. *Condorcet paradox rankings*

Alf	Betty	Charlie
P_1	P_2	P_3
P_2	P_3	P_1
P_3	P_1	P_2

principles. If Alf's ranking is $S_1 > S_2$, while Betty's is $S_2 > S_1$, then Alf may validate P' while Betty validates P''. Thus, the initial problem in justifying priority rules becomes a problem of justifying any principle or claim when it is validated by multiple evaluative standards.

4. Two Flawed Responses to Evaluative Diversity

Given the assumption of evaluative diversity, how might we endeavor to publicly justify some ranking of principles? Following Rawls, we might suppose a deliberative setting of rational and reflective moral persons evaluating proposed moral principles according to their evaluative criteria; what such people would all accept shows what is publicly justified.[49] To fix ideas, suppose that three reasonable moral persons are deliberating about how to rank three moral principles (assume for now that the evaluative perspective of each person provides some reason to accept all three principles). Their rankings are summarized in Table 2.1. Can any social ranking be justified to all three individuals?

4.1   Aggregation

Let us first consider the familiar process of collective (aggregative) commensuration: Suppose that in our deliberative setting we seek to develop some aggregation procedure that takes, as inputs, each reasonable free and equal moral person's ranking of proposed moral principles (based on his or her own evaluative standards) and generates, as outputs, a publicly justified ordering of moral principles. Now, ex hypothesi, the procedure we develop must also pass the test of public justification; moreover, the problem of evaluative diversity resulting in different rankings of principles must not

[49] "Understood in this way the question of justification is settled by working out a problem of deliberation: we have to ascertain which principles it would be rational to adopt given the contractual situation." John Rawls, *A Theory of Justice*, revised ed. (Cambridge, MA: Belknap Press of Harvard University Press, 1999), 16.

reproduce itself as a rational diversity in rankings of aggregation procedures. Given that all see themselves as equal moral persons, we might think that some aggregation procedure reflecting "one person, one vote" might be employed in our deliberative setting to decide on the publicly justified ordering of principles. The hitch, of course, is that the aggregation procedure itself must be justified, and our disputes about the rankings of principles will reproduce themselves as disputes about the rankings of procedures.[50] No candidate aggregation procedure would be ranked best by each. As we know from Arrow's theorem and related work on collective choice rules, reasonable objections can be brought against every procedure for ranking three or more options, or indeed every procedure for choosing from a set of three or more options. As Kenneth Arrow showed, given a social choice over three or more options (with two or more people choosing), there is no aggregation method that (1) is guaranteed to produce a complete and transitive social ordering and (2) meets a set of reasonable conditions.[51] Although some proponents of collective decision-making seek to dismiss the relevance of Arrow's theorem,[52] it clearly undermines any claim that there is an uncontroversial way to commensurate all diverse rankings by developing an aggregation method that rationally and fairly transforms individual rankings into a publicly justified social ranking. There are a number of such methods, but all are flawed, and there is no reason to suppose that rational and reflective people will converge on one. Moreover, equally reasonable, flawed procedures can

---

[50] As Robert Nozick reminds us: "When sincere and good persons differ, we are prone to think they must accept some procedure to decide their differences, some procedure they both agree to be reliable and fair. Here we see the possibility that this disagreement may extend all the way up the ladder of procedures." *Anarchy, State, and Utopia,* 98.

[51] The conditions are these: (1) Universal domain: There is a social ordering for every possible set of individual preference profiles. (2) Monotonicity: An individual's changing her evaluation from {y is better than x} to {x is better than y} cannot itself make x socially less preferred than y. (3) Nonimposition: The social ordering is always a function of individual orderings. (4) Pareto optimality: If everyone prefers x over y, the social ordering ranks x over y. (5) Independence of irrelevant alternatives: The social preference between x and y must depend only on individuals' preferences between x and y, and cannot be affected by the presence or absence of some third alternative, z. (6) Nondictatorship: There is no person whose individual ordering over every pair of options is decisive for the social ordering. See William Riker, *Liberalism Against Populism* (Prospect Heights, IL: Waveland Press, 1988). I evaluate Riker's criticisms of democracy in my essay "Does Democracy Reveal the Will of the People? Four Takes on Rousseau," *Australasian Journal of Philosophy* 75 (June 1997): 141–62. For an analysis more nuanced than Riker's, see Dennis Mueller, *Public Choice III* (Cambridge: Cambridge University Press, 2003). For Arrow's own version, see Kenneth Arrow, *Social Choice and Individual Values,* 2d ed. (New Haven, CT: Yale University Press, 1963).

[52] John Dryzek, for example, rejects most of Riker's analysis; see Dryzek, "Democratic Theory," in Gaus and Kukathas, eds., *Handbook of Political Theory,* 143–54.

produce different results, so the choice of aggregation procedure really does matter.[53] Table 2.1 depicts Condorcet's famous set of paradox orderings, in which pairwise majority choice between the options (options are considered in pairs, with majority vote deciding which of the pair is the social preference) results in an intransitive social ordering ($P1 > P2 > P3 > P1$). Thus, rational individual rankings yield an irrational social ranking: Arrow's theorem can be understood as a generalization of this result to all plausible aggregation procedures. More generally, the chaotic characteristics of aggregation procedures such as voting show that their outcomes can be highly unstable. As Donald G. Saari, a mathematician, observes: "*Beware!* Beware of aggregation procedures because, in an unexpected manner, they allow unanticipated behavior."[54]

This is not to say that we are never warranted in relying on democratic procedures to resolve disputes. Given the background justification of moral and political principles, it may well be that at some point we have disagreements that we all have reason to believe must be resolved, and no procedure for resolving them is better than democracy. However, no aggregation procedure is intrinsically fair, stable, and reliable; whatever the merits of aggregation procedures, they are highly objectionable as ways to produce a justified, rational social choice of basic moral principles out of diverse individual orderings.

4.2   Elimination (or Idealization)

Arrow's theorem relies on the assumption that the aggregation procedure must successfully operate for all possible individual rankings: the procedure must work for every permutation of the options. One way to respond to Arrow's theorem is, to use D'Agostino's term, "elimination": we disallow some rankings so that the paradoxical social choice implied by Table 2.1 does not occur.[55] Elimination of troublesome evaluative standards might be achieved by idealizing our deliberative moral persons so that they have "correct" evaluative systems, which thus limit the possible orderings of proposed moral principles. Thus, we might suppose that all rational and reflective moral persons have the sort of evaluative systems

---

[53] This point is emphasized by Riker, Liberalism Against Populism, chap. 2. On the importance of this for democratic choice, see Gaus, "Does Democracy Reveal the Will of the People?"
[54] Donald G. Saari, *Chaotic Elections! A Mathematician Looks at Voting* (Providence, RI: American Mathematical Society, 2000), 152; emphasis in original.
[55] D'Agostino, *Incommensurability and Commensuration*, 91–95.

devoted to the cultivation of individuality endorsed by John Stuart Mill,[56] or that they all have the same rational insight into natural law or natural rights endorsed by Locke. Those who do not have such evaluations are then eliminated from the deliberative problem. But this is just to weaken our assumption of rational evaluative diversity; such proposals seek to constrain evaluative diversity within some acceptable range and, thereby, produce significant rational consensus. However, this move is question-begging: it assumes that, prior to public justification between rational moral persons, some substantive public evaluative conclusions have been reached about suitable individual standards of evaluation. That, though, looks as if it must mean that some persons assert that, while a certain restriction of evaluative standards could not be validated by all rational reflective moral persons, nonetheless it is warranted and those dissenting can be excluded from public justification. This is to lack respect for the moral freedom and equality of others.

5. Justifying Public Morality: Arguments from Abstraction

5.1 Abstract and Full Justification

Is there some way to achieve public justification in the face of evaluative diversity? D'Agostino tells us that one of the great attractions of Rawls's original position is that it provides a device of "social commensuration":

> Rawls's problem is, indeed, one of ranking options in a social setting. The members of some society have to decide, in a way that will be collectively binding, how they are to organize their relations with one another, at least in certain fundamental ways. In particular they have to decide how to rank proposals about the so-called "basic structure of society." If each individual appeared in his own identity as a participant in discourse or negotiations about how to organize the "basic structure of society" in a collectively acceptable way, it is unlikely, in the extreme, that any agreement on substantive matters would be possible and, hence, the various options (each a specification of "the basic structure") would remain incommensurable with respect to one another. From a collective point of view, we would not know how to order them in a satisfactory way.[57]

The device of the original position aims to provide a public justification of a ranking of some moral claims (such as liberty versus equality) by

---

[56] For an explicit argument of this sort, see Jonathan Riley, *Liberal Utilitarianism: Social Choice and J. S. Mill's Philosophy* (Cambridge: Cambridge University Press, 1983).

[57] D'Agostino, *Incommensurability and Commensuration*, 100.

abstracting from our actual, full evaluative positions, and so providing a shared core perspective that yields a determinate deliberative-justificatory outcome.[58] One function of the veil of ignorance is to locate this shared basis for evaluation. "One excludes the knowledge of those contingencies which set men apart. . . ."[59] Individuals are abstracted to the common status of agents devoted to their own evaluative criteria (values, comprehensive conceptions of the good, and so on), and because "everyone is equally rational and similarly situated, each is convinced by the same arguments."[60] Indeed, abstraction allows us to avoid the problem of inter-personal justification since the problem is reduced to the choice of one person.[61] The success of an argument from abstraction depends on three key claims.

(1)   Most obviously, it must be the case that there is a shared perspective that identifies a common basis of evaluation. The aim is to show that once we abstract to a certain shared perspective (and thus, for example, we exclude our desires to dominate or rule others), we do share some evaluative standards. Arguments for abstraction need not deploy a device such as the original position: Alan Gewirth, S. I. Benn, and others have maintained that the perspective of an abstract agent devoted to acting on his or her own evaluative criteria validates basic liberty claims, though they have not utilized a hypothetical choice situation.[62]

(2)   This shared perspective must identify especially important shared evaluative standards; it will be of little avail to identify a shared perspective that does not capture really important evaluative standards. We must, as Rawls says, "give very great and normally overriding weight" to the norms prescribed by the shared standpoint.[63]

(3)   Related to this point, it must be the case that the deliberative conclusions are not overturned as the process of abstraction is undone and individuals are again understood to be guided by their full set of evaluative standards. It is, I think, seldom appreciated just how important this point is to Rawls's later work. Rawls argues that the political conception can be justified as freestanding: it is based on an abstract conception of persons as reasonable and rational, free and equal – a conception that is said to be implicit in our democratic

---

[58] Ibid., 100–01.   [59] Rawls, *A Theory of Justice*, 17.   [60] Ibid., 120.   [61] Ibid., 120–21.
[62] Gewirth, *Reason and Morality*, chap. 2; S. I. Benn, *A Theory of Freedom* (Cambridge: Cambridge University Press, 1988), chaps. 6–7. See also my *Value and Justification*, sec. 24.2.
[63] Rawls, *Political Liberalism*, 241.

society, and thus, shared by all.[64] Justice as fairness thus expresses "shared reason."[65] Rawls maintains that justice as fairness is a justified political conception because it articulates the requirements of the concepts of the person and society that all reasonable citizens in our democratic societies share. What Rawls calls "freestandingness" is a case of argument from abstraction. However, Rawls does not believe that this exhausts justification. Indeed, he says that this is simply a pro tanto (so far as it goes) justification.[66] In what he refers to as "full" justification, citizens draw on their full range of evaluative standards and find further reasons for endorsing the political conception. At this stage, Rawls tells us, the pro tanto abstract justification "may be over-ridden by citizens' comprehensive doctrines once all values are tallied up."[67] What was simply "freestanding" must, if it is to be fully justified, serve as a "module" that fits into each free and equal rational moral person's set of evaluative criteria.[68]

It is, I believe, a serious mistake to think that Rawls's basic notion of justification changed from *A Theory of Justice* to *Political Liberalism*, replacing the focus on shared reasoning in the original position with justification qua "overlapping consensus" – that all reasonable evaluative systems overlap on the basic liberal principles. Rather, the core idea throughout his work is the argument from abstraction in the original position, but Rawls increasingly worried that as the abstraction is undone and people come to know their comprehensive conceptions of value, their devotion to the principles might be "overridden." Full knowledge of evaluative standards may change what is validated from their perspectives. Hence Rawls's claim that under "full" justification the normative importance of the pro tanto argument from abstraction is preserved (i.e., condition 3 is met). Let us, then, call this third requirement the stability of abstract justification under full justification. This last requirement is immensely important: unless the conclusion of the argument from abstraction can be affirmed in light of a rational and reflective, free and equal moral person's full set of evaluative criteria, the abstract justification will be

---

[64] Ibid., 10.   [65] Ibid., 9.   [66] Ibid., 386.   [67] Ibid.

[68] Most commentators on Rawls mistakenly identify these two ideas. Rawls employs the idea of a "module" when explaining "overlapping consensus" (ibid., 12–13; 144–45), whereas "freestandingness" applies to the appeal to shared conceptions of the person, and lack of metaphysical and other commitments, of the abstract argument for the two principles (ibid., 10, 40, 133, 144). The crucial passage that confuses many readers is on pp. 144–45 of *Political Liberalism*, where Rawls argues that because the political conception is freestanding it can serve as a module; many readers suppose that Rawls is simply equating the two ideas.

defeated by these other elements of her evaluative set. When Rawls tells us his main concern in developing political liberalism was to provide an account of the stability of a society based on his principles,[69] we should not think of this as mainly a sociological concern: the fundamental concern is the stability of the abstract justification in the light of the diversity of reasonable and conflicting "comprehensive conceptions of the good."

5.2   Rawls's Two Principles of Justice

As is well known, Rawls maintains that two strictly ordered principles are justified via the argument from abstraction:

> First: each person is to have an equal right to the most extensive scheme of equal basic liberties compatible with a similar scheme of liberties for others.

> Second: social and economic inequalities are to be arranged so that they are both (a) reasonably expected to be to everyone's advantage and (b) attached to positions and offices open to all.[70]

Rawls provides a compelling case that his argument from abstraction for the first principle and its priority over other social values satisfies our three conditions. (1) We do share the perspective of rational agents devoted to our ends. (2) What we are committed to when occupying this perspective is of great importance, since it is always relevant to action based on our evaluative standards. (3) The pro tanto case for an extensive and strong scheme of liberty seems stable under full justification. The compelling arguments in Rawls's *Political Liberalism* for overlapping consensus concern basic liberties. Much less compelling is the argument for the second principle. It was notoriously controversial whether the argument from the original position actually endorses the second principle. (Let us focus simply on principle 2(a), the so-called difference principle.) Rawls's attempts to show that abstract agents would select basic institutions that must distribute universally required goods so as to maximize the share to the least-advantaged group has confronted an array of objections that this would simply not be a rational strategy for such agents. Objectors insist that the abstracted parties would do better to maximize the average payoffs, or, alternatively, to avoid distributions that are disastrous to some,

---

[69] Ibid., xix.

[70] Ibid., 53. Compare the original edition of Rawls, *A Theory of Justice* (Cambridge, MA: Belknap Press of Harvard University Press, 1971), 60.

but once those distributions are omitted choose the distribution that maximizes average payoff, and so on.[71] However, let us leave these well-hoed fields behind. Even if the difference principle is justified by the argument from abstraction, it manifestly is not stable under full justification. Once free and equal reasonable individuals become aware of their evaluative standards (comprehensive conceptions of the good), many find the difference principle highly objectionable. Many people, for example, are strongly committed to notions of desert which clash with the difference principle.[72] We need not, though, focus simply on Rawls's highly controversial difference principle. Consider the much more modest claim of Alan Gewirth that abstract agents would demand rights to welfare as well as freedom.[73] Suppose we grant that abstract agents would accept an unconditional right to welfare: because they value their agency, they would value those things that are necessary for continued agency. However, as our model deliberators become aware of the full range of their evaluative criteria (including notions of desert, responsibility, and prudence) some will rationally reject the results of the abstract justification, showing again that it is not stable under full justification. Consider two such objectors, Prudence and Sylvan.

Prudence is reasonably averse to risk, and spends a good deal of time planning for trouble and how to avoid it. Central to her evaluative criteria is that one is responsible for avoiding the pitfalls of life. Now she has good reason to value a cautious life in which she looks out for her own welfare rather than a life in which we look out for each other. For others may lead riskier lives, and thus put themselves in positions in which they are more likely to be imperiled. Prudence will see welfare-grounded claims to assistance as violating her "comprehensive conception of the good": those whom she considers irresponsible and who reject the value of prudence, or reject taking responsibility for their own lives, will have claims on her that are antithetical to her values. People get into very hot water because they seek excitement, or are careless, or are too cheap or lazy to take precautions, or simply would rather spend their time and money having a

---

[71] For evidence that ordinary reasoners tend toward this last option, and thus have non-Rawlsian strategies in original position–like situations, see Norman Frohlich and Joe A. Oppenheimer, *Choosing Justice: An Experimental Approach to Ethical Theory* (Berkeley: University of California Press, 1992).

[72] For a review of the literature on people's beliefs about justice that brings out the importance of desert, see David Miller, "Distributive Justice: What People Think," *Ethics* 102 (April 1992): 555–93. See also my *Social Philosophy*, chap. 6.

[73] Gewirth, *Reason and Morality*, chap. 2.

good time. Prudence's objection is sound. Although, say, health-care provision often has been enacted on the ground that everyone's basic welfare interests should be protected, experience has shown that the careless or reckless make inordinate demands on health-care systems. Because welfare provision is funded by all, Prudence and others like her end up paying a good deal for the recklessness of smokers and motorcyclists who ride without helmets; thus, Prudence and her like-minded fellows are forced to encourage what they see as vices.

The second objection comes from Sylvan, a nature lover. Sylvan's values are not centered on his own life or well-being, but on the wonders of nature. Although he does what he can to help and protect nature, Sylvan is under no delusion that his survival is necessary for the survival of nature. Because he so loves nature, however, he seeks to devote his life to worshipping it and understanding it; he has a religious awe when in the presence of nature. Now Sylvan may well resist incurring significant costs or transferring resources via taxation to help others; he does not cherish humans – he thinks they are not all that important in the scheme of things. Now, to respect and to cherish are not the same: Sylvan can respect others as moral persons without cherishing their flourishing. To Sylvan, devoting his resources to being near nature is tremendously more important than saving humans. Of course, Sylvan realizes that some day he may need help, and he is reasonable enough to admit that if he needs help, it would be nice to get it. But his environment-oriented philosophy indicates that it will be no great loss to the universe whether he dies in five, ten, twenty, or forty years. So Sylvan would resist the idea that significant costs should be put on him to assist others.

5.3   The Moral Right to Private Property

Political philosophers such as   Rawls and Gewirth thus contend that, if we consider simply the abstract perspective of ourselves as agents, we appreciate not only the importance we place on agency freedom, but the importance we place on the maintenance of agency, and thus we all endorse strong claims against others to help us maintain our agency. Even if the latter "agency welfare rights" are justified from the abstract perspective, I have argued, they are not stable under full justification: once Prudence and Sylvan are aware of their complete set of evaluate standards, they will reject these claims on them.[74] However, Rawls and Gewirth are

---

[74] See Loren Lomasky's argument concerning the "strains of commitment" that are induced by making us responsible for each other, and why this casts doubt on Rawls's claim that the

certainly right that the perspective of abstract agency does not simply endorse liberty rights. As Immanuel Kant argued, property rights are required for agency.[75] Think about a world without any moral rights to property. From a moral point of view, in such a world an agent can only possess: he can physically control objects and resources but never own them. And he must allow that there is nothing wrong with others' possessing what he would like to have, for there are, we are supposing, no moral rights to property (and that includes no collective moral rights vested in the community). If one rejects the very idea of a moral right to private property by refusing to assert ownership, argued Kant, one must allow that it would be no moral injury to one should others arbitrarily take what one possesses and in so doing undermine one's activity and will. "In other words, it would reduce these objects to naught from a practical point of view and make them into res nullius, although . . . the will [is] involved in the use of these things"[76] Recall that given the argument from abstract agency, we have, qua agents, a central concern with acting on our evaluative standards. By reducing the objects of his will and plans to "res nullius," one who rejects the very idea of private property rights undermines his own claim qua agent to act on his evaluative criteria: it is never a moral injury to him to "rob" his activities of those parts of the world with which they are intertwined. In sum, without true property rights defining a sphere of moral authority (see Section VII.A), an agent has no moral claims on others to allow him to employ his evaluative standards over most of social life. Thus, Kant reminds us that claims to property are part of free agency itself: when one claims property over a thing, one claims "that any interference with my using it as I please would constitute an injury to me."[77] This Kantian idea is reflected in the common law. When a thing that is simply possessed becomes integral to one's activity, the common law often supposes that claims are thereby generated. In common law, for example, possession is understood as an implicit act of communication of a claim that gives rise to rights, and often to title. Although possession qua control is understood as physical fact, it can give rise to claims. Even acts of

---

difference principle would be selected in the original position. Lomasky, "Libertarianism at Twin Harvard," *Social Philosophy and Policy* 22, no. 1 (2005): 178–99.

[75] This, of course, supposes that property rights are not freedom rights. I argue for this view in my essay "Property, Rights, and Freedom," *Social Philosophy and Policy* 11, no. 2 (1994): 209–40.

[76] Immanuel Kant, *The Metaphysical Elements of Justice*, trans. John Ladd (Indianapolis, IN: Bobbs-Merrill, 1965), 53 (Private Law, sec. 2). Res nullius is a thing belonging to no one.

[77] Ibid., 55 (Private Law, sec. 5).

possession such as killing and carrying away an unowned fox have been held to give title.[78]

Given that a free moral person has an interest in acting in accord with his own evaluative standards (see Section II), it does not seem that he can reject moral rights to property, even under full justification. This, of course, by no means justifies anything like capitalistic property rights. It merely demonstrates the importance of private property as a moral category for agency. The contours of those rights must be filled in, but however they are filled in, the property rights must be robust enough to secure the interest in agency and in doing "as I please." Moreover, it must be remembered that whatever principle of property is justified by considerations of abstract agency must be stable under full justification. To accept that there is an intrinsic tie between free agency and property rights, and thus that a system of property rights is morally necessary, also implies certain other conditions: just as only systems of basic liberties that widely distribute liberty can be justified among abstract agents, so too with property. Systems distinguishing "mine and thine" by making everything mine and nothing thine are manifestly unable to be endorsed under full justification. Adequate defenses of private property have always sought to show that, at a minimum, the benefits of property rights are universal: everyone is much better off under a system of private property than without one.[79] However, universal benefit from property may not be

---

[78] Thus the famous case of Pierson v. Post (Supreme Court of New York, 1805; 3 Cai. R. 175, 2 Am. Dec. 264). Post, the plaintiff, was pursuing a fox with his hounds while Pierson came in during the chase, shot the fox, and carried it off. Post sued (invoking something like the labor theory of value) on the grounds that he was pursuing the fox, and so had a claim to it. The court found in favor of Pierson, as he possessed the fox. See Jesse Dukeminier and James E. Krier, eds., *Property*, 5th ed. (New York: Aspen, 2002), 19–24. For a discussion, see Carol Rose, "Possession as the Origin of Property," *University of Chicago Law Review* 52 (Winter 1985): 72–96.

[79] The universal benefit of private property has been a fundamental liberal theme. Consider the following canonical liberal passages. First, Adam Smith: "[T]he accommodation of an European prince does not always so much exceed that of an industrious and frugal peasant, as the accommodation of the latter exceeds that of many an African King, the absolute master of the lives and liberties of the thousand naked savages." Adam Smith, *An Inquiry into the Nature and Causes of the Wealth of Nations*, ed. R. H. Campbell and A. S. Skinner (Indianapolis, IN: Liberty Press, 1981), vol. I, pp. 23–24. Now Locke: "There cannot be a clearer demonstration of any thing, than several Nations of the Americans are of this, who are rich in Land, and poor in all the Comforts of Life; whom Nature having furnished as liberally as any other people, with the materials of Plenty, i.e. a fruitful Soil, apt to produce in abundance, what might serve for food, rayment, and delight; yet for want of improving it by labour, have not one hundredth part of the Conveniences we enjoy: And a King of a large fruitful Territory there feeds, lodges, and is clad worse than a day Labourer in England." Locke, *Second Treatise of Government*, 314–15 (sec. 41). In both cases, the claim is that private property is a Pareto improvement over a non-property regime.

sufficient; an unimpaired opportunity to acquire property, or even something closer to a system that is conducive to universal property-holding,
may be required.[80]

6. Justifying Public Morality: The Testing Conception

6.1 Optimal Eligible Interpretations

The argument from abstraction identifies, at a minimum, the importance
of agency freedom and property rules; let us focus for now on agency
freedom, the fundamental liberal concern. As I said, the abstract argument
gives us abstract requirements; a wide range of interpretations present
themselves about just what freedoms are morally required by agents such
as ourselves. To see our way to more specific justifications, let us introduce
the concept of a set {p1 ... pn} of optimal eligible interpretations of an
abstract justified principle P. Our justificatory problem comes to this: We
need to first identify what such a set might be, and then justify identifying
one member of it as our public morality. Let us say that each interpretation
p is put forward as a fully specified scheme of agency freedoms, including
any priority rules. An interpretation p is eligible if and only if under full
justification the interpretation of P qua p would be ranked by every
reasonable moral person as better than no P interpretation at all. And let
us restrict ourselves to only optimal eligible interpretations: if p1 and p2
are both eligible interpretations of P, and if under full justification everyone's evaluative standards rank p1 > p2, then p2 is excluded from the set
of optimal interpretations.

I shall suppose, for the moment, that the set of optimal eligible interpretations contains more than one member (but see below). If the set is
null, then the abstract argument was not stable under full justification
insofar as, for every possible interpretation, at least one reasonable moral
person ranks it as worse than a morality without the principle. If the set has
one member, then the justificatory task is completed. But the assumption
that the set can be reduced to one – in other words, that abstract
philosophical argument actually justifies a unique and determinate answer
to what our morality requires – strikes me as implausible, and is indicative

---

[80] For a sensitive discussion, see Jeremy Waldron, *The Right to Private Property* (Oxford: Clarendon
Press, 1988), esp. chap. 11. Arguments for a Lockean "proviso" are also relevant here: i.e., the idea
that a condition of a justified property right is that it does not interfere with others' opportunities to
acquire property.

of disregard for current practices that Freeden (to say nothing of Hume, Hayek, and so many others) warns against. I assume, then, that we have a nested disagreement: a rational disagreement about the best choice nested within a rationally agreed upon set.[81] We disagree about the best specification of moral claims, but this disagreement is nested in a rational agreement that moral regulation of this matter is publicly validated.

B.   The Testing Conception

We seem to have landed back where we started: we have divergent rankings with no best option, though now we do rationally concur that some member of the set must be selected. Of course, we can continue on with abstract philosophical argument: we might, for instance, develop some sort of bargaining theory that would show that some member of the set is the rationally-to-be-selected option.[82] But any proposal for a rationally best solution from the set of optimal eligible interpretations will itself be evaluated differently by various evaluative standards, leading us to a second-level disagreement about the rankings of different bargaining theories. A fresh start is needed. Abstract philosophical construction has done a lot of work; we have arrived at abstract principles and an understanding of what range of interpretations is rationally admissible. But what is the next step in understanding a morality for free and equal rational agents?

An alternative conception of moral validation has been employed by philosophers such as Kurt Baier. Basic to Baier's analysis is that moralities are social facts. Anthropologists can identify a group's morality, and distinguish it from laws, taboos, and etiquette.[83] To be sure, members of a group may have sharp disagreements about some of the rules and interpretations of them, but an anthropologist could describe them in a fairly accurate way. On this conception, to validate a morality is to test the moral rules of one's group from the moral point of view: we ask whether each person's evaluative standards validate this rule. However, "validation" here does not imply "the best social moral code," "the best of all possible rules from one's perspective," or "the rules that would be arrived at in a perfectly fair bargaining situation." Because, ultimately, moralities are not

---

[81] I have given a slightly different account of nested disagreement in *Justificatory Liberalism*, 156ff. For an enlightening discussion, see Micah Schwartzman, "The Completeness of Public Reason," *Politics, Philosophy, and Economics* 3 (June 2004): 191–220.

[82] I sought to do this in *Value and Justification*, chap. 9.

[83] See Baier, "The Point of View of Morality."

philosophical creations – they are not at all the same thing as what philosophers call "moral theories" – philosophers cannot construct them by writing books, even quite long ones. They are social facts that confront us. The task of philosophical ethics is to sort out which of these social facts should be acknowledged as imposing obligations and which should be rejected as inconsistent with treating all as free and equal moral persons.[84]

Our abstract construction has provided us with the requisite critical perspective; the task of moral reflection is to apply this perspective to our actual morality. Restricting ourselves now to agency freedom, our actual morality must be within the set of optimal eligible interpretations if all are to have good reason to accept our social morality. If our current interpretation of agency freedom is within the optimal eligible set, then we are confronted with actual moral freedom rights that satisfy the requirements of abstract moral reflection, and would not be rejected by any reasonable moral person under full awareness of her evaluative standards. This does not mean, however, that each person sees this as the best specification, or even one of the best, or even better-than-average. The existing practice may not be close to most people's ideal, but if it is part of the optimal eligible set, it qualifies as publicly justified. Moral obligation is not a tight function of moral perfection. Of course, people can provide arguments to move the current morality in their ideal directions. As Baier observes, "improvements in the society's morality can occur only by changes in the members' morality and these are best brought about by the members' own efforts at convincing one another by their discussions with others (and, of course, by their own critical reflections)."[85]

In contrast, the current interpretation may fail to be justified in two ways: (1) It could be that our current interpretation of liberty rights is part of the set of eligible interpretations, but not in the set of optimal eligible moralities. In that case, there is some alternative moral practice that everyone's evaluative criteria rank as better than the current way of interpreting our agency rights. In that case, our current moral rights to agency freedom, though they represent an eligible option, are irrational because they are suboptimal: we all have reason to adopt the optimal alternative scheme. This raises complex issues. How far, for example, is the current interpretation of P from the relevant optimal interpretation? Certainly, there is a case for moral reform here, but whether one has reason to follow the current understanding of our moral liberty rights depends on the

---

[84] See Kurt Baier, *The Rational and the Moral Order* (Chicago: Open Court, 1995), 212.
[85] Ibid., 217.

details of the case. A reasonable proposal is that in personal interactions one should appeal to the optimal code, as one has the opportunity for showing that it is justified among free and equal moral persons. In relations with strangers, however, it may be morally presumptuous for one to ignore the accepted code.

(2) Secondly, it might be the case that our current moral practice is not within the set of eligible interpretations: it is not justified under some free and equal moral persons' full evaluative standards. In that case, the current interpretation is illegitimate: it does not specify moral rights to freedom. Of course, we might still have pragmatic reasons to pay attention to these positive rights, but they would not be justified elements of our public morality. However, we should not jump to the conclusion that the entire current moral practice involving agency freedom would be undermined. Even if the entire practice cannot be fully justified, some parts of it may survive the scrutiny of full justification and thus morally ground parts of our current agency freedoms. Insofar as we can partition our moral practices,[86] we can distinguish those parts that withstand critical reflection from those that do not. However, should large parts of our current practice fail to be within the set of eligible interpretations of abstractly justified principles, we would be faced with a sort of moral chaos: our current moral practice would then fail to treat each individual in a way required by his status as a free and equal moral person. We would then be faced with a deep moral problem: we are committed to some interpretation of a moral principle, but we cannot identify any publicly justified specific interpretation, so we are unable to arrive at a workable morality even though some moral principles are validated. It is tempting to suppose that democratic decision-making can offer a solution: the law might be understood as a way for us to coordinate on new practices within the eligible set.[87] However, we need to be careful: there is no good reason to suppose that majoritarian procedures will focus on practices that would be validated by all, rather than just the majority. If politics and legislation are to help us escape such moral anarchy, we would have to employ carefully constructed extramajoritarian methods to ensure that the outputs were reasonably likely to pass the test of public justification.[88]

---

[86] This partitioning raises formal problems about the possible interconnectedness of justifications that I do not pursue here.

[87] See Jeremy Waldron, *Law and Disagreement* (Oxford: Oxford University Press, 1999), 104ff.

[88] See my *Justificatory Liberalism*, 237ff. See also my essay "The Legal Coordination Game," *American Philosophical Association's Newsletter on Philosophy and Law* 1 (Spring 2002): 122–28.

C. Morality as Recognized Claims

Some object to the testing conception of moral validation because it supposes a "bias" toward current moral practice. Why select the current morality from the set of eligible codes? What could justify this bias toward the actual?

A bias toward the actual is endorsed by a certain publicity condition on morality. This requires that a morality be a social fact. To be rationally justified is not sufficient to establish a bona fide moral rule: it must be accepted, taught, and relied upon. Baier sought to capture this publicity condition by requiring as a condition for being a moral rule that a rule "be taught to all children," so that all would know what the rule is.[89] Rawls upheld a publicity condition as a formal constraint on the concept of right: our conception of what is right presupposes that justified moral principles are known to be such by everyone.[90] Some interpret the publicity condition in a weaker way, as simply mandating that the moral rules and principles could be made public, and thus their efficacy does not necessarily depend on being restricted to a few. The stronger condition endorsed here (and, I think, by Baier) is that moral principles must be public in the sense that they provide the basis of our settled expectations about each other's duties and claims. Moral duty is not simply a matter of reason, it is necessarily a practical guarantee and source of mutual recognition of each other as possessing a certain status as free and equal moral persons – in the words of T. H. Green, "a society of men who recognise each other as isoi kai homoioi [equals]."[91] If we accept the publicity condition, a necessary condition for R to be a moral right entailing obligations is that it is publicly recognized as part of morality. Only rules that are part of our current code can fulfill that condition.

7. The Rights of the Moderns

7.1 Rights as Devices of Devolution

Our fundamental moral concern, then, must be whether our current morality is at least within the set of eligible interpretations. Do we have any reason to think it is?

---

[89] Baier, "The Point of View of Morality."
[90] Rawls, *A Theory of Justice*, 115. Rawls relates this condition to Kant's justification of publicity in a note, 115n.
[91] T. H. Green, *Lectures on the Principles of Political Obligation*, in Paul Harris and John Morrow, eds., *Lectures on the Principles of Political Obligation and Other Writings* (Cambridge: Cambridge University Press, 1986), sec. 116.

D'Agostino's analysis is again helpful, providing grounds for concluding that our liberal morality does reasonably well at the crucial task of coping with evaluative diversity. Because liberal morality is a morality of rights, its main solution to the problem of divergent evaluative standards, and divergent interpretations of shared principles, is to devolve to individuals the moral authority to decide what evaluative standards to apply in specific situations. A system of rights is an efficient response to the problem of public justification given evaluative diversity. "Civil society, with its individual rights and rights of association, [and] the market, with its foundation of property rights and rights of contract," are, D'Agostino argues, devices of "commensuration" that devolve moral authority: they define spheres of authority that specify whose evaluative standards will be regulative in a social interaction.[92] "In effect, we say that in a society with n individual members, there are n separate spheres in which an answer . . . may be sought, each of which is, in theory, inviolable and particular to the individual who occupies it."[93]

Of course, because there are indefinitely many systems of rights, the devolution solution presupposes that successful arguments from abstraction have identified the eligible systems, and the testing conception confirms that our system is in the set. Granted that, however, we can see how devolution via a system of rights greatly lessens what we might call the burdens of justification. Deep evaluative diversity, we have seen, poses serious obstacles to the public justification of a common morality. The rights solution is to mitigate our evaluative disagreements by granting to each a limited sphere in which an individual's evaluative standards have public standing. This function of rights is almost always overlooked.[94] Liberals are apt to see rights as ways in which individuals are protected against others: they define morally protected zones surrounding each. While rights are certainly that, however, they are typically far more: a moral right gives a person moral authority to decide the social outcome on the basis of his own evaluative standards. If I exercise my moral right against you, my evaluative standards are given social moral standing: they become, on this issue, the voice of public morality.

7.2 The Impossibility of a Paretian Liberal?

At this point, the argument of Amartya Sen's essay "The Impossibility of a Paretian Liberal" is relevant, and seems to pose an objection to the

---

[92] D'Agostino, *Incommensurability and Commensuration*, 105.   [93] Ibid.

[94] For a notable exception, see Eric Mack, "In Defense of the Jurisdiction Theory of Rights," *Journal of Ethics* 4 (January–March 2000): 71–98.

devolution proposal.[95] Sen conceives of a person having a right R as having authority to decide the social preference over at least one pair of alternatives (x, y) such that if a person chooses x > y, that is the social preference; and if the person chooses y > x, then that is the social preference. This conception of a right has been disputed, but it perfectly captures the conception of rights as devolved ways to cope with evaluative diversity: instead of a collective choice over the pair (x, y), the social choice is devolved to a single agent.[96] However, Sen shows that attributing such rights to two persons, and assuming all possible orderings of social states are permissible, the social outcome selected by the rights can conflict with the widely endorsed Pareto principle (that if for everyone x > y, then the social preference must be x > y). More formally, Sen shows how combining rights, the Pareto principle, and no restriction of preference orderings can result in intransitive social preference. Sen nicely summarizes his argument:

> There is a book (e.g. *Lady Chatterley's Lover*) which may be read by Mr. A ("the prude") or Mr. B ("the lascivious") or by neither. Given other things, these three alternatives define social states, a, b and o respectively. Consider now the following possibility. The prude A most prefers o (no one reading it), then a ("I'll take the hurt on myself"), and lastly b ("Imagine that lascivious lapping it up"). The lascivious [Mr. B] prefers most a ("it will give that lilywhite baby a nice shock), then b ("it will be fun"), and last o ("what a waste of a good book"). On grounds of individual freedom, since B wants to read the book rather than no one reading it, b is socially preferred to o; note that in either case A does not read the book here. Similarly, since A does not want to read it, o is socially better than a. But a is Pareto superior to b, yielding a preference cycle.[97]

Thus, we get b > o (by Mr. B's right); o > a (by Mr. A's right), and a > b (by the Pareto principle, since in both Mr. A's and Mr. B's ordering, a > b); therefore, we get b > o > a > b – a cycle.

Some see this as a case against individual rights: such rights can conflict with the Pareto principle, which many see as so intuitively obvious as to be beyond dispute. After all, if everyone in society prefers a to b, then certainly that ought to be the social ordering; but if we combine this

---

[95] Amartya Sen, "The Impossibility of a Paretian Liberal," *The Journal of Political Economy* 78 (January–February 1970): 152–57. For an extended, and accessible, discussion, see Amartya Sen, "Liberty, Unanimity, and Rights," *Economica*, New Series 43 (August 1976): 217–45.

[96] Nozick, for one, criticized this conception in *Anarchy, State, and Utopia*, 165–66. Cf. Sen, "Liberty, Unanimity, and Rights," 229–31.

[97] Sen, "Liberty, Unanimity, and Rights," 218.

principle with individual rights to decide the social preference over some options, we can get a social preference – or a public morality – that is intransitive, and thus irrational. However, Sen saw this not as a case against liberal rights, but as showing "the unacceptability of the Pareto principle as a universal rule."[98] We have especially good reason to discount the Pareto principle here.[99] According to our argument from abstraction, morality is to ascribe central importance to agency freedom. Sen's case is an example where people's agency freedom conflicts with what they prefer others to do; preferences about what another does in her sphere of rights thus should be ignored by public morality.

7.3 Rights and Social Recognition

Appreciation of the importance of rights as devices of devolution leads to another consideration (in addition to the publicity condition; see Section VI.C) supporting the testing conception's "bias" toward actual morality. If a system of rights is to perform the function of devolving moral authority to individuals in society, it is crucial that these rights be socially recognized. In his *Lectures on the Principles of Political Obligation*, Green considers the distinction between de facto and de jure sovereignty.[100] Green resists the idea that de jure sovereignty is simply "rightful authority" that has no practical force, as when appeal is made simply to a "general will, or the mere name of a fallen dynasty exercising no control over men in their dealings with each other."[101] Instead, Green argues, the distinction "has natural meaning in the mouths of those who, in resisting some coercive power that claims their obedience, can point to another determinate authority to which they not only consider obedience due, but to which obedience in some measure is actually rendered..."[102] Green's point – and he seems entirely right – is that a political authority that has

---

[98] Ibid., 235.

[99] If the Pareto principle is unacceptable as a general constraint, then we must question Arrow's theorem (see Section IV.A), which also relies on it (see note 51). Does this mean that justification via aggregation is a live option again? I think not, both for the reason I explore in the text, and because the formal problems identified by Arrow's theorem are just the tip of the iceberg with aggregation procedures, which display a plethora of worrisome features such as path dependence.

[100] Green, *Lectures on the Principles of Political Obligation*, sec. 105. For defenses of "the rights recognition thesis," see Rex Martin, *A System of Rights* (Oxford: Clarendon Press, 1993); Derrick Darby, "Two Conceptions of Rights Possession," *Social Theory and Practice* 7 (July 2001): 387–417; and Gerald F. Gaus, "Green's Rights Recognition Thesis and Moral Internalism," *British Journal of Politics and International Relations* 7 (2005): 5–17.

[101] Green, *Lectures on the Principles of Political Obligation*, sec. 105.   [102] Ibid.

no practical effect is no political authority at all, as it cannot perform its main task of sorting out disagreements and harmonizing rights. To be any sort of authority at all, there must be some general recognition of it; only then can it perform its designated tasks. If it is not generally recognized as an authority, we might argue that it ought to be an authority, but we cannot claim that it now is. The job of authority is to regulate and coordinate interaction; if so, an authority that is not recognized simply is unable to perform the office of an authority, just as one who is not socially recognized as a leader is unable to fulfill the position of "group leader." We can say that a person who is not recognized – either explicitly or implicitly – as a leader ought to be the leader, but not that he is the leader.

The application of Green's analysis of sovereignty – understood in terms of the point of authority argument – to rights qua dispersed moral authority is manifest. To the extent that the function of moral rights is to localize moral authority, they cannot fulfill this function at all if they are not generally recognized. If there are no recognized moral rights, we are in a state akin to civil war, with each side seeking to construct its own preferred authority. As Green observes, however, in situations like this, there really is no sovereignty at all.[103] Rights as dispersed moral authority thus require social recognition. Without general recognition, no authority exists.

7.4   The Rights of the Moderns

Benjamin Constant's famous lecture "The Liberty of the Ancients Compared with That of the Moderns" is interesting to us insofar as he set out to compare two interpretations of the freedom principle: the one that we "moderns" have developed and a more ancient one, which still has a pull on us. The liberty of the moderns, Constant tells us, consists in people's freedom from arbitrary arrest and punishment, their freedom of association and religion, their right to exercise influence on government, their right of expression, and their right "to choose a profession and practice it, to dispose of property, and even to abuse it; to come and go without permission, and without having to account for their motives or under-takings." Constant contrasts this to the liberty of the ancients, which consisted of "exercising collectively, but directly, several parts of the complete sovereignty."[104] As I said at the outset in Section I, Rawls's

---

[103] Ibid.
[104] See Constant, "The Liberty of the Ancients Compared with That of the Moderns," 310–11.

final position was that these two types of liberties are of equal status.[105] His influential interpretation of this distinction, which he attributed to Constant, is troubling in two ways.

First, as Rawls sees it, the liberties of the moderns are, centrally, "freedom of thought and liberty of conscience, and the civil liberties generally."[106] Elsewhere, Rawls adds "certain basic rights of the person and property, and the rule of law."[107] He consistently identifies political liberties with the liberties of the ancients,[108] though Constant was explicit that the liberty of the moderns includes "everyone's right to exercise some influence on the administration of the government, either by electing all or particular officials, or through representations, petitions, demands to which the authorities are more or less compelled to pay heed."[109] For Constant, the liberty of the ancients concerned not simply political rights, but a

> collective exercise of sovereignty; in deliberating, in the public square, over war and peace; in forming alliances with foreign governments; in voting laws, in pronouncing judgments, in examining the accounts, the acts, the stewardship of the magistrates; in calling them to appear in front of the assembled people, in accusing, condemning or absolving them.[110]

Constant did not have in mind, then, simply the distinction between, on the one hand, freedom of conscience and expression, freedom of association, and basic rights of the person, and, on the other hand, political rights. Once we see that political representation is part of the liberty of the moderns, it is uncertain whether the liberty of the ancients holds any attraction whatsoever. The "collective exercise of sovereignty" resulting in a "social jurisdiction" over the commensuration of evaluative standards

---

[105] Rawls appears to change his position from a priority of the liberty of the moderns over the ancients (in his senses) to one of equal status. Compare Rawls, *Justice as Fairness*, 143, and *Political Liberalism*, 106ff. Although *Justice as Fairness* was published after *Political Liberalism*, it expresses Rawls's views from the 1980s. Constant himself held that "[i]ndividual liberty ... is the true modern liberty. Political liberty is its guarantee, consequently political liberty is indispensable." Constant concludes his essay, however, by insisting that the two sorts of liberty must be combined in free institutions. As Stephen Holmes points out, Constant wrote parts of his famous essay in the first years of the nineteenth century, with left-wing critics in his sights; much of this part of the essay is critical of the liberty of the ancients. By 1819, when he delivered his lecture, these left-wing critics had passed from the scene, and Constant, worried about overprivatization, added comments sympathetic to the liberty of the ancients. See Stephen Holmes, *Benjamin Constant and the Making of Modern Liberalism* (New Haven, CT: Yale University Press, 1984), chap. 2.

[106] Rawls, *Political Liberalism*, 299.   [107] Ibid., 5.

[108] See Rawls, *A Theory of Justice*, 176–77, 195; Rawls, *Justice as Fairness*, 143; and Rawls, *Political Liberalism*, 396ff.

[109] Constant, "The Liberty of the Ancients Compared with That of the Moderns," 311.   [110] Ibid.

cannot loom large in modern life, for the familiar reasons I have canvassed. Given (as Arrow and others have shown) the impossibility of devising a way of aggregating preferences into an overall social preference ordering (or, indeed, into a simple social choice) that does not violate reasonable conditions, collective commensuration wilts under the burdens of justification (see Section IV.A).

Second, Rawls's gloss on the distinction just barely admits the right to private property as one of the "liberties" of the moderns. As I have said, in some places Rawls includes among the liberties of the moderns "basic" rights of property, while at other times no mention at all is made of property.[111] In any event, it is clear that Rawls does not think that a just scheme of agency freedom must include any property rights in productive resources.[112] Constant gave a far more important place to property rights in his account: modern "freedom" (broadly understood here to include a range of liberties, claims, powers, and liabilities) is based on devolution of moral jurisdiction to individuals over wide areas of social life, crucially including a system of robust property rights. To be able "to choose a profession and practice it, to dispose of property, and even to abuse it; to come and go without permission, and without having to account for their motives or undertakings" is fundamental to the morality of people living in complex, evaluatively diverse modern societies. One can act within a sphere without having to account to others because one has moral authority within it. Constant's chief aim was to contrast the modern system of private jurisdictions over parts of social life to the unlimited "social jurisdiction" of the ancients.

Private property is perhaps the chief means by which the authority to employ controversial evaluative standards is devolved to individuals and associations. We thus arrive at a second fundamental argument for private property rights (in addition to the argument from agency; see Section V.C). In the absence of robust private property rights, the rights of freedom of expression and of conscience, freedom of association, and freedom of occupation ineffectively respond to the burdens of justification, as so many of our evaluative standards relate to the disposition of resources. Owners employ controversial standards with which others disagree, yet others recognize a bundle of moral duties and liabilities that give public moral standing to an owner's standard-based activity. Rights in several

---

[111] Property is included in Rawls, *Political Liberalism*, 5, and *Justice as Fairness*, 2; it is omitted in Rawls, *A Theory of Justice*, 195; *Justice as Fairness*, 144; and *Political Liberalism*, 299.
[112] See Rawls, *Justice as Fairness*, 177.

property, by devolving moral jurisdiction, thus allow for moral claims in the face of evaluative disagreement and in the absence of collective commensuration.[113] As Jeremy Waldron notes in his insightful book on the right to private property: "Ownership ... expresses the abstract idea of an object being correlated with the name of some individual, *in relation to a rule which says that society will uphold that individual's decision as final when there is any dispute about how the object should be used.*"[114] Ownership, then, implies authority over decisions about the use of objects and parts of the world.[115] A robust system of private ownership is endorsed by the very (Rawlsian) idea of public justification under conditions of far-reaching evaluative diversity. As the political theorist John Gray once observed:

> The importance of several property for civil society is that it acts as an enabling device whereby rival and possibly incommensurable conceptions of the good may be implemented and realized without any recourse to any collective decision-procedure ... One may even say of civil society that it is a device for securing peace by reducing to a minimum the decisions on which recourse to collective choice – the political or public choice that is binding on all – is unavoidable.[116]

A regime of individual moral rights, including a regime of private or "several" property, is thus a form of public justification or, perhaps better understood, a way to settle the problem of public justification in such a way that in the future it is no longer a collective problem. This point is seldom appreciated. It is, of course, widely accepted that, as the prominent libertarian philosopher Eric Mack puts it, the "organizing idea" of the "private property system ... [is] the idea of sanctioning expansion of personal spheres of authority so as to secure individuals' inviolability in their respective life projects."[117] (Or, in the words of the left-leaning Charles Reich, "[p]roperty draws a circle around the activities of each private individual or organization. Within that circle, the individual has a greater degree of freedom than without."[118]) This is the abstract

---

[113] On these points, see Mack, "In Defense of the Jurisdiction Theory of Rights"; and Randy Barnett, *The Structure of Liberty: Justice and the Rule of Law* (New York: Oxford University Press, 1998), 138ff.

[114] Waldron, *The Right to Private Property*, 47; emphasis added.

[115] The idea of ownership as a status against the whole world in relation to a thing remains important in property law. See, e.g., Armory v. Delamirie (Kings Bench, 1722, 1 Strange 505), in Dukeminier and Krier, eds., *Property*, 108–9. On the importance of property qua jurisdiction over resources, see Barnett, *The Structure of Liberty*, 64ff.

[116] John Gray, *Post-Enlightenment Liberalism* (London: Routledge, 1993), 314.

[117] Mack, "Self-Ownership and the Right of Property," 536.

[118] Charles Reich, "The New Property," *Yale Law Journal* 73 (1964): 771.

argument from agency (Section V), and it should by no means be belittled. What is less appreciated, though, is how this devolution of moral authority allows us to cope with evaluative diversity without ongoing collective commensuration.[119]

7.5   The Fatal Attraction of the Liberty of the Ancients

What Constant called the liberty of the moderns is, I believe, one of the great modern discoveries: it provides a framework for a common morality that reconciles deep differences in our evaluative standards by devolving moral authority to individuals, giving each a sphere in which her evaluative standards have authority. Yet, puzzlingly, contemporary political theory is enamored with the liberty of the ancients – collective commensuration to reach joint judgments about evaluative standards. The current fascination in contemporary political theory is "deliberative democracy" – a diverse family of views favoring enlarging the scope of democratic decision-making based on widespread public deliberation aiming at consensus.[120] "[T]he aim of the regulative idea is agreement of conviction on the basis of public reasons uttered and assessed in public discourse"[121] Even Rawls came to embrace some version of this doctrine.[122] Apparently, we are still held captive by the highly idealized picture in our mind's eye of the Athenian polis: Why can't we again be like that? (Was it ever like that?)

This attempt to emulate in practice a romantic image of the past can only lead to oppression. Deliberative democracy supposes that our differences in evaluative standards are, as it were, only on the surface. Once we reason together and talk things through, deliberative democrats hold that our value orderings will be transformed:[123] the range of disagreement will radically narrow so that the problems of social commensuration will become fairly insignificant, if not vanish altogether. Surely, though, this is a fantastic claim: in the end, deliberative democrats acknowledge, we

---

[119] See Barnett, *The Structure of Liberty*, 138ff.

[120] The core work here has been done by Jürgen Habermas. See his "Popular Sovereignty as Procedure," trans. William Rehg, in James Bohman and William Rehg, eds., *Deliberative Democracy: Essays on Reason and Politics* (Cambridge, MA: MIT Press, 1997), 44. See generally the essays in that volume. See also Dryzek, "Democratic Theory."

[121] Gerald J. Postema, "Public Practical Reason: Political Practice," in Ian Shapiro and Judith Wagner DeCew, eds., *Nomos XXXVII: Theory and Practice* (New York: New York University Press, 1995): 345–85, at 356.

[122] See note 105.

[123] See Jon Elster, "The Market and the Forum," in Bohman and Rehg, eds., Deliberative Democracy, 10–11.

must cut off discussion and take a vote, but then the majority is subjugating others to its judgment in the name of public reason – reason which is not shared by the dissenting minority. Moreover, we know that there is nothing uniquely correct about the outputs of any actual voting procedures. Once we accept that our disagreements are widespread and deep – that the range of possible value orderings is almost unlimited – democratic procedures simply are not up to the task of collective commensuration (again, we come back to Arrow-like problems; see Section IV.A).

8.   Conclusion: Our Morality of Rights

I have argued that our commitment to treating others as free and equal moral persons implies a commitment to the public justification of our moral claims. Given reasonable evaluative diversity, the public justification of a morality must, somehow, take these reasonably diverse standards and arrive at a common, justified morality. The burdens of justification are weighty. A regime of rights solves the commensuration problem by devolving moral authority. Thus, I have upheld the liberty of the moderns – understood as a system of individual rights – over the liberty of the ancients, which stressed collective decision-making as the primary mode of public commensuration.

But how can we justify a regime of rights? Before we can devolve authority, we must justify a specific rights regime. Philosophical reflection and justification, I have argued, can give us abstract answers regarding which moralities are acceptable to free and equal moral persons, but they cannot create a morality, moral rights, or moral obligations. A morality is a social fact (though not only a social fact) that cannot be conjured up by even the most potent philosophical brews: it involves real norms, which structure actual social interaction. Once we abandon the thoroughly constructivist project, we see that the main aim of normative ethics is to reflect on the moral rights that are recognized in our society, and to determine which of them free and equal moral persons ought to embrace.

CHAPTER 3

Recognized Rights as Devices of Public Reason

1. A Social Morality of Recognized Jurisdictional Rights

My concern in this essay is a family of liberal theories that I shall call "public reason liberalism." Fundamental to public reason liberalism is the commitment to the moral equality of all persons. Because we are equal moral persons, morality must be justified to all. Public reason liberalism is not to be equated with political liberalism. The latter is a specific version of public reason liberalism that seeks to restrict the set to be justified to a small number of principles of political right that are largely independent of moral principles. Rawls's earlier work – certainly his 1951 essay "Outline of a Decision Procedure in Ethics" and the famous essay on "Justice and Fairness" – understood the subject of justification more expansively, focusing on what we might call "social ethics," i.e., the moral resolution of competing claims of individuals.[1] On this view liberalism is not simply a theory of the justice of the basic structure of society, but a public moral framework by which individuals can adjudicate their conflicting claims and demands on one another. Some may call this is a "comprehensive" liberalism, but we should be wary of such a simple description.[2] Much of what we call "ethics" – including visions of the good life and conceptions of virtue and vice – lies outside social morality. As J.S. Mill saw it, the subject of "Civil" or "Social Liberty" – which is plausibly the subject of liberalism – involves the nature and limits of the moral authority of society over individuals to insist that they refrain from speaking, acting, and living as they wish.[3] It is this broader understanding of liberalism that is my focus. Public reason liberalism, as I conceive it, claims that the principles of

---

[1] John Rawls, "Outline of a Decision Procedure for Ethics" and "Justice as Fairness" in *John Rawls: Collected Papers*, ed. Samuel Freeman (Cambridge, MA: Harvard University Press, 1999), pp. 1–19, 47–72.

[2] As I have argued in "The Diversity of Comprehensive Liberalisms" in *The Handbook of Political Theory*, ed. Gerald F. Gaus and Chandran Kukathas (London: Sage, 2004), pp. 100–14.

[3] See John Stuart Mill, *On Liberty* in *The Collected Works of John Stuart Mill*, ed. J.M. Robson (Toronto: University of Toronto Press, 1977), vol. 18, chap. 1, 1.

social or public morality that allow one individual to make demands on others to act or desist from acting must be justifiable to each and every reasonable moral person within that community.

In this essay I argue that under conditions of extensive reasonable disagreement about what is valuable in life, conceptions of the good, and so on, a publicly justified social morality must be (i) a morality that gives pride of place to jurisdictional rights that are (ii) socially recognized. Re (i): given what I shall call "deep evaluative pluralism," I argue that a social morality that is publicly justified must be one in which most moral claims are based on individual moral rights. I shall argue that rights are often best understood in terms of a jurisdictional model. This jurisdictional conception has often been implicit in analyses of rights, but it has been overshadowed by focus on the way that rights involve choice or relate to interests. In his famous essay on "Are There Natural Rights?" – which is standardly interpreted as a defense of the choice theory – H.L.A. Hart pointed out that some rights grant the rightholder "authority or sovereignty in relation to some specific matter."[4] On this jurisdictional view moral rights are individualized spheres of moral authority or sovereignty, in which the rightholder's judgment about what is to be done provides moral directions for others. Although this view has obvious affinities to the choice theory, it is distinct from it, as well as from interest and benefit theories.[5] Re (ii): my second thesis is (even) more controversial: bona fide jurisdictional rights must be socially recognized.[6]

---

[4] H.L.A. Hart, "Are There Natural Rights?" *Philosophical Review*, vol. 64 (April 1955): 175–91, p. 184.

[5] For a detailed argument to this effect, see Eric Mack, "In Defense of the Jurisdiction Theory of Rights," *Journal of Ethics* 4 (January–March 2000): 71–98. I do not present the jurisdictional analysis as a theory of rights at all, at least if by "theory" we mean an account that identifies necessary conditions for well-formed rights claims. The long-running debate between "choice" and "interest" theories of rights was (for the most part) predicated on the supposition that each identified a necessary condition for a sound claim that "Entity X has right R." An advocate of the will (or choice) theory would typically insist that X must be capable of choice, or exercising her will, and R must somehow be responsive to X's choices. Thus Hart ("Are There Natural Rights?" p. 181) insisted that babies and animals did not have rights (though, of course they can be wrongly treated). In contrast, Mill (*On Liberty*, chap. IV, ¶3) and others have upheld an account of rights as necessarily protecting important interests. Given that babies and animals have interests, they can be rightholders: thus the common claim that a fetus has a right to life, though of course it cannot choose whether to exercise it. I shall put aside this search for "a theory" of rights. I very much doubt whether our concept of a moral right is sufficiently coherent to support interesting necessary conditions for well-formed rights claims. My concern is to analyze the crucial jurisdictional function of rights that has long been overlooked. I do not claim that all well-formed rights must be jurisdictional, or that justifications of specific rights cannot combine jurisdictional considerations with the importance of choice or protecting interests.

[6] The argument I advance in this essay is not the only case for the thesis that bona fide rights require social recognition. I have presented additional arguments for this conclusion in "Green's Rights

2. Morality, Authority, and Public Justification

2.1   *Morality, Authority and the Threat of Subjugation*

As I have said, social morality can be understood as a set of rules or principles that warrant individuals making moral demands on each other. As Mill recognized, when one appeals to social morality one makes a claim to be something like a moral authority over another: one is claiming that on this matter, the other is not to do as she thinks best, but as you require. Stephen Darwall has recently stressed the way in which interpersonal morality involves "authority relations that an addresser takes to hold between him and his addressee."[7] When one makes a moral claim on another, as Darwall points out, one is not making a request or calling attention to your view of morality: one is demanding that the other complies with one's demands.[8] We immediately confront a problem: how is such a claim to authority consistent with treating others as equal moral persons? At the heart of our moral relations with others is an appeal to authority, yet public reason liberalism insists that we are moral equals. How can a moral equal claim moral authority over another and demand that he is subject to your authority? Jeffrey Reiman puts the worry in a dramatic way: this assertion that one "has a higher authority" over how another should act raises the specter of "subjugation" – that "the very project of trying to get our fellows to act morally" may be "just pushing people around."[9]

When Alf makes a moral claim on Betty he may defend himself by insisting that he is not demanding that she submit to his authority, but to the authority of morality. What Darwall calls a claim to authority might be better understood as claim to have standing. Morality gives us standing to make another's action our business in the sense that we can appeal to moral principles and demand that she complies. When Betty asks "what business of yours is it whether I engage in homosexual relations?" Alf may reply that morality makes it his business, and so morality gives him standing to insist that she desist. This example, though, shows the ultimate

Recognition Thesis and Moral Internalism," *British Journal of Politics and International Relations*, vol. 7 (2005): 5–17. A revised and greatly expanded version of that essay appears as "The Rights Recognition Thesis: Defending and Extending Green," in *T.H. Green: Metaphysics, Ethics and Political Philosophy*, ed. Maria Dimovia-Cookson and Wlliam Mander (Oxford: Oxford University Press, 2006), pp. 208–35.

7 Stephen Darwall, *The Second-Person Standpoint: Morality, Respect and Accountability* (Cambridge, MA: Harvard University Press, 2006), p. 4.

8 Ibid., pp. 10–11, 76.

9 Jeffrey Reiman, *Justice and Modern Moral Philosophy* (New Haven, CT: Yale University Press, 1990), p. 1.

flaw in Alf's case that he is relying only on the authority of morality, and makes no claim to personal authority over Betty, for he is claiming that his view of morality is to be regulative for Betty. Alf's claim is that his understanding of morality gives him standing to demand that Betty desist from her activities, but this implies that she should defer to his understanding. He is not merely calling attention to a possible understanding: he is making a demand on Betty based on it. Alf, then, must be supposing that a moral inequality pertains between them. If Betty refuses to comply, he will judge her to have done wrong and to be blameworthy; if she addresses to him a contrary moral demand ("There is nothing wrong with what I am doing, so mind your own business!") he will judge himself blameless for dismissing it.

2.2 Universal Self-Legislation

Social morality presupposes that we claim authority over others, yet public reason liberals insist that we are all free and equal moral persons, and so each has a moral freedom to interpret her moral obligations for herself. As Locke put it, we suppose "the natural liberty of man is to be free from any superior power on earth, and not to be under the will or legislative authority of man, but to have only the law of Nature for his rule."[10] How can liberalism's commitment to moral freedom be reconciled with the authoritative nature of moral demands? Kant's ideal of the realm of ends provides the core insight: "A rational being belongs to the realm of ends as a member when he gives universal laws in it while also himself subject to these laws. He belongs to it as sovereign when he, as legislator, is subject to the will of no other."[11] Kant insists that for morality to be consistent with "the dignity of a rational being," a rational being must obey no law other than that which he gives himself. For morality to exist, the individual must be a subject; for it to be non-authoritarian, he must be the legislator.

Kant's depiction of the self-legislative nature of a free morality stresses that each rational being has a will that is legislative for every other will, giving laws to all which qua subject, are authoritative for her. Our moral freedom consists in being "a legislative member in the realm of ends,"[12]

---

[10] John Locke, *Second Treatise of Government*, §21, in *Two Treatises of Government*, ed. Peter Laslett (Cambridge: Cambridge University Press, 1960).
[11] Immanuel Kant, *Foundations of the Metaphysics of Morals*, ed. and trans. Lewis White Beck (Indianapolis: Bobbs-Merrill, 1959), p. 52 [Akademie, 433–34].
[12] Ibid.

but we are also subject to such legislation. Now it is important that by "realm" Kant meant "the systematic union of different rational beings through common laws."[13] So Kant does not think it is fine if you legislate in one way and I in another. Implicit in Kant's analysis of morality, then, is a unanimity requirement: we legislate common laws. The same morality thus must be legislated by all rational beings, who are in turn subjects of their own demands.

2.3 The Generic Public Justification Principle and Its Companion Deliberative Model

If we take seriously the unanimity requirement implicit in Kant, we are led to a view of moral justification along the lines of:

> The Public Justification Principle: M is a (bona fide) moral requirement only if each and every member of the public P has sufficient reason(s) R to accept M as a binding requirement on all.

Thus far this is a generic principle that all public reason liberalisms endorse. As I proceed, I will further specify some elements, identifying what I take as a plausible liberal conception.

Let us follow Rawls's lead by translating our justificatory problem into a deliberative problem. Rawls's great insight is that we can make progress in solving the justificatory problem by depicting a deliberation in which "free persons who have no authority over one another" come to unanimously endorse and accept various moral requirements to regulate their interactions.[14] Rather than proposing a complex deliberative setting (à la Rawls's later original position), let us work with a deliberative setting that closely models the justificatory problem. Suppose that each member of the public Pi (who employs some set of evaluative standards, more on this presently) deliberating under conditions C (involving, say, an information set, the absence of threats, and so on) proposes a moral requirement Mi to regulate some area of social life.[15] So there will be a set of proposals M1 ... Mn. Let

---

[13] Ibid.   [14] Rawls, "Justice as Fairness," p. 55.

[15] The idea of regulating an area of social life clearly needs further explication, but it has much in common with the idea of a social practice that Rawls employed in "Justice as Fairness." The important point is that the members of the public in the deliberative setting propose genuinely competing, alternative moral requirements. Thinking of them as proposing different ways of regulating a sphere of social life is one way to do this. Of course if we characterize spheres of social life broadly, then rather than individual moral requirements we would think of proposals as sets of moral requirements, or we might say alternative moral practices (which would bring the deliberative model closer to Rawls's 1958 essay on "Justice as Fairness"). The idea of spheres of

us also suppose that each member of the public ranks all proposals, so that at the end of the day each member of P under C has a complete, transitive ordering of all alternative proposals. Thus our deliberative problem is not a bargaining problem; individuals are not to bargain about acceptable moral requirements. As described, the deliberative problem models a collection of Kantian legislators in the realm of ends, proposing moral requirements and evaluating those of others, based simply on her own understanding of the relevant criteria.

3.   Evaluative Pluralism and Moral Disagreement

But what are the relevant criteria? To make progress we must specify the bases on which the parties generate and rank proposals. If the parties are so specified that they all reason on the basis of the same substantive moral theory, the range of moral requirements proposed by each would be highly restricted. In this case the Public Justification Principle and its companion model would do little work; most of the outputs would be determined by the shared moral theory. The Public Justification Principle becomes a substantive test of a moral requirement, and the deliberative problem becomes more interesting (and difficult), when we accept Rawls's insight that a wide range of rational disagreement is the "normal result of the exercise of human reason."[16] And liberals seem committed to significant pluralism concerning the basis of people's reasoning about what moral principles they are all to live under. Often this is put in terms of the moral relevance of differing conceptions of the good, or "comprehensive" conceptions: in evaluating proposed moral principles people draw on a wide variety of values, interests, and so on.

Suppose, then, that we accept reasonable pluralism in the sense that our characterization of the members of P deliberating under conditions C includes that members of P reason on the basis of different values, ends, goals, etc. This does not prejudge whether values are "ultimately" plural, for perhaps fully rational, omniscient beings would agree on what is valuable: the important point for public reason views is that the characterization of P under C allows for diversity in the basis of their reasoning about what moral requirements to endorse. Abstracting from the notions

social life is of course fundamental to Michael Walzer's *Spheres of Justice* (New York: Basic Books, 1983), though nothing said here presupposes the deep and extensive shared meanings that Walzer maintains characterizes the spheres.

[16] Rawls adds: "within the framework of free institutions of a constitutional regime." *Political Liberalism*, paperback edn. (New York: Columbia University Press, 1996), p. xviii.

of goods, values, moral "intuitions" and so on, let us say that b is an evaluative standard for member of the public Alf if holding b (along with various beliefs about the world) gives Alf a reason to endorse moral restraint M1 over alternative M2.[17] Evaluative standards, then, are to be distinguished from justified moral requirements: as I have characterized them they need not meet the test of Public Justification, but are the reasons for members of P to accept (or reject) M1 over some alternative.

Liberals suppose, then, some degree of plurality in the evaluative standards for P under C. But how much? Under radical pluralism we would so characterize the deliberations of P under C as to allow for just about any evaluative standard that rational agents have endorsed – including, say, those that value the suffering of others and subjugating others. But it is unlikely that a plausible conception of parties who conceive of each other as free and equal moral persons would endorse the moral relevance of such oppressive evaluative standards. In any event, the core problem of a liberal social morality under conditions of pluralism is not how we respond to, say, the Nazi, but how those who conceive of each other (and themselves) as free and equal handle their disagreements and so find a way to live under a non-oppressive social morality. How to respond to people who pursue as valuable what we think of as evil is a real problem, but the prior problem is how to deliberate with others who pursue what are recognizably human values, but who endorse very different "conceptions" of the good – how values are to be arranged into a coherent scheme. Moreover, empirical research indicates that the main source of our disagreements is not about what is valuable, but about what is more valuable. According to Milton Rokeach, a psychologist, Americans agree in affirming a set of thirty-six values; what they differ on is "the way they organize them to form value hierarchies or priorities."[18] This is a plausible take on Isaiah Berlin's claim that the range of plausible pluralism is limited by the "common human horizon" – what humans agree on as ways of living that can be intelligibly valued.[19]

---

[17] I leave aside here whether b is itself a belief about the world, or supervenes on one, as ethical naturalists would have it. Nothing in the account precludes moral realism as a metaethical or metaphysical thesis. The rationality-based constraint on justificatory reasons is the crucial principle on which the analysis rests.

[18] See Milton Rokeach, *The Nature of Human Values* (New York: The Free Press, 1973), p. 110; Milton Rokeach, "From Individual to Institutional Values" in his *Understanding Values* (London: Collier Macmillan, 1979), p. 208.

[19] See my *Contemporary Theories of Liberalism: Public Reason as a Post-Enlightenment Project* (London: Sage, 2003), pp. 27–31.

Consider, then, a less radical form of pluralism, according to which members of P under C all agree on a list of evaluative standards that are intelligible bases for the public justification of moral requirements. Now again we might consider more or less radical versions of such "intelligible value pluralism." The most radical version of this pluralism supposes that, of this agreed-upon list of intelligible values, members of P under C advance every possible ordering: every logically possible value hierarchy is represented in our deliberative setting. Assuming such unrestricted intelligible value pluralism, though, still seems too strong; public reason liberals may maintain that everyone, say, holds that not killing innocents is more important than securing personal pleasures, or (à la Rawls) liberals might suppose that all members of P under C hold that achieving fair terms of cooperation is an important desideratum. Even Berlin thinks that the "common human horizon" allows some common ranking of values: we sometimes agree that some rankings are more "humane" while others are "indecent."[20] We should not insist that liberals adopt a version of pluralism more extreme than Berlin's. Although, then, we should not require liberal public reason views to suppose entirely unrestricted rankings, a compelling liberal account nevertheless must attribute great diversity to the evaluative standards that individuals endorse. So liberals suppose that members of the public deliberating under C are characterized by great, though not entirely unrestricted, intelligible value pluralism.

The fundamental question for liberalism is how deep a pluralism is consistent with a morality of publicly justified requirements that respect all as free and equal. The problem for liberalism is manifest. If the parties in our deliberative model employ their evaluative standards to evaluate different proposed moral requirements, and if their evaluative standards are fundamentally at odds, these differences would seem to inevitably result in great disagreement in their rankings of proposed moral requirements. If member of the public P_1 holds ranking b_1 b_2 [read as "b_1 is ranked above b_2"], while P_2 maintains that b_2 b_1, then if the degree of justification of the moral requirements within a perspective is monotonic with the ranking of evaluative standards, P_1 will hold $M_1 > M_2$, while P_2 will rank the requirements $M_2 > M_1$. If evaluative pluralism is deep, since the members of the public rank proposals by appeal to their diverse standards, we would thus expect that great disagreement in evaluative rankings would result in great disagreements in the rankings of proposed moral requirements. If the

[20] See ibid., pp. 43–46; see also Jonathan Riley, "Interpreting Berlin's Liberalism," *American Political Science Review*, vol. 95 (June 2001): 283–97.

basis for judging moral requirements is diverse, so too will be evaluations of moral requirements. Deep moral disagreement would seem the inevitable result of evaluative pluralism.

4.   The Two-Step Kantian Moral Legislation Procedure

The liberal is thus confronted with the specter of deep moral disagreement, yet she is committed to the public justification of social morality. Liberals are committed to a common morality of universal self-legislation and great evaluative pluralism (of members of P under C). How can we get Kantian legislative consensus given the deep disagreement about the bases for judgment? The liberal seems to have straightforwardly incompatible commitments. How did Kant, and later Rawls, seek to solve the problem?

Kant writes:

> By "realm" I understand the systematic union of different rational beings through common laws. Because laws determine ends with regard to their universal validity, if we abstract from the personal differences of rational beings and thus from all content of their private ends, we can think of the whole of all ends in systematic connection, a whole of rational beings in themselves as well as of the particular ends which each man may set himself. This is a realm of ends ...

> A rational being belongs to the realm of ends as a member when he gives universal laws in it while also himself subject to these laws. He belongs to it as sovereign when he, as legislating, is subject to the will of no other.[21]

Kant's method for determining moral laws qua universal laws of freedom involves an individual decision procedure: each individual is to propound universal laws. Of course, as universal laws of morality regulating the realm of ends to which all free persons are subject, these laws are to be the same for all. How are different individuals, each acting as moral sovereign, to arrive at the same set of laws? Often Kant is seen simply as formalist, as if the mere universal form of the law guarantees convergence of legislation: once we universalize we will see what morality requires, and so what ends are consistent with morality. There are well-rehearsed objections to any such purely formal account of moral legislation. As we see in the above passage Kant hints at a rather more subtle idea: when united by common laws we ignore our "particular" or "private ends," and consider only universally valid

---

[21] Kant, *Foundations of the Metaphysics of Morals*, pp. 51–52 [Akademie, 433–34].

ends. For this bracketing strategy to succeed, we must have good reasons to bracket the considerations that set us apart (our private ends), and having done this, we must still have available to us some common considerations that can serve as the basis of individual deliberations about what laws to legislate. As Rawls suggests (in his discussion of the universal law formulation of the categorical imperative), we might appeal to a notion of "true human needs" which are shared by all and so are not mere private ends.[22]

Rawls's argument from the original position can be understood as a formalization of this two-step legislation procedure. First, (via the veil of ignorance) we abstract away "private ends" that would lead us to legislate different universal laws.[23] One excludes "knowledge of those contingencies which set men apart..."[24] Second, we attribute to the parties a concern with primary goods that provides a basis for their common deliberation. These primary goods can be understood as akin to "true human needs." Insofar as we consider ourselves as agents devoted to our varying (but undefined) ends, they are what we need. So we share a common perspective of agents who each pursue different ends. We thus isolate the specific evaluative standards characteristic of our (common) status of agents devoted to their own (unknown) ranking of evaluative standards (values, comprehensive conceptions of the good and so on); because "everyone is equally rational and similarly situated, each is convinced by the same arguments."[25] Consequently although the original position begins by posing a problem of collective choice, the problem is reduced to the Kantian problem of public legislation by one person.[26] However, unlike Kant, who apparently sees specific "private ends" as irrelevant considerations that can be entirely bracketed in moral legislation, Rawls's commitment to evaluative pluralism prevents him from holding that the specifics of one's conception of the good are irrelevant to moral justification. Rawls contends that the argument from the original position is free-standing: it isolates the evaluative considerations that follow from our conception of persons as reasonable and rational, free and equal – a conception that is said to be implicit in our democratic society, and so shared by all.[27] Justice

---

[22] John Rawls, "Themes in Kant's Moral Philosophy," in *John Rawls: Collected Papers*, pp. 497–528 at pp. 501ff.
[23] See Fred D'Agostino, *Incommensurability and Commensuration: The Common Denominator* (Aldershot, Hampshire: Ashgate, 2003), p. 100.
[24] Rawls, *A Theory of Justice*, revised edn. (Cambridge, MA: Belknap Press of Harvard University Press, 1999), p. 17.
[25] Ibid., p. 120.   [26] Ibid, pp. 120–21.   [27] Rawls, *Political Liberalism*, p. 10.

as fairness thus expresses "shared reason":[28] it is a justified political conception because it articulates the requirements of the concepts of the person and society that all reasonable citizens in our democratic societies share. It is partly based on the idea that we are all agents devoted to our several and divergent ends. However, Rawls does not believe that this argument from what we share exhausts justification. Indeed, he says that this is simply a pro tanto (so far as it goes) justification.[29] In what Rawls refers to as "full" justification citizens draw on their full range of evaluative standards and find further reasons for endorsing the political conception. At this stage, Rawls tells us, the pro tanto (freestanding) justification "*may be overridden by citizens' comprehensive doctrines once all values are tallied up.*"[30] What was simply "freestanding" or isolated must, if it is to be fully justified, serve as a "module" that fits into each free and equal reasonable moral person's set of evaluative standards.[31]

The Kantian legislation procedure is caught in a dilemma. If we follow Kant in entirely setting aside that which sets us apart as mere "private ends" that cannot be appealed to in moral legislation we may get a shared result, but only because we have severely restricted the role of differing values in moral justification. This restriction is objectionable: a person's value system is fundamental in her deliberations about what moral requirements she has reason to endorse. Remember, our goal is for each to follow her own reason while seeing herself as a member of the realm of ends: by preventing appeal in moral justification to so much of what a person understands as basic to her evaluative outlook, she can only see these laws as rationally self-legislated in an extremely attenuated sense. Rawls sees this, and so insists that the free-standing justification is only pro tanto – full justification must admit the full range of evaluative considerations, which might override the free-standing justification. But now it becomes doubtful that the free-standing argument is often stable under full justification; it is not, for example, in Display 1.

---

[28] Ibid., p. 9.   [29] Ibid., p. 386.   [30] Ibid. Emphasis added.
[31] Most commentators on Rawls mistakenly identify these two ideas. Rawls employs the idea of a "module" when explaining "overlapping consensus" (ibid., pp. 12–13; 144–45) whereas "freestandingness" applies to the appeal to shared conceptions of the person and lack of metaphysical and other commitments of the argument for the two principles (ibid., pp. 10, 40, 133, 144). The crucial passage that confuses many readers is on pages 144–45 of *Political Liberalism* where Rawls argues that because the political conception is freestanding it can serve as a module; many readers suppose that Rawls is simply equating the two ideas.

Display 1

	P1		P2		P3	
	Σ ranking	M ranking	Σ ranking	M ranking	Σ ranking	M Ranking
Freestanding Justification	x	M_1	x	M_1	x	M_1
(isolated perspective		M_2		M_2		M_2
of Σx)		M_3		M_3		M_3
Full Relevant Σ	x	M_1	y	M_2	x	M_1
Justification		M_2	x	M_1	y	M_3
(all Σ)		M_3		M_3		M_2
Irrelevant Σ	y		z		z	
	z					

In Display 1, we isolate the perspective that everyone shares of herself as an agent, devoted to some ends, which differ from person-to-person, but the specifics of which she does not know. Call this shared, isolated, perspective bx. If that is the only relevant evaluative standard, all concur on the ordering M1 M2 M3. But it is not clear that this will help a great deal after the full range of evaluative standards are brought into play. In Display 1 all three members of the public agree under full justification that bx is relevant to the judgment and that bz is not; yet we still can generate three different orderings of the proposed moral requirements under full justification. The moral disagreement implicit in evaluative pluralism, bracketed in the first stage, is apt to reassert itself under full justification.

5. The Burdens of Justification and Rights as Jurisdictions

5.1 *Rights as Partitioning the Moral Space*

We can conceive of all moral issues as constituting a space, and so our problem is how to regulate that space – what moral requirements we are to share that instruct us how to act in various parts of that space. Kant's and Rawls's proposals conceive of the problem of moral legislation as finding a common way of regulating the moral decision space. We can think of this as a centralizing response (which is implicit in Kant's understanding of a law). Under conditions of deep evaluative diversity, centralizing responses tend to collapse under the burdens of justification: they aim to take as inputs a large body of diverse rankings and yield as an output a determinate favored result. The Kantian-Rawlsian legislation procedure only yields results if the information pool – i.e., the relevant differences in evaluative orderings – is greatly limited. The knowledge that there is evaluative diversity is allowed, but the specifics of one's evaluative commitments are excluded from the deliberation about what moral laws to endorse. But that means in the end, we all reason in the same way, and that is how we can have common legislation despite evaluative diversity. This, though, leads to the common complaint that the Kantian-Rawlsian procedure rules out too much of what a person most deeply cares about when justifying principles to regulate our social life.

It seems as if deep evaluative pluralism simply poses too great a burden on justificatory procedures, so its influence must be greatly circumscribed. However, we can decrease the burdens posed by deep pluralism if we do not aim solely at uniform moral requirements or laws. Rather than seeking a uniform way to regulate the moral space, we may partition it. That is, we might devolve authority over different parts of the space to different individuals. As Fred D'Agostino has pointed out, "[i]n effect, we [can] say that in a society with n individual members, there are n separate spheres in which an answer ... may be sought, each of which is, in theory, inviolable and particular to the individual who occupies it."[32] If we partition the moral space in this way, for each and every person, there is some part of the moral space over which her evaluative standards have public standing. In that part of the moral space controlled by a person, her evaluative standards are sovereign, and others must respect those standards in that space.

Such partitioning yields a system of jurisdictional rights. As I noted in Section 1, Hart pointed out that some rights grant the rightholder "authority or sovereignty in relation to some specific matter."[33] Jurisdictional rights are individualized spheres of moral authority, in which the rightholder's judgment about what is to be done provides others with moral reasons to act. A regime of jurisdictional individual moral rights is thus a form of public justification – or perhaps it is better understood as a way to settle the problem of public justification in such a way that in the future it is no longer a collective problem. Benjamin Constant, I think, saw this in his famous lecture on "The Liberty of the Ancients Compared with That of the Moderns." Constant noted that liberty of the ancients consisted of "exercising collectively, but directly, several parts of the complete

---

[32] D'Agostino, *Incommensurability and Commensuration*, p. 105.
[33] Hart, "Are there Natural Rights?" p. 184.

sovereignty."[34] For the ancients, freedom manifested itself as a centralized, collective activity. In contrast, the moderns conceive of freedom in terms of individualized spheres in which their own values hold sway, such as freedom of association and religion, the right to "choose a profession and practice it, to dispose of property, and even to abuse it; to come and go without permission, and without having to account for their motives or undertakings."[35] John Gray once noted how private property rights economize on collective justification:

> The importance of several [i.e., private] property for civil society is that it acts as an enabling device whereby rival and possibly incommensurable conceptions of the good may be implemented and realized without any recourse to any collective decision-procedure. One may even say of civil society that it is a device for securing peace by reducing to a minimum the decisions on which recourse to collective choice – the political or public choice that is binding on all – is unavoidable.[36]

Property rights are quintessentially jurisdictional. To own property is to have a sphere in which one's evaluative standards have great authority for others. But we should not think that jurisdictional rights are exhausted by several property. Mill's defense of a "self-regarding sphere" in which "the individual is sovereign" is the classic liberal case for individual jurisdictions.[37] Such a sphere is composed not simply of property rights (in fact, Mill has little to say about property in *On Liberty*), but crucially, of privacy rights too. Insofar as one is acting within one's private sphere, one is authorized to act on one's controversial evaluative standards and others are bound not to interfere in certain ways, not to disseminate information about one's activities, and so on without one's permission. Also included within such a private sphere are various rights of association and rights involving the family.

It is important to stress that I am not maintaining that all of our common moral requirements – indeed, not all of moral rights[38] – are inherently jurisdictional. No doubt, under plausible depictions all members of the public under C will converge on some common moral requirements such as the wrongness of inflicting gratuitous suffering, principles of

---

[34] See Benjamin Constant, "The Liberty of the Ancients Compared with That of the Moderns" in *Political Writings*, ed. Biancamaria Fontana (Cambridge: Cambridge University Press, 1988), 311.

[35] Ibid.   [36] John Gray, *Post-Enlightenment Liberalism* (London: Routledge, 1993), p. 314.

[37] Mill, *On Liberty*, chap. 1, 9. I have argued that Mill's case takes evaluative pluralism seriously in "Controversial Values and State Neutrality in *On Liberty*" in *On Liberty: A Critical Guide*, ed. C.L. Ten (Cambridge: Cambridge University Press, 2008): 83–104.

[38] See note 5.

veracity, and so on. We should not go so far as to claim that common moral requirements are always impossible under deep evaluative diversity; the point is that the obstacles to a robust common morality that treats all as free and equal are severe, and a critical project of liberal morality must be to show that the challenge posed by these obstacles can be met. Jurisdictional rights, I maintain, are crucial to doing so.

5.2 The Liberal Limit on Evaluative Pluralism: Defending a Conception of "the Reasonable"

The jurisdictional solution to the burdens of justification is an option only if, whatever disagreements we have about evaluative standards, there is consensus that, when push comes to shove, moral requirements that give each authority to act on her own standards are generally higher ranked than moral requirements that everyone acts the same. The key to the jurisdictional solution is to allow great, but not unlimited, diversity in evaluative standards and show that this can lead to an agreement on moral jurisdictions. Deep evaluative pluralism need not engender deep moral disagreement if the parties' evaluative standards lead each to care more about living according to her values than having others conform to her values.

Recall Rawls's stylized history of European toleration, from initial insistence that all live according to one's own creed, to an uneasy standoff between churches that most highly value having all live according to their creed but accept the pragmatic impossibility of this, to the deep acceptance of toleration in the sense that one's evaluative standards simply do not endorse demanding that others live according to one's creed.[39] Now it is not necessary that members of the public go this far: they need not entirely abandon the view that their evaluative standards give them reason to make moral demands on others to adopt their creed, or vision of the good. They do, however, have to rank these proposed moral requirements lower than the moral right of each to act on her own standards. Once this becomes a characteristic of people's evaluative outlooks, a liberal morality of rights becomes possible. When Rawls supposes that the parties to the original position are "reasonable" one of the things this means is that each seeks mutually acceptable terms of cooperation in the sense that she is not devoted to requiring that others adhere to her controversial standards. But for Betty to refrain from insisting that others live according to her controversial standards, and to insist on the importance to her of her own fidelity to these standards, is simply to say that to Betty living

[39] Rawls, *Political Liberalism*, pp. xxv–xxviii.

according to her own lights is ranked higher than insisting that each conforms to her preferred evaluative standards.

Amartya Sen showed formally how a regime of jurisdictional rights is inconsistent with unanimous legislation (and, so we can see, public justification) when people care more about regulating others than being free to act as they see fit.[40] Sen conceives of a person having a right R as having authority to decide the social preference over at least one pair of alternatives (a,b) such that if a person chooses a b that is the social preference; and if the person chooses b a then that is the social preference. This conception of a right has been disputed, but it perfectly captures the conception of rights as devolved ways to cope with evaluative diversity: instead of a collective choice over the pair (a, b), the social choice is devolved to a single agent.[41] However, Sen showed that attributing such rights to two persons, and assuming all possible orderings of social states are permissible, the social outcome selected by the rights can conflict with the Pareto principle (that if for everyone a b, then the social preference must be a b). More formally, Sen demonstrated how combining rights, Pareto, and no restriction of preference orderings can result in intransitive social preference. Sen nicely summarizes his famous proof:

> There is a book (e.g. *Lady Chatterley's Lover*) which may be read by Mr. A ("the prude") or Mr. B ("the lascivious") or by neither. Given other things, these three alternatives define social states, a, b and o respectively. Consider now the following possibility. The prude A most prefers o (no one reading it), then a ("I'll take the hurt on myself"), and lastly b ("Imagine that lascivious lapping it up"). The lascivious [Mr. B] prefers most a ("it will give that lilywhite baby a nice shock), then b ("it will be fun"), and last o ("what a waste of a good book"). On grounds of individual freedom, since B wants to read the book rather than no one reading it, b is socially preferred to o; note that in either case A does not read the book here. Similarly, since A does not want to read it, o is socially better than a. But a is Pareto superior to b, yielding a preference cycle.[42]

So we get b>o (by Mr. B's right); o>a (by Mr. A's right); and a>b (by Pareto, since in both Mr. A's and Mr. B's ordering, a>b); so we get b>o>a>b – a cycle.

Some see this as a case against individual rights: they can conflict with the Pareto criterion, which can be seen as the core principle of unanimous

---

[40] Amartya Sen, "The Impossibility of a Paretian Liberal," *The Journal of Political Economy*, 78 (Jan.–Feb. 1970): 152–57. For an extended, and accessible, discussion, see Sen's "Liberty, Unanimity, and Rights," *Economica*, New Series 43 (Aug. 1976): 217–45.

[41] Nozick, for one, criticized it in *Anarchy, State, and Utopia* (New York: Basic Books, 1974), pp. 165–66. Cf. Sen's "Liberty, Unanimity, and Rights," pp. 229–31.

[42] Sen, "Liberty, Unanimity, and Rights," p. 218.

collective self-legislation. If all members of P under C rank M1 as better then M2 then certainly the collective legislation should be M1 (rather than M2). If we combine this principle with individual rights to decide the social (moral) preference over some options, we can get a social preference – or a public morality – that is intransitive, and so irrational. What is crucial here is that A's (and B's) values run counter to the scheme of jurisdictional rights because A's higher ranked standards are to get B to act as A wishes, rather than A valuing acting as he wishes in his own moral decision space. Many have accused liberals of supposing that people's aims are inherently selfish, or that their value systems are purely self-centered. This is not so, but the criticism is not totally unfounded (given that it has been so often made, that should not be surprising). The liberal ideal of a non-authoritarian morality becomes possible only when value systems generally converge on the higher importance of each living by one's own lights than having others live by one's lights. Moreover, we must remember that liberal individuals do not simply have self-interested reasons to live by their own lights: their overall evaluative standards lead them to conclude that it is more important for people to live by their own lights than for others to live according to standards one thinks are best.

The core idea, then, is that we can (i) maintain great evaluative diversity in the ways of living to which we are committed (in my more formal rendering, our orderings of evaluative standards) and yet (ii) achieve moral agreement if we (iii) converge in our evaluative standards regarding the priority of each of us living according to his or her preferred standards over having all live according to his preferred standards. This is indeed a limit on evaluative pluralism, but it is also a type of limit that, at the same time, makes it possible for a wide range (perhaps, indeed, the widest feasible range) of plural standards to be implemented. This limit of evaluative diversity is a core element of a compelling interpretation of the much criticized Rawlsian notion of "reasonable comprehensive view."

5.3   The Reasonable v. the Modus Vivendi

Now some insist that this is far too strong a supposition, and is far too much of a restriction on true pluralism. Public reason liberalism, it is charged, begins with grand pronouncements that the fundamental problem for public justification is evaluative pluralism but then admits into the relevant justificatory public only those who highly rank living according to their own evaluative standards. In Rawlsian terms this means that those who do not share this type of ranking are "unreasonable." A number of critics have insisted that this is an anemic pluralism. Gray has argued that this highly restricted notion of the reasonable renders such public reason liberalism "a species of fundamentalism, not a remedy for it."[43] To make matters worse, Gray argues, this limitation of pluralism is not necessary to justify liberal toleration: a modus vivendi – a standoff between those with deeply conflicting standards of evaluation – will suffice to ground something like liberal toleration.

In Rawls's stylized history, modus vivendi was the dominant understanding of toleration at the close of the religious wars: a conviction that others ought to live according to one's standards, tempered by a belief that it is impossible to get them to do so. Now it is important to see that even a plausible modus vivendi has to assume that, overall, individuals place a high value on living according to their own lights. Suppose for example, the relevant individuals have the evaluative orderings in Display 2. Let us say:

x, y, z = all others ought to live according to the evaluative standard x, or y, or z. (Read " x" as "for everyone, that they live according to bx.")

Ix, Iy, Iz = an evaluative standard according to which one values living according to x, y, or z. (Read "Ix" as "for me, that I live according to bx.")

Display 2

P1	P2	P3
$\forall x$	$\forall y$	$\forall z$
$\forall y$	$\forall z$	$\forall x$
$\forall z$	$\forall x$	$\forall y$
Ix	Iy	Iz

In Display 2, each individual Pi prefers that everyone lives according to Pi's evaluative standards, but each also ranks last the importance of her living according to her own lights. All three members of the public evaluate as better any way of living together under a common standard to each going it alone. Because in Display 2 each member of the public's primary concern is that we all live according to a common evaluative standard, there is no reason to think that a modus vivendi will arise. "Me, living according to my preferred standard" is ranked by everyone as lower than all living under some (any) common standard: it is Pareto-dominated by all other options. It might be replied that none of the other options stand a chance of adoption, but it is by no means clear that this is a relevant rejoinder. The core point is not what stands a

---

[43] John Gray, *The Two Faces of Liberalism* (Oxford: Polity, 2000), p. 21.

chance of being accepted by everyone, but one's evaluative ranking; even if everyone will not accept that they ought to live according to my preferred evaluative standard, this in itself does not show that I should not rank universal conformity to it as the best option. However, let us suppose that the individuals are concerned not simply with what they evaluate as the best outcome, but also its feasibility – whether it can become the common standard for society. This still will not lead them to a modus vivendi. Assuming the orderings in Display 2, in which all the individuals hold that coordinating on some common standard is more important than being able to live according to one's own preferred evaluative standard, they have a reason to coordinate on some common standard (x, y, or z) rather than risking failure to coordinate. Each going their own way is not favored by anyone. To better see why a modus vivendi will not arise in Display 2, consider a special case of the orderings in Display 3.

Display 3

Alf	Betty	Charlie
∀*Windows*	∀Mac-OS	∀*Linux*
∀Mac-OS	∀*Linux*	∀*Windows*
∀*Linux*	∀*Windows*	∀Mac-OS
I-*Windows*	I-Mac-OS	I-*Linux*

In this case each highly values using the same operating system as do others; going it alone is again Pareto-dominated. In Display 3 – where each wishes to do as others do – should one option (perhaps simply because of some random event) become slightly more popular than the others, people will gravitate to that option (as it stands the best chance of universal acceptance), and we witness a "bandwagon" effect based on the increasing returns for everyone of adopting the more popular option.[44]

The point here is that a plausible case for even a modus vivendi must itself suppose a restricted pluralism of evaluative rankings. Display 4 gives the quintessential ordering that many think would give rise to a modus vivendi:

---

[44] For an important analysis, see W. Brian Arthur, *Increasing Returns and Path Dependency in Economics* (Ann Arbor: University of Michigan Press, 1994).

Display 4

P1	P2	P3
$\forall x$	$\forall y$	$\forall z$
Ix	Iy	Iz
$\forall y$	$\forall z$	$\forall x$
$\forall z$	$\forall x$	$\forall y$

In Display 4, each ranks as most important that everyone lives according to her preferred evaluative standard, but next most important is the value of her (perhaps alone) living by her standard. Even the orderings in Display 4, however, do not immediately lead to toleration or a modus vivendi; so long as the first option for each is a moral requirement that everyone lives according to her preferred standard, there may be moral conflict and attempts at imposition. A modus vivendi can come about, though, by each eliminating her favored option from the feasible set ("I'd like everyone to be a Catholic, but others continue to successfully resist, and given their probability of success, further attempts to impose my standards are too costly; so I will simply no longer consider it as a feasible option"), thus producing the orderings of Display 5:

Display 5

P1	P2	P3
Ix	Iy	Iz
$\forall y$	$\forall z$	$\forall x$
$\forall z$	$\forall x$	$\forall y$

Once we have the orderings of Display 5, a modus vivendi in the form of jurisdictional rights can arise. P1 says to P2: "if you allow me a sphere to live according to x, I will allow you a sphere to live according to y," and so with P3, etc. Let us say:

Mx, My or Mz = a moral requirement that everyone acts on x, or y, or z. (Read "Mx" as "for all, a moral requirement that she acts on standard x.")

R(x,y,z) = a right of each to act on her preferred evaluative standard, x, y or z.

So we now have (Display 6) a ranking of moral requirements based on Display 5's ranking of evaluative standards.

Display 6

P1	P2	P3
$R(x,y,z)$	$R(x,y,z)$	$R(x,y,z)$
$\forall My$	$\forall Mz$	$\forall Mx$
$\forall Mz$	$\forall Mx$	$\forall My$

Display 6, however, is essentially the sort of ordering of moral requirements that liberal reasonable people have – not, of course, simply on feasibility grounds, but because they have come to embrace the primary importance (to be sure, within a range) of each living according to her own understanding of what is important. The "reasonable" liberal ranks the possible moral requirements as:

Display 7

P1	P2	P3
$R(x,y,z)$	$R(x,y,z)$	$R(x,y,z)$
$\forall Mx$	$\forall My$	$\forall Mz$
$\forall My$	$\forall Mz$	$\forall Mx$
$\forall Mz$	$\forall Mx$	$\forall My$

The difference between the liberal and the simple modus vivendi ranking of possible moral requirements, then, is that whereas the "reasonable liberal" ranks (1) everyone being able to live on the evaluative standard she adheres to as better than (2) everyone being required to live on my own preferred standard – based, say, on the importance of reciprocity – the modus vivendi argument simply drops (2) (i.e., everyone being required to act on my standards) from the feasible set. But in both cases jurisdictional spheres are the best option in the remaining set. The line between modus vivendi and reasonable accommodation is thus a fine one. This strengthens Rawls's conjecture that reasonable accommodation can arise out of a modus vivendi. The distinction indeed is far less important than either Gray or Rawls supposes. Some may have Display 7 orderings because they think they are the only fair and reciprocal orderings, or because they possess evaluative grounds for thinking that each should find salvation in his own way, while yet others have Display 6 orderings on pragmatic grounds. The important point is not agreement in evaluative standards, but in orderings of moral regulations. And while there is much to say for the greater stability of a moral order that does not rely on merely pragmatic considerations, those who uphold the requisite ordering on pragmatic grounds nevertheless have good reasons to accept the jurisdictional solution. Liberal "reasonable" orderings of moral requirements are thus not especially "sectarian" when compared to orderings that lead to a modus vivendi. They are, rather, the sort of orderings that are generally required for a non-authoritarian morality (or, we might say, mutual accommodation) under conditions of deep evaluative pluralism.

6. Jurisdictional Rights as De Jure Authority

Let us recall our problem and where we have traveled thus far. A moral claim on others is a claim to a sort of authority over their actions; liberalism, however, is premised on a non-authoritarian conception of the moral order. Such a moral order is possible only if each person – to employ Kant's depiction – is both legislator and subject. If each has reason to endorse a moral requirement, then when others make demands on the basis of such a requirement one is requiring the action of oneself. This proposal, which shows how a liberal moral order is possible, seems to run aground on the second pillar of liberalism, evaluative pluralism. If free and equal moral persons employ different evaluative standards, then it is dubious that they will often converge in their universal legislation. We thus confront the specter of deep moral disagreement. I have argued that one way to maintain a common morality in the face of disagreements in evaluative standards is to partition the moral decision space so that each person has authority, based on her own evaluative standards, within her sphere. A system of jurisdictional rights accomplishes this; so long as members of the public are conceived of as primarily valuing living their own lives by their own lights, the jurisdictional proposal provides the key to understanding how a common non-authoritarian morality is possible under evaluative pluralism.

A morality of rights that delimits the jurisdictions of individuals is, as I have been arguing, one that, as Hart said, gives an individual authority or sovereignty over some "matter." To be part of a genuine liberal morality, this must, of course, be de jure authority: no simply de facto authority will do. We are concerned with a system of authority that meets the test of public justification. It is thus of first importance to grasp what is implied by the idea of de jure authority or sovereignty. In his *Lectures on the Principles of Political Obligation* T.H. Green resists the idea that de jure sovereignty is simply "rightful authority" that has no practical force, as when appeal is made simply to a "general will, or the mere name of a fallen dynasty exercising no control over men in their dealings with each other."[45] Instead, Green argues, the distinction between de facto and de jure sovereignty "has natural meaning in the mouths of those who, in resisting some coercive power that claims their obedience, can point to another determinate authority to which they not only consider obedience due, but to which obedience in some measure is actually rendered..."[46] Green's general point, and he seems entirely right, is that a political authority that has, or is likely to have, no practical effect is no political authority at all, as it cannot perform its main task of sorting out actual disagreements and coordinating activities. To be any sort of authority at all there must be some general recognition of it; only then can it perform its designated tasks. If it is not generally recognized as an authority, we might argue that it ought to be an authority, that it alone could qualify as a justified authority, but we cannot claim that it now is such an authority. The job of authority is to regulate and coordinate social interaction; if so, an authority that is not recognized simply is unable to perform the office of an authority, as one who is not socially recognized as a leader is unable to fulfill the position of "group leader." We can say that a person who is not recognized – either explicitly or implicitly – as a leader ought to be the leader, that she would be a wonderful leader, or even that she would be the only leader worth having; but we cannot say that a person no one pays attention to is now the leader.

To be sure, difficult issues arise here concerning how effective, or potentially effective, a justified authority must be before we can say that it is the de jure authority. We might say that it has to have significant following, or that it has some reasonable prospect of gaining such a following. All these are complicated issues, but the crucial point is that on Green's analysis, "A is the de jure authority over M" is not established simply by a moral or philosophical argument that submitting to the direction of A in M-matters is justified, or even uniquely justified. A de jure authority must meet both the (1) justification and (2) minimal effectiveness conditions.[47] If, as Green says, we claim that rightful obedience is to be rendered only to some forgotten fallen dynasty, or a fantasized one, exercising no control over men in their dealings with each other, we are claiming that there simply is no de jure

---

[45] T.H. Green, *Lectures on the Principles of Political Obligation* in *Principles of Political Obligation and Other Writings*, ed. Paul Harris and John Morrow (Cambridge: Cambridge University Press, 1986), §105.
[46] Ibid.
[47] This is not to claim that a de jure authority must be de facto authority; that is a significantly stronger claim.

authority – no one has sovereignty – since no party has both minimal effectiveness and a justified claim.

Now given that bona fide jurisdictional rights define spheres of individual de jure authority over parts of social life, and given that de jure authority requires some minimal effectiveness or recognition, we can see that one of Green's most controversial claims is partially vindicated: viz., that a right must be socially recognized. Green's claim is too sweeping as, like so many others, he holds that our concept of rights is fully captured by a single "model" of rights, and so he gives necessary and sufficient conditions for all rights claims. If we abandon the idea that all moral (or political) rights ascriptions must conform to a single model,[48] we will not be led to such a sweeping claim. But we can say that (1) a fundamental role of rights in liberal social morality is to define jurisdictions over which, as Mill said, individuals are sovereign, (2) such rights can serve their function of allowing us to live together in mutual respect only if they are a de jure authority, and so (3) to be such de jure authority some degree of social recognition is required.

7.   What Scheme of Rights? – Rational Indeterminacy and Social Recognition

As Gray correctly claimed, a system of rights reduces to a "minimum" the recourse to collective choice. However, no system of jurisdictional rights can do away with collective justification. Most important for our purpose is that we require collective moral justification to partition the moral decision space in some particular way. We cannot do without a common view about which, of the large set of potential partitioning systems, we shall live under. Of course, not all systems of jurisdictional rights pass the test of public justification. For the first two hundred years of its existence American society upheld a system of jurisdictional rights in which the moral domains of some whites included the lives and bodies of African-Americans. To say that only a system of jurisdictional rights can cope with the burdens of justification is not to claim that any such system will suffice. Some partitions of the moral space clearly fail the test of the public justification. On the other hand, it seems that a number of schemes of rights will be acceptable to all members of the public, though they will disagree about which is best. It looks that we are back where we began, with moral disagreement and indeterminacy.

I have argued that liberal "reasonable" members of the public will put some rights schemes at the top of their ordering of possible moral

---

[48] Again, see note 5.

requirements. We can expect rational disagreement about the rankings of different schemes of rights, but given what we have said about the nature of liberal (and modus vivendi) orderings, there will be a number of rights schemes ranked higher than common moral requirements, as in Display 8.

Display 8

P1	P2	P3
$R_1(x,y,z)$	$R_2(x,y,z)$	$R_3(x,y,z)$
$R_2(x,y,z)$	$R_3(x,y,z)$	$R_1(x,y,z)$
$R_3(x,y,z)$	$R_1(x,y,z)$	$R_2(x,y,z)$
$\forall Mx$	$\forall My$	$\forall Mz$
$R_4(x,y,z)$	$\forall Mz$	$\forall Mx$
$\forall My$	$R_4(x,y,z)$	$\forall My$
$\forall Mz$	$\forall Mx$	$R_4(x,y,z)$

Now in Display 8, rights schemes R_1, R_2, R_3 Pareto dominate all universal moral requirements and R_4, but none (of R_1–R_3) Pareto dominate the others in the optimal set. So, we can say that all members of the public agree that any member of the set R_1, R_2, R_3 is better than any proposal outside the set. If they are to maximize, they must select from this optimal set.[49]

Suppose that one member of the set is presently socially recognized; it is the scheme of rights that actual moral persons generally accept and act on. Given that social recognition is a necessary condition for an effective scheme of de jure jurisdictional authority, the socially recognized scheme has a decisive advantage over the other members of the justified set: it meets the justification condition as well as the others do, but it alone meets the minimal effectiveness condition. It thus weakly dominates the other members of the optimal set: on no dimension does it do worse, and on some dimension it does better. Both the justification and minimal effectiveness conditions are necessary for the jurisdictional solution to work, and only if the jurisdictional solution works can we treat each other as free and equal moral persons under conditions of evaluative pluralism. Everyone thus has a decisive moral reason to conform to the de jure authority of the existing scheme of rights.

The other possibility is that the current scheme is not within this optimal set of rights. In this case people need to find a way to come to converge on a member of the justified set. Now we have seen (e.g., in

---

[49] See Amartya Sen, "Maximization and the Act of Choice" in his *Rationality and Freedom* (Cambridge, MA: Belknap Press of Harvard University Press, 2002): 158–205.

Display 8) that each individual will rank the various rights schemes. We have also seen (section 6) that a scheme of rights only has moral value if it is socially recognized. So we can generate (from Display 8):

Display 9 translates P1–P3's ordinal rankings of possible rights schemes into an ordinal utility function, which tells how well the social recognition of each proposed scheme satisfies a person's evaluative standards. We

Display 9

social recognition of	P1	P2	P3
R_1	3	1	2
R_2	2	3	1
R_3	1	2	3
None	0	0	0

suppose that no one wants a morality outside the optimal set (remember, this set Pareto dominates all other proposals), so an outcome outside of the optimal set is 0; the best outcome is a utility of 3. It is crucial to stress that by "utility" here I simply mean a measure of how well an option satisfies the evaluative standards of each member of the public. Utility here does not mean "self-interest" nor is it an independent value: it is simply a summary measure of how highly the option satisfies the person's overall evaluative standards.[50] Now at this point our members of the public face an impure coordination game along the lines of Display 10 (which concerns simply P1 and P2).

Display 10

P1	R1	R2
R1	3	0
P2	1	0
R2	0	2
0	3	

Suppose that R1 and R2 are alternative moral rights (P2's utility is in the lower left, P1's in the upper right, of each cell). The uncoordinated outcomes indicate no socially recognized moral rights at all on this matter. Looked at ex ante, P1's evaluative standards give her reason to endorse right R1; P2's lead

---

[50] I defend this claim in "Reasonable Utility Functions and Playing the Cooperative Way," *Critical Review of International Social and Political Philosophy*, vol. 11 (June 2008): 215–34.

him to endorse R2. Ex ante, P1 does not have reason to endorse R2 as legitimate over R1, nor does P2 have reason to endorse R1 rather than R2. They do, however, have reason to coordinate on either R1 or R2 in this game.

Should P1 and P2 find themselves at R1, R1 neither would have reason to act on R2. Given each of their rankings of the possible schemes (and their absence), they have the most reason to act on R1. If either refuses to act on R1, instead of acting on recognized jurisdictions, they act on conflicting views of their rights: there is then no de jure authority and no one has moral sovereignty. On the other hand, should they instead find themselves at R2, R2 each will then have most reason (given each of their evaluative rankings) to act on R2. Note that in neither case is the individual being induced by some external consideration to conform to a right that is not, from his or her perspective, optimal: consulting simply his or her own evaluative standards, each has decisive reason to freely endorse whichever jurisdictional right they have coordinated on. At right R1 P1 can cite the requirements of R1 to P2 and, consulting only his own evaluative standards, P2 will have a reason to conform to R1; and at right R2 P2 can cite R2, and P1's standards instruct her to act on it. And this even though, from the initial deliberative perspective, neither had reason to act on the other's preferred right. Thus, once a common morality has arisen each person, consulting only her own evaluations of the moral possibilities, sees that she has reason to freely conform to this right if it is in the optimal set.

A one-shot two-person game can give us an insight, but it is clearly an inadequate way to model the adoption of a scheme of rights. The coordination problem is not simply between two people but among many, and it is not a single-play game, but an iterated game. We have a number of encounters with others, and each can be understood as a play in a series of impure coordination games. Now in an iterated game a person's utility (again, remember this is defined solely in terms of her evaluative criteria) is a combination of her utility in this play, plus her expectations for utility in future games. Thus P1 might sacrifice utility in one instance to "punish" P2, seeking to get P2 to act in the future in ways preferred by P1. We know that in iterated impure cooperation games based on Display 10, the play can move back and forth from one equilibrium to another.[51] However, in large N-person games with multiple coordination equilibria such alternating solutions are much harder to sustain. As I have shown elsewhere,[52] the

[51] See Peter Vanderschraaf and Brian Skyrms, "Learning to Take Turns," *Erkenntis*, vol. 59 (2003): 311–46.
[52] In "The Demands of Impartiality and the Evolution of Morality," in *Partiality and Impartiality*, ed. Brian Feltham and John Cottingham (Oxford: Oxford University Press, 2010).

key here again is increasing returns: the more people play, say, R1, the more it makes sense for others to act on R1, even those who prefer coordinating on R2. To go back to Display 3, the same reasoning that shows why I am now using Microsoft Windows (the increasing returns of shared operating systems) shows how we can all come to accept the same moral rights despite beginning with diverse rankings of proposed rights.

In our N-person iterated coordination game, coordinating on any rights in the optimal set is a Nash equilibrium. This can be easily seen: since everyone prefers common action of any right in the optimal set to failure to coordinate, once we have arrived at a common action based on one of the rights in the optimal set, unilateral defection would make a person worse off in terms of her own evaluative standards and her resultant moral rankings. We thus arrive at a striking result: in this sort of moral game, coordination on any member of the optimal set is a Nash equilibrium, and so any member of the set can constitute a right that is freely followed by all, and so respects everyone's moral freedom. The reasons to follow the right are generated by what one considers the proper evaluative standards.

8.   Conclusion: Recognized Rights and Non-authoritarianism

Rights are necessary to cope with the burdens of justification. But ex ante no scheme of rights is best in everyone's evaluative perspective. From the ex ante perspective, for every candidate right, it would be authoritarian to impose it on some. But ex post, once others are acting, if one consults only one's own evaluative standards, a rational moral agent will freely act on any socially recognized right that is in the optimal set. Only a socially recognized right can overcome the problems of evaluative pluralism and the indeterminacy of public justification and allow us all to respect each other as morally free persons. This, I think, is of the highest importance. We normally think of moral theory and rational reflection as seeking to provide determinate answers to what morality rationally requires. We first reflect on what a rational justified morality is and then examine our actual morality to see if it measures up. The history of this way of thinking has, I think, given us ample cause to doubt whether such rational determinacy is to be had, at least in a way that takes seriously deep evaluative diversity. Rational reflection can narrow the field, but socially recognized moral rights are needed to complete the story: to give us a common morality that, consulting only our own standards, we have reason to endorse.

CHAPTER 4

The Moral Foundations of Liberal Neutrality

Section 1 of this essay explicates the concept of neutrality. Section 2 provides two arguments supporting a conception of Liberal Moral Neutrality. Given a certain understanding of moral and rational persons, I argue, moral neutrality is a fundamental and inescapable commitment. Section 3 shows how liberal moral neutrality leads to Liberal Political Neutrality. Fully grasping the nature of this liberal political neutrality, I argue in Section 4, has radical implications for our understanding of the proper limits of government.

1. The Concept of Neutrality

For the last few decades political theorists have vigorously debated whether liberalism is committed to some doctrine of "neutrality," and whether neutrality provides a plausible constraint on legitimate laws and policies. In my view, this long-running controversy has been disappointing: theorists tend to stake their claim as advocates or critics of neutrality, yet the precise contours of the concept and its justification remain vague. To be sure, we have witnessed some important advances. Discussions of neutrality are now careful to distinguish: (i) the idea that a justification (say, of a policy) should be neutral; (ii) the claim that the aims of policymakers should be neutral; (iii) the claim that the effects of policy should be neutral.[1] Yet interpretations of neutrality are far more diverse than most analyses recognize.[2] Neutrality is sometimes understood as a doctrine about:

---

[1] See Charles Larmore, *Patterns of Moral Complexity* (Cambridge: Cambridge University Press, 1987), pp. 43ff.; Will Kymlicka, "Liberal Individualism and Liberal Neutrality," *Ethics* 99 (Jul. 1989): 833–905; Simon Caney, "Consequentialist Defenses of Liberal Neutrality," *The Philosophical Quarterly* 41 (Jan. 1991): 457–77.

[2] The most careful discussion is George Sher, *Beyond Neutrality: Perfectionism and Politics* (Cambridge: Cambridge University Press, 1997), Ch. 2.

constraints on legislation or legislators,[3] the proper functions of the state,[4] the prohibition of the state "taking a stand" on some issues,[5] the prohibition of the state enforcing moral character,[6] or the requirement that the state take a stance of impartiality.[7] Alternatively, neutrality can be understood as a requirement of a theory of justice rather than state action.[8] There are also differences about whether neutral states (or theories of justice, or legislators) are supposed to be neutral between conceptions of the good,[9] controversial conceptions of the good,[10] conceptions of the good that citizens may rightfully adopt,[11] comprehensive doctrines and conceptions of the good,[12] particular sets of ends,[13] particular or substantive conceptions of the good,[14] ways of life,[15] or final ends.[16] And it is unclear whether every principle of neutrality is inherently one of liberal neutrality, or whether liberal neutrality is a specific sort of neutral principle.[17]

To make a start at clarifying just what the debate is about, I propose the following general definition-schema:

> A's φ-ing is neutral between X and Y concerning X's and Y's difference D iff φ does not treat X and Y differently on the basis of D.

[3] See Jeremy Waldron, "Legislation and Moral Neutrality" in his *Liberal Rights* (Cambridge: Cambridge University Press, 1993), pp. 149ff.

[4] Peter Jones, "The Ideal of the Neutral State" in Robert E. Goodin and Andrew Reeve, eds., *Liberal Neutrality* (London: Routledge, 1989), p. 9; Govert Den Hartogh, "The Limits of Liberal Neutrality," *Philosophica* 56 (1995): 59–89 at p. 61.

[5] Colin M. MacLeod, "Liberal Neutrality or Liberal Tolerance?" *Law and Philosophy* 16 (Sep. 1997): 529–59 at p. 532; Paul Rosenberg, "Liberal Neutralism and the Social-Democratic Project," *Critical Review* 8 (1994): 217–34 at p. 218.

[6] Wojciech Sadurski, "Theory of Punishment, Social Justice and Liberal Neutrality," *Law and Philosophy* 7 (1988/89): 351–74 at p. 371.

[7] See Jones, "The Ideal of the Neutral State," p. 9.

[8] See Philippe van Parijs, *Real Freedom for All* (Oxford: Oxford University Press, 1995), p. 28.

[9] Bruce A. Ackerman, *Social Justice in the Liberal State* (New Haven, CT: Yale University Press, 1980), p. 11.

[10] Larmore, *Patterns of Moral Complexity*, pp. 53ff.

[11] Robert Talisse, *Democracy After Liberalism* (London: Routledge, 2005), p. 33.

[12] See John Rawls, *Justice as Fairness: A Restatement*, ed. Erwin Kelly (Cambridge, MA: Belknap Press of Harvard University Press, 2001), p. 152.

[13] Jones, "The Ideal of the Neutral State," p. 9.

[14] See Brian Barry, *Justice as Impartiality* (Oxford: Clarendon Press, 1995), pp. 139–45; Ronald Dworkin, "Liberalism" in his *A Matter of Principle* (Cambridge, MA: Harvard University Press, 1985), p. 191; Roger Paden, "Democracy and Liberal Neutrality," *Contemporary Philosophy* 14 (1): 17–20.

[15] Kymlicka, "Liberal Individualism and Liberal Neutrality," p. 886.

[16] J. Donald Moon, *Constructing Community: Moral Pluralism and Tragic Conflicts* (Princeton, NJ: Princeton University Press, 1993), p. 55.

[17] See Barry, *Justice as Impartiality*, pp. 125ff. Robert E. Goodin and Andrew Reeve, "Liberalism and Neutrality" in their edited collection, *Liberal Neutrality*, pp. 1–8.

The definition-schema is, I think, fully general about claims concerning neutrality. It must be stressed that the definition-schema is not intended to resolve substantive disputes about the proper interpretation of neutrality; the aim is to get clearer about the variables around which controversy centers. Each conception of neutrality provides a different interpretation of the variables. The most familiar controversy, which I mentioned above, concerns the proper interpretation of "treatment." Varying conceptions proffer different explications: those who think that neutrality requires neutrality of effect hold that unless A's φ-ing has the same effect on X and Y with respect to D, A's φ-ing treats them differently; those who uphold neutrality of justification maintain that A treats X and Y the same when A has a justification for φ that does not appeal to D. To better see how the definition-schema is to be applied, consider the classical case of a government that is neutral between two combatants. The government (A) is neutral between the combatants (X and Y) concerning the differences in their war aims (D) when A's decision, say, about shipments of arms or war-related matters (φ) does not treat X and Y differently on the basis of their war aims, alliances, etc. Note a few points. (i) The range of φ – what sorts of actions must be neutral – is in dispute between different notions of state neutrality in war (just as it is in liberal neutrality). In 1914 President Wilson insisted that

> The United States must be neutral in fact, as well as in name. We must be impartial in thought, as well as action, must put a curb upon our sentiments, as well as upon every transaction that might be construed as a preference of one party to the struggle before another.[18]

But that is an extreme interpretation of φ (and was not lived up to). The Swedish Government in 1941 declared that

> Neutrality does not demand that nations not participating in an armed conflict should be indifferent to the issues of the belligerents. The sympathies of neutrals may well lie entirely with one side, and a neutral does not violate his duties as long as he does not commit any unneutral acts that might aid the side he favors.[19]

Adopting this, let us call φ such acts by the state. (ii) Notice that the Swedish doctrine explicitly allows that A (the neutral government) need not always refrain from different treatment of X and Y on the basis of their

---

[18] Woodrow Wilson, *Message to Congress*, 63rd Cong., 2d Session, Senate Doc. No. 566 (Washington, DC, 1914), pp. 3–4.
[19] http://lawofwar.org/Neutrality.htm.

war aims (D): A's public schools might still favor X's aims, and treat X and Y differently in its curriculum, but this would not impair A's neutrality regarding φ – e.g., arms shipments or war materials. (iii) Note also that the definition-schema does not require a neutral A to always treat X and Y the same when φ-ing. Suppose A sells arms to both X and Y, but X has paid and Y has not (international law allows neutrals to sell arms). Then A may treat X differently than Y even regarding φ, because the difference in treatment is not grounded on D (their war aims), but on whether payment has been made.

Moving a little closer to our concern, think about a neutral umpire. The neutral umpire (A) does not treat the players (X and Y) differently with regard to what team they are on or whether she personally likes them (D), when making calls in the game (φ). But, of course, A does treat them differently in making calls in the game (φ) depending on whether one has violated the rules. And A can still be a neutral umpire if, when buying Christmas presents, she selects her hometown team's jersey, so does sometimes base her differential treatment on D (but not when φ-ing).[20]

Philosophy differs from mystery writing: in philosophy we can give the ending away without ruining the story. It may help to give a general description of the conceptions of neutrality that I defend here.

> Liberal Moral Neutrality: A [a free and equal reasonable moral person] making φ [a moral demand] addressed to Y [a free and equal reasonable moral person] must be neutral between X and Y [where A is also person X; that is where A is one of the relevant parties]: the justification of A's moral demand must not treat Y and A differentially based on the differences (D) in their evaluative standards.

> Liberal Political Neutrality: A [an agent of the state] when φ-ing [exercising coercion on citizen X who is also a free and equal reasonable moral person, or participating in the authorization of such coercion] must be neutral between X and Y [where Y φ any other rational citizen/moral person]: the justification of A's coercion must not appeal to X's and Y's differences (D) in their evaluative standards.

Liberal Moral and Political Neutrality, as I explicate them, are not concerned with neutrality between conceptions of the good (or, more broadly, what I will call "evaluative standards"). Liberalism, I shall argue, is neutral

---

between persons, and this neutrality requires not treating them differentially on the basis of their differing evaluative standards (or, loosely, conceptions of the good). Liberalism is not concerned with neutrality between conceptions of the good, as if conceptions of the good themselves had claims to neutral treatment. It is only because citizens hold such conceptions that neutrality between citizens has consequences for the way conceptions of the good can enter into moral and political justification. This might seem to be a distressingly pedantic point, but, I think, it helps us avoid confusion. Suppose at time $t1$ there are two conceptions of the good in society, $C1$ and $C2$ but at time $t2$, everyone has come to embrace $C1$. It would seem that, if liberalism is really committed to neutrality between conceptions of the good per se, then even at $t2$, it must be neutral between $C1$ and $C2$. But this seems implausible. As I understand liberal neutrality, since it is a requirement to be neutral between persons, appealing at $t2$ to $C1$ does not run afoul of neutrality, since there are no differences between citizens on this matter. So it is not in itself non-neutral to appeal to conceptions of the good; it all depends on the differences that obtain among moral persons and citizens.

2. Liberal Moral Neutrality

2.1 Free and Equal Moral Persons

I take as my starting point the supposition that we conceive of ourselves and others as (i) moral persons who are (ii) free and equal. Although these features are assumed in this essay, we should not suppose that these assumptions cannot themselves be defended. John Rawls rightly argues that this general conception of moral persons is implicit in our public culture.[21] In much the same vein, I have argued that our commitment to the public justification of our moral demands on each other follows from our present conception of ourselves and others.[22] Let me briefly explain each of these two fundamental characteristics.

A moral person is one who makes, and can act upon, moral demands. Moral persons thus conceive of themselves as advancing moral claims on others. Alternatively, we can say that moral persons understand themselves

---

[21] See John Rawls, "Kantian Constructivism in Moral Theory," in Samuel Freeman, ed., *John Rawls: Collected Papers* (Cambridge, MA: Harvard University Press, 1999), pp. 303–58, esp. 305ff. This is not to say that Rawls and I advance precisely the same conception of free and equal moral persons, as shall become clear in what follows.

[22] See my *Value and Justification* (Cambridge: Cambridge University Press, 1990), pp. 278ff.

to be owed certain restraints and acts.[23] Not all humans – not even all functioning adult humans – are moral persons: psychopaths do not appear to understand themselves as pressing moral claims on others that demand respect, nor do they see others as moral persons.[24] As well as advancing moral claims, moral persons have the capability to act on justified moral claims made on them. In this sense moral persons are not solely devoted to their own ends; they have a capacity to put aside their personal ends and goals to act on justified moral claims. Moral persons, then, are not simply instrumentally rational agents;[25] they possess a capacity for moral autonomy. Insofar as moral autonomy presupposes the ability to distinguish one's own ends from the moral claims of others, the idea of a moral person presupposes some cognitive skills.[26]

In the *Second Treatise* John Locke held that "The natural liberty of man is to be free from any superior power on earth, and not to be under the will or legislative authority of man, but to have only the law of Nature for his rule."[27] To conceive of oneself as morally free is to understand oneself as free from any natural moral authority that would accord others status to dictate one's moral obligations. This is not at all to say that one sees oneself as unbound by any morality; as Locke suggests, we may have the law of nature as our rule. Although we are by no means committed to a natural law conception of morality, the crucial point, again one in the spirit of Locke, is that free moral persons call on their own reason when deciding the dictates of moral law. A free person employs her own standards of evaluation when presented with claims about her moral liberties and obligations. A free person, we can say, has an interest in living in ways that accord with her own standards of rightness, value and goodness. At a minimum, to conceive of oneself as a morally free person is to see oneself as bound only by moral requirements that can be validated from one's own point of view.[28] This conception of freedom has much in common with

---

[23] See here J.R. Lucas, *On Justice* (Oxford: Clarendon Press, 1980), p. 7. For a development of this conception of morality, see Thomas Scanlon, *What We Owe Each Other* (Cambridge, MA: Belknap Press of Harvard University Press, 1998), esp. pp. 177ff.

[24] I argue this in *Value and Justification*, pp. 281ff.

[25] See John Rawls, *Political Liberalism*, paperback edition (New York: Columbia University Press, 1996), p. 51.

[26] I argue for this claim in "The Place of Autonomy in Liberalism," in John Christman and Joel Anderson, eds., *Autonomy and the Challenges to Liberalism* (Cambridge: Cambridge University Press, 2005), pp. 272–306.

[27] John Locke, *Second Treatise of Government* in *Two Treatises of Government*, ed. Peter Laslett (Cambridge: Cambridge University Press, 1960), §22.

[28] It also provides the basis for understanding morality as self-legislated. I develop this idea further in "The Place of Autonomy in Liberalism."

Rawls's notion of the rational autonomy of parties to the original position, according to which "there are no given antecedent principles external to their point of view to which they are bound."[29]

Now to say that moral persons are equal is to claim, firstly, that qua moral persons they possess the minimum requisite moral personality so that they are equal participants in the moral enterprise and, secondly, that each is morally free insofar as no one is subjected to the moral authority of others. The equality of moral persons is their equality qua free moral persons: it is not a substantive principle of moral equality but is a presupposition of the practice of moral justification insofar as it defines the status of the participants in moral justification. While a modest conception of moral equality, it rules out some conceptions of moral justification. Rawls not only conceives of moral persons as advancing claims on each other, but stresses that they view themselves as "self-authenticating sources of valid claims."[30] It would seem, and apparently Rawls agrees, that those who understand themselves as authenticating their own claims would not see themselves as bound to justify their claims on others – they would not suppose that only claims justified to others are valid.[31] But to advance a self-authenticating claim on others is not to respect their moral freedom, for others are bound only by moral claims that they can validate through their own reason: "there are no given antecedent principles external to their point of view to which they are bound." The supposition of equal moral freedom thus requires that one's moral claims can be validated by those to whom they are addressed.

Many have advanced stronger conceptions of moral equality. Some have claimed, for example, that the very practice of morality presupposes an "equal right of each to be treated only with justification."[32] In a similar vein S. I. Benn and R. S. Peters defended the principle that "The onus of justification rests on whoever would make distinctions presume equality until there is a reason to presume otherwise."[33] Such a principle of moral

---

[29] Rawls, "Kantian Constructivism," p. 334.

[30] Rawls, *Justice as Fairness*, p. 23. The importance of the idea of self-authentication is easily overlooked in Rawls's thinking. It first appeared in his 1951 paper on an "Outline of a Decision Procedure for Ethics," which conceived of ethics as adjudicating the claims of individuals, which he clearly saw as self-authenticating. See section 5 of that paper in Rawls's *Collected Papers*, Ch. 1.

[31] Hence, because of this, parties to Rawls's original position are not required to advance justifications for their claims. Rawls argues this in "Kantian Constructivism," p. 334.

[32] Hadley Arkes, *First Things: An Inquiry into the First Principles of Morals and Justice* (Princeton, NJ: Princeton University Press, 1986), p. 70. Italics omitted.

[33] S. I. Benn and R. S. Peters, *Social Principles and the Democratic State* (London: George Allen and Unwin, 1959), p. 110.

equality does not simply require us to justify our moral claims to others: it requires us to justify all our actions that disadvantage some. Now, leaving aside whether some such presumptive egalitarian principle could be morally justified,[34] this conception of moral equality is not presupposed by the very idea of a justified morality among free and equal moral persons. If I accept this principle, I claim that others act wrongly if they disadvantage me without good justification. But unless this non-discriminatory principle itself can be validated by others, I disrespect their moral freedom, as I am making a moral claim on them to non-discriminatory action that is not validated by their own reason.

Validation from the rational and reflective perspective of another, however, is not the same as her actual consent. To treat another as a free and equal moral person is to accept that moral claims must be validated from her perspective when she employs her rational faculties in a competent manner and reflects upon them. Now, although as John Stuart Mill noted, there is a strong presumption that each knows her own perspective best, this is not necessarily so.[35] Just as others can make sound judgments about a person's beliefs and principles, and be correct even when the person disagrees, so can others be correct, and the moral agent wrong, about what is validated from her perspective when she reflects on it. Knowledge of oneself is generally superior to others' knowledge of one, but it is not indefeasible. People may withhold assent for a variety of reasons, including strategic objectives, pigheadedness, confusion, manifestly false beliefs, neurosis, and so on. Nevertheless, respect for the equal moral freedom of another requires that the presumption in favor of self-knowledge only be overridden given strong reasons for concluding that she has misunderstood what is validated from her own point of view. Suppose that Alf and Betty reasonably disagree about whether some moral principle P is validated from Betty's rational and reflective perspective. Say that Alf has good reasons to conclude that Betty has misunderstood what is validated from her point of view: P, he says, really is validated from her point of view. Betty has reason to insist it isn't. For Alf to insist that his merely reasonable view of Betty's commitments override her own reasonable understanding of her moral perspective constitutes a violation of her

---

[34] I argue that it cannot in *Justificatory Liberalism* (New York: Oxford University Press, 1996), pp. 162ff.

[35] J. S. Mill, *On Liberty*, in *On Liberty and Other Essays*, ed. John Gray (New York: Oxford University Press, 1991), pp. 84–5 (ch. IV, para. 4). Mill also was aware that this assumption does not always hold true. See his *Principles of Political Economy*, in J. M. Robson, ed., *The Collected Works of John Stuart Mill* (Toronto: University of Toronto Press, 1963), vols. II and III, Book V, Ch. xi, §9.

moral freedom, for Alf is claiming authority to override her own reasonable understanding of her moral commitments with his merely reasonable view.[36] Crucial to moral freedom is that, over a wide range of deliberative competency, one's moral deliberations lead you to conclude φ authorizes you to believe φ.[37]

2.2 Morality as Giving Others Reasons

We can reach much the same conclusion by a different route. Rather than relying directly on respecting the equal moral freedom of others, we can appeal to a theory of moral reasons. Morality is inherently a rational and practical enterprise insofar as addressing moral claims to others is to give them reasons to comply. To say that I have valid moral claims but these give others – even rational others – no reason to comply with them seems to undermine the point of advancing moral claims. If we are not simply concerned with calling others names – criticizing them for "doing wrong," "being guilty," "violating the rights of others," and so on – what is the point of advancing moral claims that do not appeal to their rational nature? To be sure, views of morality that attenuate its practical or rational nature in this way are often defended. Some see moral judgments as essentially descriptive and so not essentially practical ("φ is best described as a right action"). And some understand moral statements as a way to express disapproval at what others are doing, and so not essentially rational ("Boo to φ!", "I disapprove of φ and you should too!"). Such views do not capture the crux of moral practice: it is a way for us to relate to each other as rational agents, who can give each other reasons to perform, or refrain from, actions of certain types.

If we accept that morality is necessarily about giving reasons to others, then our understanding of moral justification will be deeply influenced by our understanding of what constitutes a reason. We cannot enter here into the complexities of different accounts of reasons; consider, however, a plausible view. To give someone a reason is to give her a consideration to φ that, if she employs her rational faculties in an informed, careful, competent, and reflective way, she can see as counting in favor of φ. Suppose Alf claims that R is a reason for Betty to φ, but Alf admits that

---

[36] I deal with this complex question more formally in *Justificatory Liberalism*, Parts I and II.

[37] Again, I recognize the complexities of this matter. I try to shed a little more light on it in "Liberal Neutrality: A Radical and Compelling Principle," in Steven Wall and George Klosko, eds., *Perfectionism and Neutrality: Essays in Liberal Theory* (Lanham, MD: Rowman & Littlefield, 2003), pp. 136–65, at pp. 150ff., and *Value and Justification*, pp. 399–404.

even were she to be fully informed about information that is relevant, and she carefully and competently reflects on R, she still could not see how R is a consideration in favor of φ-ing. It is hard to see in what way Alf can say that R is a reason for Betty to φ; he has admitted that it really cannot be grasped by her reflective deliberation, and given that, it cannot be a reason for her to do anything. The idea of a reason that is unable to play a role in deliberation is surely odd. Perhaps it would be good for Betty to φ, but it seems implausible to say that she has any considerations that count in favor of φ.

If we accept this plausible view of what it is to give another a reason, combined with our practical and rational conception of the moral enterprise, we are again led to the view that, for Alf to make a valid moral claim on Betty that she φs, this claim must be validated from Betty's perspective: there must be a reason for her.

2.3   Liberal Moral Neutrality

Given the requirements for treating others as free and equal moral persons and the requirements of moral justification, the task of publicly justifying a moral principle P requires that P be validated from the perspective of each rational and reflective free and equal moral person. To publicly justify a moral principle is to justify it to all rational and reflective free and equal moral persons within some public, who confront each other as strangers.[38] I shall assume that the relevant public here is something like a society; we could also define the public in terms of all persons (a universalistic cosmopolitan morality) or a smaller community. As our main concern is with morality insofar as it relates to political justice, focus on the notion of a society's morality is appropriate.

Abstracting from the notions of goods, values, moral "intuitions" and so on, let us provisionally say that φ is an evaluative standard for moral person Alf if and only if holding φ, along with various sound beliefs about the world, is a reason for or against a purported moral principle, etc. from Alf's rational and reflective point of view.[39] So a person's evaluative standards are to be distinguished from justified moral requirements. Suppose, then,

---

[38] On the concept of the public, see S. I. Benn and G. F. Gaus, "The Liberal Conception of the Public and Private," in S. I. Benn and G. F. Gaus, eds., *Public and Private in Social Life* (New York: St. Martin's, 1983), pp. 31–66.

[39] I leave aside here whether Σ is itself a belief about the world, as ethical naturalists would have it. It is important to stress that nothing in my account precludes moral realism as a meta-ethical or metaphysical thesis; the epistemic constraint on moral reasons is the crucial principle on which the analysis rests.

that Alf attempts to justify some moral principle P on the basis of his evaluative standard φa, which is not shared by Betty. He clearly has not justified P. For P to be justified it must be validated from Betty's viewpoint. Thus, appealing to an evaluative standard about which Alf and Betty rationally and reflectively disagree cannot be justificatory: if Betty's careful and rational reflection cannot endorse φa as a consideration in favor of P, then P has not yet been justified as a moral principle at all. Even if a careful, rational and reflective Betty can see φa as a consideration in favor of P, this is still not enough to show that P is validated from her view. She might also have reason to embrace φb and that may be a consideration against P; the matter then turns on which consideration defeats the other in her overall ranking of evaluative standards.

It is crucial to appreciate that this argument does not show that Alf has a moral obligation to justify his claims on Betty.[40] On such a view, although Alf may have a moral obligation not to insist on P without justification, he might have an overriding moral obligation to act on P even if it cannot be justified to her. On the account I have articulated here, unless P is validated from Betty's perspective, it is not a moral principle at all, and so cannot ground any moral reasons. Its status as a reason-giving moral principle applying to society depends on its validation from the public perspective. Morality supposes impartiality, and impartiality requires that the principle be validated by all members of the moral public.

If Alf is to respect others as free and equal moral persons and provide them with genuine moral claims, he is committed to:

> Liberal Moral Neutrality: Alf's moral demands addressed to Betty must be neutral between his and Betty's evaluative standards: the justification of Alf's moral demands must not rely on relevant differences between his and Betty's evaluative standards.

Let us consider more carefully why Alf is committed to Liberal Moral Neutrality.

(i)   We are supposing that Alf is committed to treating others as free and equal moral persons, and he is a moral person committed to making moral demands on others. If this is so, he must advance moral demands on others, and for these to be valid moral demands (i.e., to actually be moral demands) they must be justified to those others.

(ii) Liberal Moral Neutrality does not require that Alf present, or even be aware of, the justifications for his moral demands – he may be

---

[40] This interpretation is advanced by Christopher Eberle, *Religious Convictions in Liberal Politics* (Cambridge: Cambridge University Press, 2002), Ch. 3.

unable to articulate arguments about what others have reason to accept. But for his moral demands to be genuine, they must provide considerations for all reflective and rational others. Now given this, it cannot be the case that their justification either favors his evaluative standards or theirs on a relevant difference between them. If there is a relevant difference (a difference that affects the justification of P), then if Alf is biased towards his own evaluative standards he will not be providing Betty with adequate reasons; should for some reason he favor Betty's, then the moral demand would not be validated from his view: it would not provide him with a sufficient reason. Note that if their evaluative standards converge on P, then the justification of the demand may be based in their different evaluative standards because it would not then be exploiting a difference between them, but appealing to their commonality. This is important. Public justifications may be based either on consensus or convergence of evaluative standards.[41] A consensus justification maintains that P is justified because everyone has grounds to endorse it on the basis of the same evaluative standard; a convergence justification maintains that P is justified because Alf has grounds to endorse it on the basis Σa, Betty on the basis of Σb, etc. Now a consensus justification is perfectly neutral: the justification does not rely on our disagreements about evaluative standards but, instead, on our agreement about the implications of our standards. Thus, we must reject the plausible idea that liberal neutrality prohibits appeal to "controversial conceptions of the good"; we see here that in some cases such appeals treat all as free and equal moral persons to whom we owe reasons.

(iii)   It should be clear why "treatment" is to be understood in terms of justification. The reason we are led to Liberal Moral Neutrality is a conception of free and equal moral persons who are committed to making moral demands on others that provide reasons from everyone's perspective. The grounding of morality is impartial treatment qua moral justification. Any more robust requirement of non-differential treatment – say, that every state policy should equally impact each conception of the good life – would have to be justified within the moral or political enterprises. Such robust conceptions of non-differential treatment are surely not presuppositions of the moral enterprise itself.

---

[41] On convergence as a mode of justification, see Fred D'Agostino, *Free Public Reason: Making It Up As We Go* (New York: Oxford University Press, 1996), pp. 30–1.

3. Liberal Political Neutrality

3.1 The Non-coercion Principle

I deem this conception of moral neutrality "liberal" because it starts from the quintessentially liberal conception of moral persons as free and equal, rational and reflective, agents. It is not, however, liberal in any more substantive sense. In order to move toward Liberal Political Neutrality, we must first make a basic, and I think fairly uncontroversial, claim within morality. If any claim can be justified within the constraints of Liberal Moral Neutrality, it is surely:

> The Non-coercion Principle: (i) It is prima facie morally wrong for Alf to coerce Betty, or to employ force against her. (ii) With sufficient justification, Alf may have a moral right to use of coercion or force against Betty.

Almost every liberal political philosopher has understood the Non-coercion Principle as a basic moral commitment of liberal political philosophy. The principle's core claim is that, other things equal, the use of force or coercion against another is wrong. To show that other things are not equal, and so that the use of force and coercion is morally permissible, a moral justification is required.[42]

It is hard to see a plausible case against the Non-coercion Principle.[43] Whatever one's evaluative standards, so long as one has any reason to act on them, and so be an agent, one must have strong reason to object when others exercise force or coercion to thwart one's agency. Someone who seeks to coerce you (without justification) to make you do as he wishes is attacking your fundamental interest in acting on your own evaluative standards. The wrongful coercer supplants your evaluative standards with his own as the grounds for your action. Jeffrey Reiman aptly describes this as a case of "subjugation": i.e., "the judgment of one person prevails over the contrary judgment of another simply because it can and without adequate justification for believing it should."[44] As Reiman suggests, the "suspicion of subjugation" can be dispelled – we can distinguish "might from right" – if there is adequate justification:[45] to say that coercion is

---

[42] In order to simplify, I will henceforth refer to "coercion" rather than the more cumbersome "force and coercion."

[43] I have considered some possible objections in "Liberal Neutrality: A Radical and Compelling Principle."

[44] Jeffrey Reiman, *Justice and Modern Moral Philosophy* (New Haven, CT: Yale University Press, 1990), p. 2.

[45] Reiman, *Justice and Modern Moral Philosophy*, p. 2.

"prima facie" wrong is to say that reasons can be provided to vindicate some instances of coercion. Suppose someone denies this: she says that coercion can never be justified: she accepts part (i) of the principle but denies (ii). Such an objector must, then, see self-defense as always wrong: in response to the wrongful force by another, it would still be wrong for her to employ force to resist. Though some have advanced such extreme pacifist views, the claim that one is never justified in employing any degree of coercion to repel any wrongful aggression against oneself is highly counterintuitive; I will not pause to consider it further. If our agency is of fundamental importance to us, then we must accept that, at least in some cases, we have reason to endorse a principle that allows coercion – at the very least, to counter coercion against us.

3.2   The Moral Claims of, and Constraint on, Liberal Governors

Government officials participate in the authorization of coercion; unjustified coercion is wrong, so if officials are not to act wrongly their coercion must be justified. Consider first the two-person case: official Alf is coercing citizen Betty, say, by imposing a law. So, at a minimum, Alf must have a justified moral liberty to coerce Betty: it must be, morally, not wrong for him to coerce her.[46] And, of course, this justification must meet the demands of Liberal Moral Neutrality: he cannot favor his own evaluative standards. But for the same reason, the justification cannot favor the evaluative standards of some third party, Charlie, when coercing Betty. Now take any law that applies to both Betty and Charlie: the justification of the law means Alf cannot exploit differences in Betty and Charlie's evaluative standards, since then one of them will have inadequate reason to accept that Alf has a moral right to impose the law. So Alf's act of imposing the law is only morally permissible if there is a justification for the imposition that meets Liberal Political Neutrality.[47]

This all supposes that the Non-coercion Principle applies to governments and its agents (qua agents). This is not entirely uncontroversial; a

---

[46] According to Wesley Hohfeld, Alf has a liberty to φ, if and only if Betty has no claim against Alf that he not φ. For Hohfeld's classic analysis, see his "Some Fundamental Legal Conceptions as Applied in Judicial Reasoning," *Yale Law Review* 23 (1913): 16–59.

[47] Note that should the law not apply to some other party, the law would not have to be justified to him: a law might apply to only a "section of the public." Think, for example, of a law that regulates motorcycle use: it may not require justification to some class of citizens (say, those who do not drive). Stanley Benn and I explore the idea of a "section of the public" in "The Liberal Conception of the Public and Private."

recurring view in the history of political philosophy insists that the "normal" moral restraints that apply to individual actors do not apply to the state; "the State, as such, certainly cannot be guilty of personal immorality, and it is hard to see how it can commit theft or murder in the sense in which these are moral offenses."[48] More generally, what has been called "political realism" insists that the constraints of "ordinary" morality are not applicable to politics. As Machiavelli famously observed, "A man who wishes to make a profession of goodness in everything must necessarily come to grief among so many who are not good."[49] If governors have a duty to protect the interests of their citizens, it has seemed to many that in the unpredictable and morally lax environment in which politicians often operate, they must ignore the normal precepts of everyday morality and look to promote the good of their people. As the realist sees it, to insist that the Non-coercion Principle applies to those in government fails to appreciate the distinctive character of the political.

We need to distinguish three different conceptions of the special nature of politics.[50] (i) The "realist" insists that there is an "ineluctable tension between the moral command and the requirements of successful political action."[51] On this conception successful politics requires immorality: one must often have morally "dirty hands" to be a successful politician. The liberal tradition in politics rejects such realism: politics is neither above nor outside the claims of morality. (ii) The first view is puzzling: why should the fact (if it be a fact) that political success requires immorality be a reason to ignore morality rather than to forgo political success? If a trade union official told us that success for the union requires immorality, we would hardly think that this excuses her immorality. A moral plausible view is that while morality applies to the government, it is an entirely different morality: the state, we are told by some, cannot be guilty of personal immorality – it is held accountable to a higher morality: "successful

[48] Bernard Bosanquet, "The Philosophical Theory of the State," in *The Philosophical Theory of the State and Related Essays*, ed. Gerald F. Gaus and William Sweet (Indianapolis, IN: St. Augustine Press, 2001), p. 285. Even Bosanquet, however, insisted that, while the state as such could not be guilty of immorality, "if an agent, even under the order of his executive superior, commits a breach of morality, bona fide in order to do what he conceives to be a public end desired by the State, he and his superior are certainly blamable..." (p. 284).
[49] Niccolò Machiavelli, *The Prince* in *The Prince and the Discourses* (New York: Modern Library, 1950 [1515]), p. 56.
[50] I consider these issues in more detail in "Dirty Hands" in R. G. Frey and Kit Wellman, eds., *The Blackwell Companion to Applied Ethics* (Oxford: Basil Blackwell, 2003), pp. 169–79.
[51] Hans J. Morganthau, *Politics Among Nations*, 5th edn (New York: Alfred A. Knopf, 1973), p. 10. See also Reinhold Niebuhr, *Moral Man and Immoral Society* (London: Student Christian Movement Press, 1963).

political action" is "itself inspired by the moral principle of national survival," and so politicians have no "moral right" to sacrifice their state in the pursuit of fidelity to the principles of individual morality.[52] This special "morality of the state" is also rejected by the liberal tradition: there is not one morality for persons and a different one for states, as if states were not composed of individuals with commitments to respect the moral personality of others. (iii) However, to deny that there is a special morality of the state is not to deny that that the special circumstances of politics may allow for justifying acts that otherwise would be wrong. Liberals (although not perhaps libertarians) accept that the conditions under which the agents of the state can justifiably employ coercion differ from the conditions under which private individuals may. This, of course, is the fundamental concern of political philosophy: how does the state come to be authorized to employ coercion (such as to punish) while private individuals are not so authorized? To accept that the agents of the state are justified in employing coercion when non-state agents are not does not mean that the Non-coercion Principle fails to apply to governors: the liberal claims that there are arguments that meet the test of Liberal Moral Neutrality that, in some cases, allow only agents of the state to justifiably coerce.

The upshot is that unless we wish to join the realist in withdrawing politics from the purview of morality, or allow that the state is subject to its own special morality of national interest, the actions of those who are agents of the state must conform to requirements of morality, specifically the Non-coercion Principle, and the only way to overcome the presumption against coercion is through a justification that conforms to the demands of Liberal Moral Neutrality. We thus have:

> Liberal Political Neutrality: An agent of the state when coercing a citizen, or participating in the authorization of such coercion, must be neutral between that citizen and any other citizen: the justification of the state official's coercion must not treat differentially reasonable and reflective citizens' differences in their evaluative standards.

Notice that we have switched our focus from moral persons to citizens. For the most part, I shall leave open the relation between these two classes. We do need to suppose that all members of the class of citizens are also free and equal moral persons, since the moral foundations of Liberal Political

---

[52] Morganthau, *Politics Among Nations*, p. 10. Note that Morganthau seems to advocate both positions (i) and (ii). It is often difficult to know whether "realists" are arguing against applying moral considerations to politics, or are arguing for a special political morality.

Neutrality lie in Liberal Moral Neutrality. Perhaps all moral persons residing within a jurisdiction should be considered as citizens (I am certainly sympathetic to this proposal); however, I shall leave open the possibility that some moral persons within a jurisdiction (i.e., resident aliens) might be excluded from the class of citizens. This is an important issue in political theory, but we cannot pause to discuss it here. Nothing I say in what follows turns on this point.

3.3   The Coercive Nature of the State

Does Liberal Political Neutrality apply to all, or only some, action by state officials? John Stuart Mill distinguished authoritative from non-authoritative interventions by government; while the former take the form of a command backed by enforcement, the latter give advice and information, or establish an agency to deal with a problem while allowing others to compete.[53] Although the government threatening drug users with prison sentences is indeed an act of coercion, drug education programs, on Mill's view, would not be coercive. George Sher makes much of this point. In order to promote certain aims, governments might offer rewards, engage in economic policies that favor the aim, fund educational programs, and so on.[54] If these policies are not coercive, then they do not fall under the Non-coercion Principle.

What is sometimes called the "libertarian" response must be right here: each of the supposedly non-coercive measures is only possible because of a prior act of coercion, be it threats associated with the tax code, threats that back up banking regulations (relevant, say, to setting interest rates), and so on. The action "conduct an educational program" presupposes the action "raise via taxation the revenues to conduct the program." Assuming the former is impossible without the latter, it is inappropriate to separately evaluate them. An act that depends on having certain resources or powers cannot be evaluated without consideration of the legitimacy of obtaining those resources or powers. Here at least is a case where the dictum that "He who wills the end must also will the means" is appropriate: to insist that there is nothing coercive about the end, when the only way to achieve the end is through a coercive means, is disingenuous. To say that it is not coercive to spend your money, even though I must use coercion to get my hands on it, hardly seems convincing. The object of evaluation should be the complex act {raise revenues through taxation & spend them on an

---

[53] Mill, *Principles of Political Economy*, Book v, Ch. XI.   [54] Sher, *Beyond Neutrality*, pp. 34–7.

educational program}. That the complex should be the focus of evaluation is by no means simply a libertarian view: the American Civil Liberties Union sues public authorities that use tax money to advertise religion (say, by using public workers to erect signs saying "Jesus is Lord").[55] The idea is that this is not a mere educational measure that does not impose burdens on some; it does impose burdens that must be borne by dissenting citizens because of threats of punishment by the taxation department.

It can, though, plausibly be maintained that some state actions are less coercive than others. Just as a threat of a short prison sentence is less coercive than threat of a long one, and threat of a small fine is less coercive than threat of a moderate jail term, so too the coercion involved in an extra one percent marginal tax rate is typically less coercive than the threat of jail.[56] Thus, if we concern ourselves with the strength of the justifications required to legitimate the coercion, then a distinction between stronger and milder forms of coercion will be relevant.[57] But that distinction is not relevant to the Non-coercion Principle, which concerns the set of actions that require justification.

4. The Implications of Liberal Political Neutrality

4.1 The Demanding Nature of Liberal Political Neutrality

To paraphrase Robert Nozick, so strong and far-reaching is Liberal Political Neutrality that it raises the question of what, if anything, the officials of the state may do.[58] It is unclear whether much in the way of public policy survives the neutrality test. Since we have seen that whenever state officials act they participate in a coercion-authorizing process, to implement any such policy would require a justification that does not exploit differences in the evaluative standards of reasonable and reflective citizens – i.e., is neutral between them. Some may think that this is not terribly demanding. It is reasonable to suppose that, after all, citizens do share many evaluative standards. Although we may not have consensus on a full-fledged conception of the good, we might still identify "a public conception of the good": there might be substantive shared values that are

---

[55] *The Times-Picayune* (New Orleans), Sunday Feb. 24, 2002, Metro Section, p. 1.
[56] See Daniel M. Weinstock, "Neutralizing Perfection: Hurka on Liberal Neutrality," *Dialogue* 38 (1999): 45–62.
[57] I explore the problems of degrees of coercion and strength of justification in "Coercion, Ownership, and the Redistributive State," *Social Philosophy & Policy* 27(2010): 233–75.
[58] Nozick, *Anarchy, State, and Utopia*, p. ix.

a matter of overlapping consensus of everyone's conceptions of the good –
say, health, security and happiness.[59] Suppose, for example, that some
evaluative standard Σ is shared by all. Then it would seem that an appeal to
Σ in a justification for policy P would not run afoul of Liberal Political
Neutrality: implementing policy P treats all citizens neutrally since the
justification for it does not appeal to their reasonable differences in
evaluative standards. But this moves too quickly, for we need to take
account of different citizens' rankings of their evaluative standards.
Reason R does not justify a policy consistent with neutrality unless it
would be accepted by all fully rational and reflective citizens. Now
although a rational Betty might reject R as a reason because it appeals to
an evaluative standard that she does not share, she will also reasonably
reject it as a good reason in favor of P when it appeals to a ranking of
evaluative standards that she does not share; R may be a reason in favor of
P, but it is overridden in her ranking by R*, which is a reason against
P. According to Milton Rokeach, a psychologist, Americans agree in
affirming a set of thirty-six values; what they differ on is "the way they
organize them to form value hierarchies or priorities."[60] If so, our main
disagreements are not about what is of value (what is an evaluative
standard), but the relative importance of our evaluative standards. Even
if everyone agrees, say, that smoking causes cancer and that this is a reason
for a policy discouraging smoking, rational people clearly do disagree about
whether the pleasures are worth the risk of death. Given that rational
people weigh the relative values of pleasure and safety differently, coercive
acts that can only be justified on the grounds that the pleasure does not
outweigh the risk to health fail to provide a neutral case. Thus, although
the badness of ill health caused by smoking can be invoked in a neutral
justification, that its badness outweighs the goodness of the pleasure of
smoking cannot; and without that, no state policies discouraging smoking
will be justified. This has direct relevance to United States drug policy,
which is based on certain middle-class value rankings, and which results in
policies that place inordinate costs on the poor.[61]

   This fundamental point deserves emphasis. Political philosophers are
usually insensitive to what economists call "opportunity costs": the cost of

---

[59] Weinstock, "Neutralizing Perfection," p. 55.
[60] See Milton Rokeach, *The Nature of Human Values* (New York: The Free Press, 1973), p. 110;
Milton Rokeach, "From Individual to Institutional Values," in his *Understanding Values* (London:
Collier Macmillan, 1979), p. 208.
[61] See J. Donald Moon, "Drugs and Democracy" in Pablo De Greiff, ed., *Drugs and the Limits of
Liberalism* (Ithaca, NY: Cornell University Press, 1999), pp. 133–55.

getting one thing you value is that you must forgo something else you value.[62] It is often assumed that once we recognize a shared value, we have the basis for a neutral policy: but everything depends on whether achieving this shared value requires that some give up something of greater value. If it does, then for those citizens pursuing this shared value is irrational: they are giving up something more important for something they prize less. So it does no good to simply point to shared value: we must point to a shared ranking of values, so that all rational and reflective citizens will agree that achieving this value is more important than any other values that might be achieved. But this is a daunting task: rational and reflective, free and equal persons appear to disagree deeply on the rankings of their evaluative standards (what is a "conception of the good" but a scheme in which values are weighted?). It looks as if almost any collective pursuit of values will involve some citizens being coerced into pursuing a value that is less important to them than a value they had to give up (say, because they were taxed for the collectively pursued value).

Some try to blunt the radical implications of Liberal Political Neutrality by restricting the range of the neutrality principle (the class of cases covered by φ) to a small set of basic political matters.[63] Rawls, for example, appears to restrict φ to constitutional issues or matters of basic justice: unless an issue concerns a "constitutional essential" neutrality does not apply – apparently non-neutral justifications can be employed in everyday (non-constitutional) politics. Can they? Suppose that we have a neutral justification of a constitution, and now are advocating policy P, which is not itself about a constitutional matter. There are two possibilities. It might be that the constitution, which is, ex hypothesi, neutrally justified, authorizes P. In this case P does have a neutral justification insofar as it is

---

[62] George Klosko is something of an exception. He acknowledges that people disagree in their rankings, but he insists that somehow this is not a problem for justification. Thus, he tells us that it is not "forbidden that government policy priorities reflect some conceptions more than others. Neutrality requires only that public policies be intended to realize nonsectarian values and that the relevant means be similarly defensible." "Reasonable Rejection and Neutrality of Justification" in Steven Wall and George Klosko, ed., *Perfectionism and Neutrality: Essays in Liberal Theory* (Lanham, MD: Rowman & Littlefield, 2003), pp. 167–89 at p. 178. Klosko's position seems to be that so long as policy is justified on "non-sectarian" grounds, it is neutrally justified, even if the policy "reflects" some citizens' ranking over others. I cannot see the motivation for restricting justification to the kinds of reasons advanced but not their importance; unless a more complicated account is offered, a person has no reason to accept a policy that is based on a ranking of evaluative criteria that she reasonably rejects. Klosko thus defends motorcycle helmet laws as "neutral" even though he admits that they presuppose rankings of values that are rationally rejected by some citizens. Klosko's main motivation, I think, is simply to ensure that liberal neutrality does not have radical implications; see §4.3.

[63] Weinstock, "Neutralizing Perfection," p. 54.

justified through the constitution which is neutrally justified. The issue, though, is whether a constitution with extensive authorizations of this sort could be neutrally justified. It seems doubtful indeed that, for example, a constitution that allows the government to use taxation to discourage smoking, encourage a healthy life-style, regulate drugs, fund the arts, go to war to spread democracy, seek to advance human flourishing, protect the family, or promote community is capable of neutral public justification. Given what has been said above, there is a strong presumption that all coerced citizens could not be given impartial reasons of the requisite sort for granting the state authority over these matters. The other alternative is that the constitution is neutrally justified, but only the constitution; there is no indirect neutral justification via the constitution for policy P. The case for P is another matter entirely, outside of the scope of Liberal Political Neutrality. But this implies that P is a coercive act without adequate justification and so wrong. Neutrality cannot be restricted to a certain "level" because the Non-coercion Principle is a fully general principle, applying to all coercive acts.

4.2 The Specter of Anarchism?

If Liberal Political Neutrality is that demanding, is any law justified? Do we end up with anarchism? Everything I have thus far said about public policies that seek to advance values such as health would seem to apply to matters of basic political justice, such as a regime of property rights. While every rational and reflective citizen may agree that some system of property rights is better than none (for then we avoid the state of nature, where there is no "mine and thine"), no argument for a specific system of property can function as a neutral justification of the requisite sort, as it will be rationally rejected by some. Some will, say, rank a libertarian system of property higher than a welfare state system, while others will have evaluative standards that lead them to the reverse ranking. The difference between the smoking case and the property rights case lies in where the option "no policy at all in this matter" is on each rational citizen's rankings. Suppose that all rational citizens endorse or prefer systems of property {Pr1, Pr2, Pr3} over no system of property rights, but some prefer no system of property rights over {Pr4, Pr5}. If so, there is a Liberal Political Neutralist justification for selecting from the set of {Pr1, Pr2, Pr3}; our evaluative standards converge on the conclusion that any member of that set is better than no property regime at all. What is required next – and this is where democracy enters in – is a justified procedure to select from that set.[64] If we have such a procedure, then we will have a fully justified system of property rights despite the disagreements about what is the best system – disagreements on the relative merits of {Pr1, Pr2, Pr3}. In contrast, in the typical public policy case, at least over a very wide range of issues, for each and every policy P in the set of options, a number of citizens rank P as inferior to "no policy at all on this matter." No policy whatsoever will be preferred, first, by those who prefer no policy to every policy, and so rank P and all other policies behind no policy at all (e.g., classical liberals regarding pornography regulation). Second, P will also be ranked worse than no policy at all by those who prefer some other policy P* to no policy at all, but prefer no policy at all to P.[65] Thus on issues where some rational citizens fall into one of these two groups no public justification of P can be advanced. Of course, if there is a public justification for some policy on this matter (for example, regarding a public good such as pollution control), and P is in the set of admissible policies, then we move to a case like that of property rights. It is very likely, though, that once we take account of comparative judgments, Liberal Political Neutrality precludes a great deal of contemporary legislation.

4.3   Liberal Political Neutrality: Critical or Apologetic?

Liberal Political Neutrality is a radical principle: it expresses a suspicion that coercion threatens subjugation and, based on our understanding of others as free and equal moral persons, advances a demanding test to overcome this suspicion. Pace almost all contemporary advocates of Liberal Neutrality, I have argued that Liberal Political Neutrality is genuinely liberal in the sense that it is suspicious of all coercion and drastically limits the scope of government. Many of the things that contemporary states do fail the test of Liberal Political Neutrality – which is to say that contemporary states are not genuinely liberal. Some advocates of "liberal neutrality" see this conclusion as a reductio ad absurdum.[66] To these liberals, any adequate conception of liberal neutrality must show that most of what contemporary governments do is justified. Thus, some tell us that if a conception of liberal neutrality excludes, say, public school classes in

---

[64] I have argued that constitutional democracy is such a procedure in *Justificatory Liberalism*, Part III.

[65] I explore this problem in much more depth in "The Legal Coordination Game," *American Philosophical Association's Newsletter on Philosophy and Law* 1 (Spring 2002): 122–8.

[66] See, e.g., Klosko, "Reasonable Rejection and Neutrality of Justification," pp. 175ff.; Weinstock, "Neutralizing Perfection," p. 47.

drama and music, it is shown to be an absurd conception.[67] This common view presupposes what liberals must question: that state coercion is justified. I see no good reason to accept what amounts to a conception of political philosophy as an apology for the current state. To appropriate a contemporary if not pellucid term, in the eyes of liberals the state is problematic. That is why the classic social contract theories begin with the state of nature – a condition without any government – and seek to show that construction of a limited government is consistent with moral principles. Current advocates of neutrality work the other way around: they start with government as we know it and test moral principles by showing that they justify it.

Even supposing it is true that "daily politics is irretrievably perfectionist" – that the aim of politics is to make people more autonomous, or healthier, or wiser, or more family-oriented, or more God-fearing – this would by no means show that anti-perfectionism is absurd or misguided.[68] If compelling moral claims show that most state coercion is unjust, then the loser is state coercion, not these fundamental moral convictions. Liberal moral principles are indeed "self-stultifying"[69] when what is being stultified is unjustified coercion of some by others. Morality stultifies a host of things that we may wish to do, including making others more perfect in our own eyes.

---

[67] See Klosko, "Reasonable Rejection and Neutrality of Justification," p. 175. Klosko is reporting, but apparently concurring with, the views of Richard Kraut.
[68] Den Hartogh, "The Limits of Liberal Neutrality," p. 59.   [69] This term is Weinstock's.

CHAPTER 5

Coercion, Ownership, and the Redistributive State
Justificatory Liberalism's Classical Tilt*

I. Justificatory Liberalism and Substantive Liberal Conceptions

In the last few decades, a new conception of liberalism has arisen –
"justificatory liberalism"[1] – which developed out of the social contract
tradition. The social contract theories of Thomas Hobbes, John Locke,
and Jean-Jacques Rousseau all stressed that the justification of the state
depended on showing that everyone would, in some way, consent to it. By
relying on consent, social contract theory seemed to suppose a voluntarist
conception of political justice and obligation: what is just depends on what
people choose to agree to – what they will. As David Hume famously
pointed out, such accounts seem to imply that, ultimately, political justice
derives from promissory obligations, which the social contract theory
leaves unexplained.[2] Only in the political philosophy of Immanuel Kant,
I think, does it become clear that consent is not fundamental to a social
contract view: we have a duty to agree to act according to the "idea" of an
"original contract" to which all agree.[3] John Rawls's revival of social
contract theory in *A Theory of Justice* did not base obligations on consent,
though the apparatus of an "original agreement" of sorts persisted. The
aim of his famous "original position," Rawls announced, was to settle "the

---

* The ideas explored in this essay derive from discussions at a workshop on public reason, held in
Tucson in November 2007, and were further developed at a talk to the Manchester Centre for
Political Theory. I would like to thank all the participants, and especially Andrew Lister. His
criticisms of my previous work led me to think about a number of matters in a new way. My
thanks also to Fred D'Agostino, Tom Christiano, Steve Macedo, Jonathan Quong, Dave Schmidtz,
Peter Vallentyne, and Kevin Vallier for their very helpful comments.
[1] Christopher J. Eberle applies this term to a family of liberal views I describe in the text, which stress
that the basic requirement of a just and legitimate state is that it can be justified to all reasonable
citizens. See Eberle, *Religious Conviction in Liberal Politics* (Cambridge: Cambridge University Press,
2002), 11–13.
[2] See David Hume, "Of the Original Contract," in his *Essays Moral, Political, and Literary* (Oxford:
Oxford University Press, 1963), 452–73.
[3] See Immanuel Kant, *The Metaphysical Elements of Justice*, 2d ed., trans. John Ladd (Indianapolis:
Hackett, 1999), secs. 42–43 (pp. 114–17), sec. 50 (p. 146).

question of justification ... by working out a problem of deliberation."[4] As the question of justification takes center stage (we might say: as contractualist liberalism becomes justificatory liberalism), it becomes clear that posing the problem of justification in terms of a deliberative problem or a bargaining problem is a heuristic: the real issue is "the problem of justification"[5] – what principles can be justified to all rational and reflective persons seeking to live under impartial principles of justice.

Justificatory liberalism rests on a conception of members of the public as free and equal. To say that each individual is free implies that each has a fundamental claim to determine what are her obligations and duties. To say that each is equal is to insist that members of the public are symmetrically placed insofar as no one has a natural or innate right to command others or to impose obligations on them. Free and equal persons thus recognize no claims to natural authority over them. As Locke insisted, "the natural liberty of man is to be free from any superior power on earth, and not to be under the will or legislative authority of man, but to have only the law of Nature for his rule."[6] Given this conception of persons as free and equal, it follows that laws, because they use (and threaten to use) force, are deeply problematic: state functionaries employ power to force others to conform to the law, or they employ threats of force for the same purpose. On what grounds could anyone exercise such power and yet still claim that he is respecting the person (as free and equal) who is imposed upon?

In Kant's eyes, a crucial and necessary condition is that the person imposed upon by the law endorses the law as the thing to do: it is what her own reason instructs her to do, and so, as a rational person, it is what she wills to do. In Kant's terms, the person who is subject to the law may also be the legislator: because the law is endorsed by her own reasoning, she wills that the law be imposed, and is in this sense the legislator as well as a subject. A law that is rationally willed by a person, Kant and his followers have insisted, treats her as free and equal (qua legislator) even though (qua subject) she is bound to obey. "A rational being belongs to the realm of ends as a member when he gives universal laws in it while also himself subject to these laws. He belongs to it as sovereign when he, as legislator, is subject to the will of no other."[7] Justificatory liberalism thus starts out with

---

[4] John Rawls, *A Theory of Justice*, rev. ed. (Cambridge, MA: Belknap Press of Harvard University Press, 1999), p. 16 (p. 17 of the original edition).
[5] Ibid.
[6] John Locke, *Second Treatise of Government*, in *Two Treatises of Government*, ed. Peter Laslett (Cambridge: Cambridge University Press, 1960), sec. 21.
[7] Immanuel Kant, *Foundations of the Metaphysics of Morals*, ed. and trans. Lewis White Beck (Indianapolis: Bobbs-Merrill, 1959), 52 [Akademie ed., 433–34].

the idea of "free persons who have no authority over one another"[8] and seeks to see how their reason can lead each of them to freely accept common laws to which they are subject.

When the state issues a law, it typically commands citizens to act and, further, threatens them with fines and imprisonment unless they obey. Such laws are clearly not simply pieces of advice or guidelines: they are required courses of action that the state insists upon whether or not a citizen agrees. As such, it seems that the citizen is simply subject to the authority of the state, and is certainly not treated as free and equal in relation to the will of the governors. If, however, qua impartial, rational, and reflective agents (which may not be the same as actual citizens with all their biases and short-sightedness), the citizens rationally endorse the law and its penalties, then the citizens also can be seen as its legislators. Only laws that are "publicly justified" in this way – those that can be shown in some way to be endorsed by the reason of all members of the public (see Section III) – can respect all citizens as free and equal. Laws that cannot be endorsed by the reason of some citizens are authoritarian: some individuals claim the right to rule others and determine their obligations, and thus do not respect those others as free and equal persons. "*Respect for others requires public justification of coercion*: that is the clarion call of justificatory liberalism."[9]

My concern in this essay is not to provide a case for justificatory liberalism, but to investigate its relation to what we might call "substantive" liberalisms. Justificatory liberalism is liberal in an abstract and foundational sense: it respects each individual as free and equal, and so insists that coercive laws must be justified to all members of the public. The liberal tradition, however, is typically associated with an enumeration of substantive commitments. Or rather, the liberal tradition evinces enduring disputes about the nature of its substantive commitments. Most fundamentally, since the end of the nineteenth century, liberals have disagreed about the proper extent of the state. On the classical view, the main tasks of the justified state are to protect individual freedom and secure a regime of extensive private property rights – that is, an economic system in which owners have an extensive bundle of rights over their property and in which the range of resources and assets subject to private ownership is

---

[8] John Rawls, "Justice as Fairness," in Samuel Freeman, ed., *John Rawls: Collected Papers* (Cambridge, MA: Harvard University Press, 1999), 55.
[9] Eberle, *Religious Conviction in Liberal Politics*, 54 (emphasis in the original).

extensive.[10] While in classical liberalism these are the core functions of the justified state, it is by no means a dogma of classical liberalism that they are the sole functions: classical liberals also typically endorse the provision of public goods and improvements, education, poor relief, as well as financial, health, and safety regulations.[11] Still, though classical liberalism is not committed to a "minimal state,"[12] it certainly endorses a far less extensive state than most contemporary "egalitarian" or "social justice" liberals insist is required. It is widely thought today that core liberal values require that the state regulate the distribution of resources or well-being to conform to principles of fairness, that all citizens be assured of employment and health care, that no one be burdened by mere brute bad luck, and that citizens' economic activities must be regulated to ensure that they do not endanger the "fair value" of rights to determine political outcomes.[13] In John Rawls's canonical formulation of this expansive version of liberalism, a variety of new "branches" of government are added to the liberal state: a branch to keep the price system competitive, a branch to bring about full employment, a transfer branch to ensure that the least well off have the resources demanded by justice, and a distribution branch that adjusts the rights of property "to prevent concentrations of power detrimental to the fair value of political liberty and fair equality of opportunity."[14]

It is widely thought that all forms of justificatory liberalism must endorse this latter, expansive understanding of the liberal state. No doubt this partly can be explained by the fact that Rawls's theory is both the most

[10] I explore these dimensions in more detail in my essay "The Idea and Ideal of Capitalism," in Tom Beauchamp and George Brenkert, eds., *The Oxford Handbook of Business Ethics* (Oxford: Oxford University Press, 2009).

[11] The classic work on the economic policy of classical liberal political economy is Lionel Robbins, *The Theory of Economic Policy in English Classical Political Economy* (London: Macmillan, 1961). Perhaps the most sophisticated classical analysis of the functions of government is Book V of John Stuart Mill, *The Principles of Political Economy* (1848), in J. M. Robson, ed., *The Collected Works of John Stuart Mill* (Toronto: University of Toronto Press, 1977), vol. 3. See also my essay "Public and Private Interests in Liberal Political Economy, Old and New," in S. I. Benn and G. F. Gaus, eds., *Public and Private in Social Life* (New York: St. Martin's, 1983), 192–93.

[12] It is thus unfortunate that so many have viewed Robert Nozick's somewhat doctrinaire defense of the "night-watchman state" as definitive of the classical liberal tradition. See his *Anarchy, State, and Utopia* (New York: Basic Books, 1974), 25–27. On the relation between libertarianism and classical liberalism, see Eric Mack and Gerald Gaus, "Classical Liberalism and Libertarianism: The Liberty Tradition," in Gerald F. Gaus and Chandran Kukathas, eds., *Handbook of Political Theory* (London: Sage Publications, 2004), 115–30.

[13] See Rawls, *A Theory of Justice*, rev. ed., 197ff.

[14] Ibid., 242–51. Rawls also believes that a just society would seek reasonable ways to limit wasteful forms of advertising: "the funds now devoted to advertising can be released for investment or for other useful social ends." John Rawls, *Political Liberalism* (New York: Columbia University Press, 1996), 365.

prominent instance of justificatory liberalism and the preeminent defense of the expansive conception of the liberal state. Moreover, both Rawls and his followers have insisted that the more extreme, "libertarian," versions of the classical view are not genuinely liberal, reinforcing the supposition that the justificatory liberal approach is hostile to substantive liberalisms that endorse wide-ranging limits on government authority.[15] Indeed, Rawls condemns classical liberalism and welfare state capitalism as unjustifiable political-economic systems.[16] According to Rawls, "laissez-faire capitalism" (or, as he sometimes calls it, "the system of natural liberty") is unjust: its regulative principles would not be agreed to by free and equal persons seeking impartial principles of justice. Because laissez-faire capitalism (1) does not require constitutional guarantees of "the fair value of the equal political liberties," so that all have real political power (more on this in Section IV.A), and (2) allows only "a low social minimum" and thus does not have institutions in place that aim to maximize the long-term prospects of the least well-off, it follows that less-advantaged free and equal persons do not have reasons to endorse it. More surprisingly, Rawls holds that even "welfare-state capitalism" fails the test of justifiability. It too allows for inequalities of wealth that, in Rawls's eyes, undermine the fair value of citizens' political rights. "It permits very large inequalities in the ownership of real property (productive assets and natural resources) so that the control of the economy and much of the political life rests in a few hands." Of the five political-economic systems he discusses – laissez-faire capitalism, welfare-state capitalism, state socialism, liberal (market) social-ism, and a "property-owning democracy" – Rawls rejects as unjust both systems that he describes as "capitalist." He allows as possible just regimes one form of socialism (market socialism) and a "property-owning democra-cy" that allows private property but works "to disperse the ownership of wealth and capital, and thus to prevent a small part of society from controlling the economy and, indirectly, political life as well."[17]

Classical liberals who are also justificatory liberals must address two questions. First, is there a sound case for the classical version in justifica-tory liberal terms, or is classical liberalism somehow at odds with the justificatory project, so that all reasonable versions of justificatory

---

[15] John Rawls, *The Law of Peoples* (Cambridge, MA: Harvard University Press, 1999), 48; Samuel Freeman, "Illiberal Libertarians: Why Libertarianism Is Not a Liberal View," *Philosophy and Public Affairs* 30 (2001): 105–51.

[16] Rawls, *Justice as Fairness: A Restatement*, ed. Erin Kelly (Cambridge, MA: Harvard University Press, 2001), 135ff.

[17] Ibid., 138.

liberalism must reject what Rawls calls "the system of natural liberty"? In a previous essay, I have argued that there is a strong justificatory liberal case for classical liberal rights.[18] This, I think, defeats the claim that justificatory liberalism necessarily endorses a strongly egalitarian theory of justice or even (what Rawls considers insufficiently egalitarian) an expansive welfare state. It may appear, however, that the upshot of this is that justificatory liberalism is an entirely neutral framework with respect to this long-running dispute within liberalism – the very nature of the justificatory project, it may be thought, does not incline toward either view, but reasonable defenses of both versions can be accommodated within justificatory liberalism. Hence the second question that classical liberals who are also justificatory liberals must address: Is justificatory liberalism a neutral framework, or does it incline toward, or tend to favor, some substantive liberalisms?

In this essay I argue for two main claims. (1) Rawls and his followers are fundamentally mistaken when they claim that free and equal persons seeking impartial principles of justice would reject all forms of "capitalism" (either the system of natural liberty or the welfare state). Quite the opposite: there is an overwhelming case that such persons would insist on either some form of capitalism or, perhaps, a property-owning democracy (it is hard to know precisely what such a system would look like).[19] They would conclusively reject all forms of socialism, including market socialism. (2) The core principles of the justificatory project, I shall argue, incline toward the classical end of the continuum regarding the redistributive functions of the state. The very nature of the project does not exclude the welfare state or even more egalitarian versions of capitalism, but, pace Rawls, those versions are more, not less, difficult to justify than a more limited governmental authority.

I begin in Sections II and III by reviewing the core commitments of justificatory liberalism, understood as a family of political views: the presumption in favor of liberty (Section II), and the principle of public

---

[18] Gerald F. Gaus, "On Justifying the Moral Rights of the Moderns: A Case of Old Wine in New Bottles," *Social Philosophy and Policy* 24, no. 1 (2007): 84–119.

[19] Rawls was greatly influenced here by J. E. Meade, *Efficiency, Equality, and the Ownership of Property* (London: Allen & Unwin, 1964), chap. 5; and Richard Krouse and Michael McPherson, "Capitalism, 'Property-Owning Democracy,' and the Welfare State," in Amy Gutmann, ed., *Democracy and the Welfare State* (Princeton, NJ: Princeton University Press, 1988). For a discussion of possible policies of such a system, see Richard Dagger, "Neo-Republicanism and the Civic Economy," *Politics, Philosophy, and Economics* 5 (2006): 151–73.

justification (Section III). Section IV examines an ambitious thesis: properly understood, justificatory liberalism only justifies the classical version of liberalism and its stress on the primacy of ownership. I argue that, while this ambitious thesis involves an important insight, it fails. Section V builds on this insight and establishes a more moderate thesis: while justificatory liberalism admits as reasonable both classical, welfare-statist, and some egalitarian liberalisms, it inclines toward classical formulations. Section VI argues that the spirit of justificatory liberalism is neither egalitarian nor libertarian, but Millian.

II. The Political Liberty Principle

A. The Presumption in Favor of Liberty

A wide variety of philosophers have held that basic to any genuinely liberal view of politics is a general presumption in favor of liberty and, thus, against legal restrictions. As Joel Feinberg puts it, "liberty should be the norm, coercion always needs some special justification."[20] Stanley Benn states the principle even more expansively, in terms of a presumption against all "interference," not simply coercion by the law. His grounding principle of morality is that one who is simply acting as he sees fit is under no standing obligation to justify his actions to others, while those who interfere with his actions are under an obligation to justify their interference.[21] Rawls agrees with Feinberg in focusing on the law (though perhaps making room for Benn's concern with non-legal interferences) but clearly follows Benn in extending the principle beyond mere coercion, identifying legal "restrictions" as requiring justification: "there is a general presumption against imposing legal and other restrictions on conduct without sufficient reason."[22] Since we are concerned here with liberalism as a political doctrine, and in particular with the legitimacy of state activities, it will help if we restrict our attention to the presumption in favor of liberty as it applies to the law; and let us further restrict our attention to the law's use of force and coercion. Let us, then, focus on liberalism's commitment to the Political Liberty Principle:

[20] Joel Feinberg, *Harm to Others* (New York: Oxford University Press, 1984), 9.
[21] Stanley Benn, *A Theory of Freedom* (Cambridge: Cambridge University Press, 1988), 87.
[22] Rawls, *Justice as Fairness*, 44.

(1) A citizen is under no standing obligation to justify her actions to the state.

(2) All use of force or coercion by the state against the persons of its citizens requires justification; in the absence of such justification, such force or coercion by the state is unjust.

The Political Liberty Principle regulates political justification, and deems state force or coercion without the requisite justification to be a case of injustice.[23] As Benn says, "justifications and excuses presume at least prima facie fault, a charge to be rebutted."[24] If I have no justificatory burden, I am permitted to act without justification – I have no charge to rebut, no case to answer. If the onus is on you, the failure to justify condemns your act. Conceivably, a conception of political morality might place the onus on the actor: "Never act unless one can meet the justificatory burden by showing that one is allowed to act."[25] The liberal insists that citizens have no such general burden to bear, though of course they may bear the onus of justification in special contexts in which a restriction already has been established (say, trusteeships).

Now as Rawls rightly insists, "this presumption creates no special priority for any particular liberty": it does not serve to identify some liberties as especially important. To identify a particular liberty as having a priority in the sense of an enforceable right itself requires justification. Suppose Alf claims to possess an enforceable right to speak in a political forum, and Betty exercises her freedom to play loud music at the same time and place. By claiming that his freedom is a right, Alf claims a ground to interfere with Betty's playing of music – he claims that she can be made to stop, by the police if necessary. But that, of course, is to call on the state to coercively interfere with her actions, and, like all such interferences, claims of rights must be justified.[26] The presumption in favor of liberty does not, then, identify special liberties as deserving special protection. Nevertheless, Rawls acknowledges that even when a basic protected liberty is not at stake, "liberties not counted as basic are satisfactorily allowed for by the general presumption against legal interference."[27] There is always a standing presumption against legal interference: those who endorse a legal

[23] This is not to say that the presumption in favor of liberty does not itself have to be argued for. See my *Value and Justification* (Cambridge: Cambridge University Press, 1990), 379ff.
[24] Benn, *A Theory of Freedom*, 87.
[25] I consider such a presumption in some detail in *Value and Justification*, 381–86.
[26] Loren E. Lomasky and I argue this point in more detail in "Are Property Rights Problematic?" *The Monist* 73 (October, 1990): 483–503.
[27] Rawls, *Justice as Fairness*, 112.

interference must bear a justificatory burden, not those who wish to remain free.

The presumption in favor of liberty, and thus against coercive laws, is easily misunderstood. Some view it as a libertarian principle because it "privileges" liberty. But this is to confuse liberalism with libertarianism. Libertarianism is a wide-ranging doctrine about the strength and priority of certain liberty or property rights in relation to other claims. The presumption of liberty does not imply that liberty always, or even usually, trumps other values: the presumption identifies what does, and what does not, stand in need of justification. The liberal does not remain neutral between those who would use the law to regulate the lives of others and those who wish to remain unregulated: it is the would-be regulator who must bear the justificatory burden. (That Benn, Feinberg, and Rawls – none of whom are remotely libertarian – advocate the principle itself should make us doubt the force of the claim that the presumption pre-supposes a libertarian view.)

Others dispute the presumption on the grounds that "there is no standing duty to justify morally relevant actions."[28] We might interpret this objection as involving four different claims:

(1)   If the state has shown that φ is a morally required or permitted action, the state is under no burden to show that φ-ing is justified.
(2)   If, as a matter of fact, φ is a morally required or permitted action, there need not be a justification for the state φ-ing.
(3)   If the state believes that φ is a morally required or permitted action, the state need not have a justification for its belief and for acting on it.
(4)   If the state reasonably believes that φ is a morally required or permitted action, the state need not show it has a justification for φ-ing.

Interpretation (1) is not a coherent challenge to the presumption: to show that one has a morally relevant ground for interference simply is to justify one's action, so this does not dispute the presumption. This is important: showing that something is morally permitted simply is showing that one has a justification of doing it. Nor does interpretation (2) offer a plausible basis for disputing the presumption. If, as a matter of fact, φ is morally

[28]   Rainer Frost, "Political Liberty: Integrating Five Conceptions of Autonomy," in John Christman and Joel Anderson, eds., *Autonomy and the Challenges to Liberalism* (Cambridge: Cambridge University Press, 2005), 240 n. 24.

required, then there is, in principle, a justification for φ – viz., the reasons why it is morally required. To be sure, one might hold that φ is required but no one knows why, and so there is no justification for it, but this is hardly a compelling view of political morality. Interpretation (3) involves, I think, a genuine substantive disagreement. Here it is being said that, if the state holds that φ is morally permitted or required, it may go ahead and φ even if it has no justification for its belief or for acting on that belief. For the state to have no justification for φ-ing amounts to it not having access to good reasons for its conclusion that φ is morally required or permitted. Here, I think, the liberal parts ways with the objector, if the objector holds that there is nothing wrong when the state goes ahead and uses coercion on the grounds that doing so is morally permitted, even though it does not itself have access to the considerations that establish why it is morally permitted. It is not enough that there be some unknown moral grounds that allow coercion. At least some state actors – those who have authorized the act – must be cognizant of the grounds. The point of morality is essentially practical: we seek to employ it as the basis for our reasoning and choices. Unless the state has access to these reasons when it makes choices, it acts with manifest disrespect for the freedom and equality of its citizens. Recall Rawls's key insight: we start out with the assumption of free and equal persons who have no authority over one another, and thus all claims to authority – including the authority to interfere with others on moral grounds – are subject to the requirement that they be justified.[29] Interpretation (4) is more reasonable. Of course, the state (all the agents of the state involved in the action) need not always show each and every person that the relevant actors have good moral reasons for what they are doing whenever they are challenged. Certainly, however, a government of free citizens – a government that respects citizens as free and equal persons – must include forums where citizens are shown these justifying reasons.

It is also important to stress that the presumption in favor of liberty does not ignore the fundamental truth that state force and coercion often prevent a great deal of private force and coercion. Some argue that, if the state does not act through coercive laws, there will be great private coercion, and thus the presumption in favor of liberty does not really protect liberty: people will simply be subject to private rather than public

---

[29] The way in which morality involves claims to authority over others is a central theme of Stephen Darwall, *The Second-Person Standpoint: Morality, Respect, and Accountability* (Cambridge, MA: Harvard University Press, 2006).

coercion. The great insight of the social contract theorists was that preventing unjustified private force and coercion is the main justification of state force and coercion. As Kant understood it, the state replaces private force and coercion with "public lawful coercion."[30] That state coercion must be justified only requires that a sufficient reason for it be advanced: that it is the best way to prevent a great deal of unjustified private coercion is certainly such a reason.

B.   Coercion and Rights of the Person

The Political Liberty Principle supposes that we can make sense of the idea of legal force and coercion. Many, though, are skeptical that this can be done. The last forty years have witnessed a number of fundamentally divergent accounts of coercion.[31] It is widely agreed that coercion typically involves some sort of threat of harm by which the "coercer" gets (or aims at getting) the "coercee" to do as he wishes, but there is considerable disagreement about what constitutes a threat of harm, whether all such threats are coercive, and so on. Now it might be thought that if we cannot agree on a general account of coercion, we cannot usefully employ the idea in the Political Liberty Principle. But this would be far too skeptical a conclusion: philosophical theories that seek to provide a biconditional analysis of a concept (i.e., A is an act of coercion if and only if conditions C1 ... Cn are met) are notoriously subject to counterexamples and controversy; we typically have a far better grasp of the use of an idea than we have of the philosophical analysis of it. Moreover, the Political Liberty Principle does not require a general analysis of coercion, but only an analysis of its application to the actions of the state against its citizens.

What makes the state – even a legitimate one – especially morally problematic to the liberal is that it employs force, or threatens to use force, against the persons of its citizens.[32] This is certainly only a subset of the many ways in which one can coerce another. If Alf threatens to destroy Betty's beloved painting – which he owns – if she does not agree to move

[30] Kant, *The Metaphysical Elements of Justice*, 115–16 [Akademie ed., 311–13]. See also the "Translator's Introduction," xxxv–xxxix.
[31] For an excellent survey, see Scott Anderson's entry on "Coercion" in *The Stanford Encyclopedia of Philosophy* (Spring 2006 edition), ed. Edward N. Zalta, http://plato. stanford.edu/archives/spr2006/entries/coercion.
[32] This is not to say that coercion against noncitizens does not require justification; it simply falls outside the scope of the Political Liberty Principle, which specifies a necessary, not a sufficient, condition for justified coercion.

to Australia with him, he may plausibly be said to coerce her into moving without threatening her person (he threatens to harm his own property). To be sure, some states do employ similar means (we are tempted to label them as "blackmail"): they threaten, for example, a dissident's family or friends with harm to get her to conform, or they threaten to banish her children from university if she does not cooperate with the regime. These uses of coercion are subject to special condemnation: they are not the modus operandi of the liberal state. Liberal legal restrictions require compliance, and if compliance is not forthcoming the citizen is typically threatened with the use of force against his person, not simply a harm to what he cares for. The police will come and use force against his person, and may imprison him. This, indeed, is a quintessential case of coercion. A reason to reject the claim that all instances of coercion involve a threat to violate the rights of another[33] is that, even in a condition such as Hobbes's state of nature (in which everyone has a blameless liberty to do as he thinks necessary, and thus no one has claim-rights to noninterference), we can sensibly and importantly say that people are coercing each other.[34] Indeed, the idea of replacing such private, lawless coercion with public, lawful coercion is an important theme in Kant's social contract theory.[35] Applying the concept of coercion (and, of course, force) makes sense even in relations among purely "natural persons" – those whom we do not consider bearers of rights.

However, coercion by the state typically does involve a threat against a citizen's rights, for in political society one's person is largely defined – and expanded – by one's rights. This idea of the expansion of legal personhood through rights was central to Kant's analysis of property. To own a thing is not simply to have possession of it, or even stable, secure, recognized possession. It is to enter into a juridical relation such that "any hindrance of my use of it would constitute an injury to me, even when I am not in [physical] possession of it (that is, when I am not a holder of the object)."[36] Once property rights are justified, a threat by the state to take my property is a threat against me: to take my property is to do an injury to me as a juridical person. Without property rights, you only do injury to me by

---

[33] See Alan Wertheimer, *Coercion* (Princeton, NJ: Princeton University Press, 1987), 277ff.

[34] I defend this interpretation of Hobbes in *Value and Justification*, 275ff.

[35] Kant's view is complex; though we have private rights in the state of nature, because there is no impartial judge about their contours, the state of nature also is characterized by an absence of public claims of justice; the idea of the social contract is to establish public justice and rights. Kant, *Metaphysical Elements of Justice*, 115–16 [Akademie ed., 312].

[36] Ibid., 45 [Akademie ed., 249].

taking my possession if you use force against my person (narrowly construed), or threaten to, when taking it. If I should put it down and walk away, it would be no injury to me for you to take it, and so it would be no threat against my person to threaten to take it away under these circumstances.[37] However, if it is my property, the injury is done not by reason of physical possession but by an extension of the bounds of my person to include my relation to it. Thus, when the state threatens to fine me for noncompliance, it threatens me, just as surely as if it threatens imprisonment.

C.   The Order of Justification

If our core concern is the state's use of force or the threat of force against the person of the citizen, and if the juridical boundaries of the person expand with her set of rights, then what constitutes a coercive threat against her person will also expand. This implies that the order of justification may affect the outcome of what is justified. On the one hand, if we assume, say, only natural personhood, or even simply rights of bodily integrity narrowly construed, then the state's demand that you conform to law L or else it will take away your "property" (qua stable, recognized possessions) will not involve a direct threat against your person, since you have no juridical relation to such "property." Thus, there would be no onus of justification on the state: it could, say, tax away those possessions at will (see Section IV.D). On the other hand, if we understand you to have a justified property right, then the state would bear such an onus, and it must justify this threat against you.

Despite first appearances, this is not, I think, a counterintuitive implication of the Political Liberty Principle. We will see in Section IV that many of the disagreements between classical and egalitarian liberals stem from disputes about the order of justification, and, in particular, about where the justification of the rights of ownership enters into an account of liberal justice. All liberals agree that at the core of their theory are persons with rights to bodily integrity, freedom of association, and freedom of conscience and speech. As we will see, the question is: At what point does the person include her property?

---

[37] To be sure, there may be an intelligible sense in which I still might be said to coerce you: "If you don't do what I want, I will pick up your possession the next time you put it down!" Again, though, a general account of coercion (if one is to be had) is not my aim.

III.   Public Justification and the Deliberative Model

A.   *The Public Justification Principle*

The Political Liberty Principle places the onus of justification on the state for the use of force and coercive threats against the persons of its citizens. The (Generic) Public Justification Principle determines how this onus can be met:

> L is a justified coercive law only if each and every member of the public P has conclusive reason(s) R to accept L as binding on all.

An unjustified law fails to treat each person as free and equal.[38] Our question is: When, if ever, does a coercive law treat all as free and equal?

Because I am concerned with a family of justificatory liberalisms, I focus on a generic formulation of the Public Justification Principle. Because this is a generic principle, I leave open the crucial problem of just how to specify P (whether the members must all be reasonable, fully rational, etc.). The Public Justification Principle supposes that the relevant justificatory public is an idealization of the actual citizenry (throughout, I will use "member of the public" as a term of art to identify this idealized public). Whereas many in the actual citizenry may act on pure self-interest, hate, or spite, or may reason on the basis of obviously false empirical theories, or may make manifestly invalid inferences, the idealized members of the public make sound inferences from appropriate and relevant values, drawing on sound empirical claims. Justificatory liberals differ in just how far

---

[38]   The Public Justification Principle supposes that a justified law must be genuinely authoritative: it is endorsed by all members of the public as binding – as generating obligations to obey. A bona fide law is not simply an act of state coercion, but an act of state authority, and so binds citizens. This is the legal expression of Kant's notion of the realm of ends, in which recognizing the law's authority over us is consistent with each person's acting on her own reasons. Contemporary political philosophy is deeply skeptical that the law generally has justified authority to direct citizens' acts. To many, the most the law could hope to achieve is a certain legitimacy, in the sense that the laws of the state are morally permissible acts of coercion, but do not in general bind citizens to obey. Thus, in place of the Public Justification Principle, we might adopt a Weak Public Justification Principle: "L is a justified coercive law only if each and every member of the public P has conclusive reason(s) R to accept that coercive acts enforcing L are morally permissible." The Weak Public Justification Principle does not suppose that laws are acts of self-legislation which all citizens have reason to obey, but simply that force and coercion by the state are permissible – though resisting them may be permissible too. For many, that is enough – indeed, the most that can be hoped for. I am dubious. The concept of law implied by this view renders laws too much like coercive demands in Hobbes's state of nature: they are not wrong, but neither is it in principle wrong to ignore them, or even fight back. However, I leave this matter unresolved in this essay. If one is convinced that the most we can hope for is such "legitimacy," one can substitute the weak version of the Public Justification Principle in what follows: the essence of the analysis is not affected.

they press this idealization. One Kantian specification of P is highly idealized – the realm of rational beings – and insofar as we act as members of P, we act fully in accord with our status as rational moral beings. Rawls relies on a more modest idealization: a conception of persons who, as reasonable, recognize the severe limits of human reason. In filling out a justificatory view, it is critical to provide a compelling specification of P; because our interest here is in a family of justificatory views, we can for the most part leave this issue open (see, though, Section III.B).

Note that the Public Justification Principle maintains that a coercive law L applying to public P is justified only if every member of P has conclusive reason to endorse L as binding. This is crucial. To sees its motivation, assume that Alf and Betty are both members of P, and Alf proposes law LA. Suppose that Alf can advance a reason R1 for Betty to endorse LA, but Betty's system of beliefs and values is such that while as a member of P she acknowledges that R1 is a reason for endorsing LA, she also holds that she has reason R2, which is a reason to endorse LB over LA (where LA and LB are incompatible alternatives). Suppose that, exercising her reason as a free and equal member of the public, Betty concludes that R2 outweighs (or defeats) R1, and thus she concludes that LB is better than LA. Now some insist that, nevertheless, Alf has provided a justification of LA insofar as he has offered a nonsectarian reason R1 in support of LA – a reason that, as a free and equal member of the public, Betty can appreciate.[39] Yet, exercising her capacities as a free and equal person, Betty has concluded that, when compared to LB, LA is inadequately justified in the sense that it is not choice-worthy; as she understands it, she has more reason to endorse LB. For Alf (even if Alf is the head of state) to simply impose LA on Betty is inconsistent with treating her as a free and equal member of the public. The critical question is not whether Betty has some reason to endorse LA, but whether, all things considered, she has reason to endorse LA over the alternatives, or even over no law at all. If she has some reason to endorse LA, but more reason to endorse an alternative, then what economists call the "opportunity costs" of choosing LA exceed the benefits: she would be opting for a law that achieves less of what she values over one that achieves more. Therefore, only a justification that showed she had conclusive reasons – the benefits outweighed the opportunity costs – would show that she has reason to endorse the law.

[39] See George Klosko, "Reasonable Rejection and Neutrality of Justification," in Steven Wall and George Klosko, eds., *Perfectionism and Neutrality: Essays in Liberal Theory* (Lanham, MD: Rowman & Littlefield, 2003), 178.

B. Reasonable Pluralism

Most political theories can endorse the Public Justification Principle as I have stated it: if the members of the public are so specified that they all accept, say, a certain substantive moral theory, the laws justified by that theory would also be justified by the Public Justification Principle. The principle would do little or no work. The Public Justification Principle becomes an interesting test – and also more obviously part of the liberal tradition – if we accept Rawls's claim that a wide range of rational disagreement is the "normal result of the exercise of human reason."[40] Suppose, then, that we accept pluralism in the sense that our characterization of P's deliberation includes the fact that the members of the public reason on the basis of a wide variety of different values, ends, goals, etc. This does not prejudge whether values are "ultimately" plural, or whether some values are truly "agent-neutral." Perhaps fully rational, omniscient beings would agree on what is valuable, or recognize agent-neutral values. The important point is that, at the appropriate level of the idealization, members of P will be characterized by diversity in the basis of their reasoning about what laws to accept. That, after all, models the core problem of our pluralistic liberal societies.

Abstracting from the notions of goods, values, moral "intuitions," and so on, let us say that Σ is an evaluative standard for Alf qua member of P if holding Σ (along with various beliefs about the world) gives Alf a reason to endorse some law L. Again, different justificatory liberalisms advance different characterizations of evaluative standards: some may focus largely on self-interest; others on conceptions of the good or value; and others will also allow members of P to employ "moral intuitions" (though these will only provide reasons for those members of P who hold them). Evaluative standards are to be distinguished from justified laws. Evaluative standards need not meet the test of Public Justification, but they are the reasons for some member of the public to endorse or reject a law. Our problem is how to achieve the public justification of uniform coercive laws based on disparate individual evaluative standards.

Any plausible liberal justificatory account must acknowledge the diversity of evaluative standards in political justification (and thus recognize the importance of reasonable pluralism), but it also must limit the range of considerations that may be drawn upon in justification. Some limits are

---

[40] Rawls adds: "within the framework of free institutions of a constitutional regime" (*Political Liberalism*, xviii).

implicit in the very idea of public justification. Our concern is not simply whether the government and its officials respect each citizen as free and equal, but whether each citizen respects her fellows when she calls on the coercive force of the law. If each citizen is to respect her fellows as free and equal, each must have reason to suppose that the Public Justification Principle is met when calling on the force of the law; but that means that each citizen must think that the relevant evaluative standards, which are the grounds of each member of the public's deliberation, provide her with conclusive reasons to endorse the law. Qua member of the public, I cannot think that your deliberation based on standard ΣX provides you (as another member of the public) with a reason to endorse a law as binding unless, in my view, ΣX is an intelligible and reasonable basis for deliberation. That your unreasonable standard leads you to endorse L cannot lead me to think you have a reason to endorse L: garbage in, garbage out. Plausible justificatory liberalisms, then, must at least accept what we might call "mutually intelligible evaluative pluralism" at the level of members of P. Members of P will see themselves as deeply disagreeing about the basis for a law's acceptance, but will acknowledge that the basis of others' reasoning is intelligible and is appropriate to the justificatory problem.

C.   The Deliberative Model

One of Rawls's fundamental insights was that the justificatory problem – what legal requirements (or social principles) do members of P have reason to endorse? – can be translated into a deliberative problem.[41] Suppose we understand a member i of P as consulting her relevant evaluative standards – the full set of considerations that are relevant to her decision about whether to endorse a law as binding. After consulting her evaluative standards, i proposes her preferred law, Li – the law that, on her (somewhat idealized) reasoning, best conforms to her evaluative standards. (This procedure parallels the one utilized by Rawls in his essay "Justice as Fairness.")[42] At no point do the parties bargain: each member of P consults her evaluative standards and proposes what she understands to be the best law. Suppose that, having each proposed her preferred candidate, each then (sincerely) employs her evaluative standards to rank all proposals.

---

[41] Rawls, *A Theory of Justice*, rev. ed., 16.
[42] "Their procedure ... is to let each person propose principles ..." (Rawls, "Justice as Fairness," 53).

This simple statement of the deliberative problem has decisive advantages over more familiar formulations. One of the shortcomings of much contemporary contractualism is that it employs a notion of reasonable acceptability (or rejectability) without being clear about the option set: to ask what one can reasonably accept (or reject) without knowing the feasible alternatives is an ill-formed choice problem. The crucial question is: "Rationally rejectable in relation to what options?" In our deliberative problem, the feasible set is defined by the set of all proposals. Rawls never made this common contractualist mistake: the parties to his original position in *A Theory of Justice* choose among a small set of traditional proposals, so their choice problem is well-defined. However, Rawls built into his later and more famous formulations of the deliberative problem a host of controversial conditions. In contrast, we can depict the deliberative problem as a straightforward articulation of the Political Liberty Principle and the Public Justification Principle, which it is meant to model: if one accepts that these principles pose the correct justificatory problem, there is strong – indeed, I think compelling – reason to accept this deliberative model. The only element the model adds is the interpretation of what one has a reason to accept in terms of a ranking of the proposals advanced by each member of P, translating the idea of having "a reason to accept" as "each member of P's ordinal rankings based on her evaluative standards."

Because justificatory liberalism is committed to a widespread evaluative pluralism among members of P, we should expect that their deep disagreements in their evaluative standards will usher in deep disagreements about which law is best – that is, which law is conclusively justified. If members of the public employ plural evaluative standards to evaluate different proposed laws, and if their evaluative standards are fundamentally at odds, these differences will inevitably result in great disagreement in their rankings of proposed laws. But given such deep disagreements in the rankings of the members of the public, it looks as if nothing can be conclusively justified, since for every proposal there will be someone who evaluates it as worse than another alternative.

The problem is this: If justificatory liberalism (i) adopts a strong standard of justification to each member of the public (some version of conclusiveness) while also (ii) insisting that members of the public have diverse bases for deliberations about what is justified, then it is hard to see how we can get a determinate result. Justificatory liberals have tended to generate determinacy either by weakening (i) – the balance of values specified by a justified political conception must be only "reasonable,"[43] and so need not be conclusively justified – and/or by weakening (ii) and maintaining that, in the end, we share a common basis for reasoning about political right, say, based on a shared index of primary goods, thus greatly qualifying the pluralism underlying the parties' deliberations. Rawls himself acknowledges that his restrictions on particular information in the original position are necessary to achieve a determinate result.[44] Suppose we refuse to take either of these routes, and allow each member of the public to rank all proposals, resulting in a set of options. Is there any way for them to agree to reduce the set of acceptable proposals? Members of P would unanimously agree to apply the Pareto principle: if in every member of P's ordering LX is ranked higher than LY, all would agree that LX is better than LY. Being strictly dominated by LX, LY can be eliminated from the set of options to be considered. Once all such dominated proposals are eliminated, the members of the public would be left with an optimal set of proposals. Can they eliminate any other proposals? In the eyes of each member of P, some of the remaining proposals may be marginally worse than her favored law; other proposals she may find highly objectionable. But how objectionable is too objectionable? All members of P accept our two liberal principles (Political Liberty and Public Justification), so they believe that liberty is the norm unless coercion can be justified. What this means, then, is that in evaluating a proposal in terms of her evaluative standards, a person will find a proposal unacceptable if it is worse than a condition of liberty. For a law to be acceptable to a member of the public, it must be a net improvement on liberty. Consulting her own standards, each must hold that the law, in comparison to a condition of liberty, brings more benefits than costs. If a condition of liberty – no law at all – would be better, given her evaluative standards, then she has no reason to accept the law. Self-legislating such a proposal would be manifestly irrational: it would create net losses as judged by her evaluative standards.

On the one hand, no member of the public can have reason to accept a law that is worse than no law at all. On the other hand, a member of the public does have some reason to accept laws that are better than no law at all: all things considered, her evaluative standards are better advanced by such laws than by "anarchy" over this area of life. Our members of the

[43] Rawls, *Political Liberalism*, 224ff.   [44] Rawls, *A Theory of Justice*, rev. ed., 121.

Table 5.1. *Orderings distinguishing eligible from ineligible proposals*

	Alf		Betty		Charlie		Doris	
	Σ*	Law	Σ	Law	Σ	Law	Σ	Law
Eligible proposals	x	L_1	y	L_2	z	L_3	w	L_4
	y	L_2	w	L_1	x	L_1	x	L_1
	w	L_3	x	L_4	y	L_2	y	L_2
	z					L_4	z	
Ineligible proposals	No L		No L		No L		No L	
	L_4		L_3				L_3	

* *Evaluative standards*

public will thus divide the proposals into eligible and ineligible sets, as in Table 5.1. In this case either member of the set {L1, L2} is preferred by every member of P to no law at all on this matter.[45] They all have conclusive reason to select from this set, for both L1 and L2 are, from everyone's evaluative standards, improvements on the absence of legislation or the condition of liberty. We now have an optimal eligible set: some choice from this set is justified, though (until more is said) no choice of any single option is justified. When we are faced with an optimal eligible set, there is still justificatory work to be done: members of the public need to arrive at some procedure for selecting one of the options. While I do not want to minimize the problem of selecting one option from the set, I have argued elsewhere that certain formal and informal procedures may justifiably do the job.[46] My concern here is the extent of the optimal eligible set in matters concerning ownership and redistribution: what is the range of possible laws from which citizens may legitimately choose? Rawls believed that it included property-owning democracy and socialist systems, but no capitalist systems.[47] I believe that Rawls implausibly constrains the range of systems in the optimal eligible set while extending the set implausibly far in a statist direction.

[45] The deliberative problem supposes that we can identify laws that regulate an "area" of social life, or as Rawls termed it, a "practice" ("Justice as Fairness," 47). I set aside for now how to identify these areas in any precise way.

[46] For the informal, social procedure, see Gaus, "On Justifying the Moral Rights of the Moderns"; for the formal, political procedure, see Gerald Gaus, *Justificatory Liberalism* (New York: Oxford University Press, 1996), Part III.

[47] Rawls, *Political Liberalism*, 338; Rawls, *A Theory of Justice*, rev. ed., 242.

IV.   The Ambitious Case for Classical Liberalism

A.   Relevant Information about the Liberty Effects of Economic Systems

An adequate deliberative model must include a specification of the information set available to members of P. Given the canonical liberal order of justification, in which rights of the person and civil liberties are prior to the justification of property arrangements, in ranking property regimes members of the public must have available to them sound information about the effects of property regimes on maintaining schemes of civil rights. If, for example, we know that some economic systems tend to undermine the effective establishment of civil rights, this is relevant and important to the deliberators' choices. However, to say that it is important for the deliberators to have knowledge of the effects of economic systems on effective schemes of civil liberty does not itself tell us the rational response of deliberators to such knowledge. Contrast two cases. In case A, a deliberator knows that economic scheme S1 has some small advantage in protecting civil liberties over S2 in the sense that, given probabilistic information, S1 has a slightly higher chance of performing a little better in protecting civil liberties than S2. For example, S1 may have a higher probability of faster economic growth rates than S2, and there may be evidence that, say, richer societies tend to better ensure a right to a fair trial. Even if this were so, some deliberators could hold that S2 still has advantages that more than compensate – say, it better conforms to their idea of economic justice. There is nothing unreasonable about such a judgment. In case B, by contrast, there is evidence that S2 has a very high probability of doing much worse than S1 in protecting the broad range of civil liberties, such that it is extremely likely that S2 will be characterized by widespread violations of civil liberties. Here, given the order of justification, reasonable deliberators must reject S2. It almost certainly will fail to honor already justified civil liberties. It would do no good to first insist on a regime of civil liberties and then admit economic systems that have a very high probability of undermining them.

To be sure, there will be many cases that fall between A and B, where the probability that an economic system may endanger civil liberties is significant, but not so high that it would be unreasonable for a deliberator to decide that the significant dangers are compensated by perceived benefits. The order of justification does not establish a lexical priority such that no possible costs to a regime of civil liberty could ever be justified by, say, economic benefits. At the same time, rational deliberators must, in

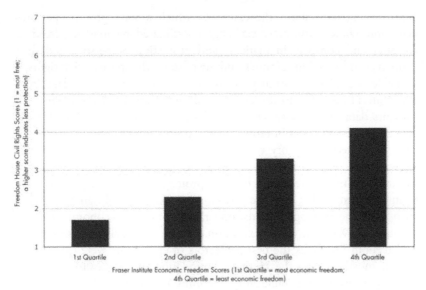

Figure 5.1.   The general relation between economic freedom and protection of civil rights

cases like B, reject economic systems that pose not only some probability, but a very high one, that the core personal and civil liberties will be threatened.

B.   The First Step: Private Property Regimes Dominate Socialist Regimes

There is powerful evidence that extensive private ownership – including private ownership of capital goods and financial instruments and institutions – is for all practical purposes a requirement for a functioning and free social order that protects civil liberties. It is, I think, astounding that Rawls never appreciates this, and simply assumes, on the basis of economic theory, that well-functioning markets can be divorced from "private ownership in the means of production."[48] There has never been a political order characterized by deep respect for personal freedom that was not based on a market order with widespread private ownership in the means of production. Figure 5.1, drawn from James D. Gwartney, Robert Lawson, and Seth Norton's *Economic Freedom of the World: 2008 Annual Report*, gives the summary relation between economic freedom (an index

---

[48] Rawls, *A Theory of Justice*, rev. ed., 239.

summarizing data about the extent to which a state protects personal economic choice; voluntary exchange coordinated by markets; freedom to enter and compete in markets; and protection of persons and their property) and Freedom House's ranking of states that protect civil rights.[49]

Table 5.2 gives a country-by-country breakdown, using data from Freedom House, Gwartney et al., and the Heritage Foundation.[50] It presents data on thirty-six countries that, according to Freedom House, ranked highest in 2008 in terms of their protection of civil rights (that is, they were rated in category 1 on Freedom House's 1–7 scale). As the table shows, none of these thirty-six countries scored less than 50 on the Heritage Foundation's rating of their protection of property rights (column 2). No state that does the best job in protecting civil rights scores less than 59 in the Heritage Foundation's ratings of overall economic freedom (column 4). With the (close) exception of Cape Verde, all states recognized by Freedom House as the best protectors of civil rights were classified as free or mostly free in the Heritage Foundation scores. Gwartney et al.'s rankings show a comparable story (columns 1 and 3).

Rawls, it will be recalled, argues that welfare-state capitalism should be grouped along with state socialist systems as socioeconomic arrangements that do not adequately protect the fair value of political rights (see Section I). Of course, it is hard to evaluate Rawls's claim that such systems do worse than his preferred alternatives, since none of his preferred systems have ever existed. As Figure 5.2 and Table 5.3 show, however, in the world as we have known it, the protection of economic liberty and private property is associated with states that do a better job of institutionalizing effective political rights (as well as civil rights).[51]

---

[49] Adapted from James D. Gwartney and Robert Lawson, with Seth Norton, *Economic Freedom of the World: 2008 Annual Report* (Economic Freedom Network, 2008), p. 21. Digital copy available from www.fraserinstitute.org; www.freetheworld.com. Used with permission of the Fraser Institute. For information on Freedom House, see www.freedomhouse.org.

[50] Sources: Freedom House, "Freedom in the World, 2008: Subscores (Civil Rights)"; Gwartney, Lawson, and Norton, *Economic Freedom of the World: 2008 Annual Report*; Heritage Foundation, "Index of Economic Freedom," 2008 data, http://www.heritage.org/Index. Used with permission of Freedom House, the Fraser Institute, and the Heritage Foundation. Note that the scores in columns (2) and (4) are on a scale from 100 (highest protection of property rights/most overall economic freedom) to 0 (lowest protection/least economic freedom).

[51] Figure 5.2 is adapted from Gwartney, Lawson, and Norton, *Economic Freedom of the World: 2008 Annual Report*, p. 21. Digital copy available from www.fraserinstitute.org; www.freetheworld.com. Used with permission of the Fraser Institute. The data in Table 5.3 are from Freedom House, "Freedom in the World, 2008: Subscores (Civil Rights)"; and Heritage Foundation, "Index of Economic Freedom," 2008 data. Used with permission of Freedom House and the Heritage Foundation.

Table 5.2. *Economic freedom in thirty-six states that best protect civil rights*

Country	(1) Property and legal protection: Gwartney ranking (1–141)	(1) Property rights protection score: Heritage Foundation (100–0)	(3) Overall economic freedom: Gwartney ranking (1–141)	(4) Overall economic freedom score: Heritage Foundation (100–0)
Finland	1	90	14	75
Denmark	2	90	13	79
Norway	3	88	23	69
New Zealand	4	90	3	80
Iceland	5	90	12	77
Australia	6	90	8	80
Austria	7	90	15	71.2
Switzerland	8	90	4	80
Germany	9	90	17	71
Netherlands	10	90	16	77
Sweden	13	90	33	70
Canada	14	90	7	80
United Kingdom	15	90	5	80
Luxemburg	17	90	21	75
Japan	18	70	27	72
Ireland	19	90	10	82
United States	21	90	8	81
France	22	70	45	65
Estonia	26	90	11	78
Portugal	28	70	47	64
Belgium	30	80	44	72
Chile	31	90	6	80
Barbados	35	90	98	71
Lithuania	37	50	31	70
Costa Rica	39	50	21	65
Spain	40	70	32	70
Hungary	41	70	28	67
Taiwan	42	70	18	71
Greece	43	50	54	70
Italy	48	50	49	62
Israel	49	70	76	66
Czech Republic	52	70	63	69
Slovenia	57	50	88	61
Poland	62	50	69	60
Ghana	65	50	66	57
Cape Verde	NA	70	NA	59

Table 5.3. *Civil rights scores and economic freedom in remaining socialist states*

Country	Civil rights score (all "not free")	Political rights score (all "not free")	Property rights protection score: Heritage Foundation	Overall economic freedom score: Heritage Foundation
China	6	7	20	53 (*mostly unfree*)
Cuba	7	7	10	28 (*repressed*)
Laos	6	7	10	50 (*mostly unfree*)
Vietnam	5	7	10	50 (*mostly unfree*)
North Korea	7	7	Not graded	3 (*repressed*)

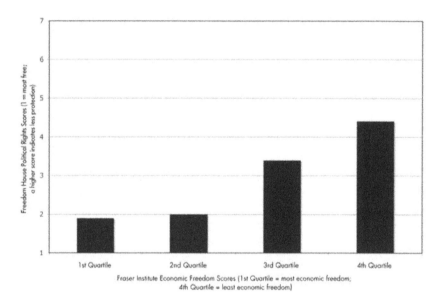

Figure 5.2. The general relation between economic freedom and protection of political rights

Table 5.3 presents the scores of the remaining state socialist regimes on the protection of civil and political rights and economic freedom. The evidence indicates that private property-based regimes that protect property rights and overall economic freedom are the best protectors of civil liberties and, indeed, of political rights. Given the evidence, because our deliberators have a deep commitment to civil liberties, they must reject socialism in favor of private property regimes and, further, must favor private property regimes with considerable economic freedom.

It might appear that Rawls and his followers have an effective rejoinder to this line of argument. Rawls consistently claims that large inequalities in wealth allow situations in which the fair value of political liberty is undermined.[52] So even if private property regimes are necessary for protecting civil liberty, private property systems that allow economic inequalities are a grave danger to political liberty. It is seldom appreciated how important this claim is to Rawls's case for equality: he believes that inequalities allowed by his "difference principle" – which requires that a just social order must maximize the economic prospects of the least advantaged citizens – may threaten the fair value of political liberty, and thus further equalization may be required.[53] As we saw in Section I, Rawls went so far as to propose a branch of government to readjust property rights, partly to ensure the "fair value" of political liberty. But while it may seem obvious to some that large inequalities of income and wealth undermine the worth of the "least advantaged" citizens' political liberties, this claim is in fact conjectural. Whether citizens have real input – whether their political rights actually have "fair value" – is a matter of complex sociology, involving the features of political culture, including levels of civic participation, institutional structures governing the relations between business and government, the existence of power centers outside of government, levels of overall wealth, and so on. Table 5.4 shows some of this complexity, charting the relation between income inequality and political rights in selected countries in the Organization for Economic Cooperation and Development (OECD).[54]

Table 5.4 offers little ground for accepting a strong relation between income inequality and a lesser value of political rights. To be sure, there is some positive correlation: below average income inequality countries always score in the high or middle range on political rights, while above average income inequality countries scored both high and low. The United States, though, scores high on OECD income inequality, but also high on political participation/political pluralism, outperforming more egalitarian countries. In any event, the differences between the Czech Republic,

[52] Rawls, *Justice as Fairness*, 139.   [53] Rawls, *Political Liberalism*, 329.
[54] Sources: Jean-Marc Burniaux, Flavio Padrini, and Nicola Brandt, *Labour Market Performance, Income Inequality, and Poverty in OECD Countries*, OECD Economics Department Working Paper No. 500 (ECO/WKP, 2006), 44; Freedom House, "Freedom in the World, 2008: Subscores (Political Rights)."

Table 5.4. *The relation between income inequality and effective political rights in selected OECD countries*

	Below average income inequality OECD countries	Above average income inequality OECD countries
*High political pluralism/ participation score (16)**	DENMARK	UNITED STATES
Middle political participation score (15)	CZECH REPUBLIC, FRANCE	JAPAN
Lower political participation scores (12–14)		MEXICO, TURKEY
High electoral process score (12)	CZECH REPUBLIC, DENMARK, FRANCE	JAPAN
Middle electoral process score (11)		UNITED STATES
Lower electoral process score (10)		MEXICO, TURKEY
High functioning government scores (11 & 12)	DENMARK (12), CZECH REPUBLIC, FRANCE	UNITED STATES
Middle functioning government score (10)		JAPAN
Lower functioning government scores (7–8)		MEXICO, TURKEY

* *Raw scores*

Denmark, France, Japan, and the United States are very slight. The real outliers are Mexico and Turkey, countries that score low on the protection of political rights and have high income inequality combined with significantly lower overall levels of wealth and income.

Perhaps the real danger to political rights is not income inequality but wealth inequality. Calculating wealth inequality is a difficult task, mainly because the idea of "wealth" is open to numerous interpretations. However, income and wealth inequality appear to be strongly correlated in OECD countries,[55] so we should not expect a great deal of difference. Table 5.5, employing a different data set from selected OECD countries

---

[55] Daniela Sonedda, "Wealth Inequality, Income Redistribution, and Growth in Fifteen OECD Countries," Royal Economic Society Annual Conference (2003), Royal Economic Society, 21; http://ideas.repec.org/e/pso158.html.

Table 5.5. *The relation between wealth inequality and effective political rights in selected OECD countries*

	Lower wealth inequality OECD countries	Higher wealth inequality OECD countries
High political pluralism/ participation score (16)	FINLAND, SWEDEN	UNITED STATES, CANADA
Middle political participation score (15)	JAPAN, GERMANY	AUSTRALIA, ITALY
Lower political participation scores (12–14)		MEXICO
High electoral process score (12)	FINLAND, GERMANY, JAPAN, SWEDEN	AUSTRALIA, CANADA, ITALY
Middle electoral process score (11)		UNITED STATES
Lower electoral process score (10)		MEXICO
Highest functioning government score (12)	FINLAND, SWEDEN, GERMANY	AUSTRALIA, CANADA
Higher-middle functioning government score (11)		UNITED STATES, ITALY
Middle-lower functioning government score (10)	JAPAN	
Lower functioning government score (8)		MEXICO

concerning wealth inequality, arrives at results comparable to those in Table 5.4.[56]

In light of Figures 5.1 and 5.2 and Tables 5.2 through 5.5, we must view as unfounded Rawls's claim that laissez-faire capitalism, welfare-state capitalism, and state socialism with a command economy all are unjustifiable partly because they fail to secure the fair value of political liberties.[57] The most we can discover is a modest real correlation between wealth and income inequalities and political rights protection scores. Welfare capitalist states such as the United States and the United Kingdom score "1" (the best at protecting rights) and all socialist states score "7" (the lowest possible score) on Freedom House's scale of effective political rights. Table 5.5, of course, does not include market socialist systems, which

---

[56] Sources: Markus Jäntti and Eva Sierminska, Survey Estimates of Wealth Holdings in OECD Countries: Evidence on the Level and Distribution (United Nations University, World Institute for Development Economics Research, 2007); Freedom House, "Freedom in the World, 2008: Subscores (Political Rights)," http://www.freedomhouse.org/template.cfm? page=414&year=2008.
[57] Rawls, *Justice as Fairness*, 137–38.

are one of Rawls's favored alternatives (since none exist). However, the only large-scale market socialist system in history – Yugoslavia under Tito – also repressed civil liberties and political rights. Of course, this data is merely indicative, and much work needs to be done, but it is dubious indeed that there is any powerful empirical evidence for a strong correlation in wealthy countries between economic inequalities and less than a fair value of political liberty. Again, this is not to say that there is no correlation at all, but excluding a whole set of economic arrangements on the basis of a modest correlation over a small range of variance is unjustified.[58] There is good reason to think that, in the countries of the OECD, the most important variable explaining high political rights scores is simply high levels of wealth and income, and that the degree of equality is a relatively minor factor.

This knowledge must be relevant to the deliberations of members of P. We suppose that they have already justified civil rights and rights of the person: such rights are basic for all liberals, and thus would be prior in the order of justification (see Section II.C). Knowing the importance of these rights, when selecting schemes of economic cooperation, the members of the public will rank all systems with extensive private ownership and economic freedom as superior to socialist systems. Not only does everything we know about economic prosperity indicate that private ownership is far superior to socialist systems,[59] but, as we have seen, the shared commitment of all liberals to civil rights provides a decisive reason to rank such systems above socialism. Moreover, as we have seen, the Rawlsian counterclaim that strong private ownership systems endanger political rights is questionable. Socialist systems would be dominated by private ownership systems and, thus, would not be in the optimal set.

C.   The Second Step: Redistribution Is Not in the Optimal Eligible Set of All Members of P

Once it has been concluded that systems with private ownership in the means of production (with great economic freedom to invest, start

---

[58] Even less compelling is the claim that inequalities in the value of political rights are simply allowed under capitalism: the question is what economic systems are conducive to a free society. Cf. Rawls, *Justice as Fairness*, 139.

[59] For the relation of economic freedom and income per capita growth, see James D. Gwartney and Robert Lawson, with Seth Norton, *Economic Freedom of the World: 2008 Annual Report*, p. 18. Economic Freedom Network. Digital copy available from www.fraserinstitute.org; www .freetheworld.com.

businesses, and so on) are in the optimal eligible set of all members of P, it looks as if the proponent of classical liberalism has won the day. Egalitarian, redistributive proposals will not be in the eligible set of all members of the public. We must suppose that some members of the public have egalitarian intuitions (evaluative standards) and some are welfare statists, while others are more strictly classical liberal. The classical liberal members of P are apt to hold that almost every redistributive plan or scheme of social justice is worse than no redistributive/social justice laws at all. Recall that, given the basic Political Liberty Principle, the baseline for liberals must be the absence of legislation (see Section III.C). Unless a law is endorsed by every member of the public as an improvement (from the perspective of her own evaluative standards) over no law at all, the law cannot possibly be one that all members endorse as free and equal persons. But citizens who are inclined toward classical liberalism will rank few if any redistributive laws as better than no laws at all, and so such laws will be excluded from the eligible set. It seems, then, that the optimal eligible set will contain only laws with a strong commitment to private ownership and economic freedom.

It is important to stress that once an extensive system of private ownership has been justified, redistributive proposals are manifestly coercive. To take away one's property infringes one's rights; the threat to do so is coercive. This is not, of course, to say that taxation cannot be justified; but as an exercise of coercion by the state, it stands in need of justification. This "everyday libertarian" view of ownership – that when the government taxes me, it takes away my property – is criticized by Liam Murphy and Thomas Nagel as a "myth":

> There is no market without government and no government without taxes; and what type of government there is depends on laws and policy decisions that government must make. In the absence of a legal system supported by taxes, there couldn't be money, banks and corporations, stock exchanges, patents, or a modern market economy. . . .
>
> . . . It is therefore *logically impossible* that people should have *any* kind of entitlement to all their pretax income. *All* that they can be entitled to is what they would be left with after taxes under a legitimate system.[60]

This is an error. I logically can have an entitlement to all my pre-tax income in the sense that taking away any of it must be publicly justified:

---

[60] Liam Murphy and Thomas Nagel, *The Myth of Ownership: Taxes and Justice* (New York: Oxford University Press, 2002), 32–33; emphasis added.

since my pre-tax income is something I have a right to, any infringement of that right must be justified. Murphy and Nagel are certainly correct that some activities of the state are necessary for my property rights to exist: funds required for those activities are justified claims against my property. But that someone has a justified claim against some of my property does not show that I do not have "any kind of entitlement" to that part of my property. Alas, my creditors have claims against a good deal of my current income, but it hardly follows that I have no entitlement to that income: even my creditors may not simply raid my bank account. They have claims that can justify overriding my entitlements if so authorized by a justified law, but having liabilities is not the same as not having the property needed to discharge those liabilities.

D.   Property, Redistribution, and the Order of Justification

Murphy and Nagel suggest a rather more comprehensive criticism of the "everyday" conception of ownership. Property rights are really simply conventional arrangements defined by governments, so governments cannot possibly violate them. As Kant was well aware, even if there is a basic moral right to have private property, this right cannot be implemented without a political order that specifies it, provides the economic institutions necessary for it be effective, and so on. Kant held that, although we can have a "provisional" right to property in the state of nature, justified rights to property only become actual in a juridical condition which determines the shape of property rights.[61] The aim of jurisprudence, Kant says, is to precisely specify "what the property of everyone is"; only in civil society is property adequately defined through public law.[62] Now if the state is in the business of determining the shape of property, it may seem that everything it does – including taxing as it sees fit – is part of this job of specifying property rights. If so, it might appear that nobody could be in a position to argue that the state is taking away his property, since until the state specifies the right, there really is no effective right to property. There is, on this way of thinking, no Archimedean point outside of the state's determinations of your property rights (or any other rights?) from which to criticize the state's activity as taking away what is yours; for its decisions determine what is yours.

---

[61] Kant, *Metaphysical Elements of Justice*, 46ff. [Akademie ed., 250ff].
[62] Ibid., 33, 41 [Akademie ed., 233, 238]. See also Hillel Steiner, "Kant, Property, and the General Will," in Norman Geras and Robert Walker, eds., *The Enlightenment and Modernity* (New York: St. Martin's, 2000), 71ff.

This conclusion does not follow from recognizing that effective property rights are conventional and depend on the state. As I have stressed, all laws are to be justified. This justification occurs against a background of one's already justified rights, what I have called the order of justification. Property rights, if not the most basic rights in the liberal order of justification, are certainly prior to many state laws and policies, such as, say, funding museums. Hobbes, Locke, Rousseau, and Kant all recognized that distinguishing "mine" and "thine" is one of the first requisites of an effective social order. In seeking to fund museums, representatives of the state cannot simply say that citizens have no entitlement to their incomes because they, the representatives, determine property rights, and thus they may tax for these purposes without justification. "Without us, there would be no property, so you have no property claims against us!" Once property rights have been justified, they form the background for further justifications; they can be overridden in order to tax, but this must be justified.

All political theories must recognize an order of justification: some things are settled, and that settlement provides a background for further justification. Of course, "settled" does not mean that we cannot go back and rethink the answers we have given, but we must decide the more basic issues before going on to others. That is the key insight of Rawls's focus on "constitutional essentials": once we have justified these essentials, we have a fixed point for further justification. The problem with the case for classical liberalism that we have been examining is not that it relies on an order of justification in which determining property rights is fairly basic, but that it insists that we first justify ownership rights and then, taking these as settled, look at the justification of all redistributive proposals. It is only because the classical liberal first fixed private ownership that she was able to eliminate redistributive proposals. That is arbitrary. The history of debate about economic justice and redistribution has been about the shape of a justified system of private ownership. Many members of P could not possibly evaluate and rank schemes of private ownership unless they knew their distributive implications:[63] for many members of the public, these issues are tightly bound together. If the classical liberal is not to beg the question, she must show that even when we justify private property and redistributive proposals at the same time (i.e., at the same point in the order of justification), justificatory liberalism still favors the classical view.

---

[63] This is certainly Mill's view in his discussion of private property in Book II of *Principles of Political Economy*.

V. Coercion, Taxation, and the Redistributive State

A. *The Political Liberty Principle, Degrees of Coercion, and the Costs of Coercion*

Recall our two foundational principles – Political Liberty and Public Justification. Liberalisms based on these principles hold that the first problem of a morally acceptable legal regime is that its coercion must be justified to everyone; in the absence of such justification, people are to be left free. Now if coercion requires justification – if, as Benn says, one who coerces others has a case to answer – then those who engage in more coercion must have a greater case to answer.[64] The more coercive the law, the greater must be the gains from the law if it is to be justified. A law that instructs all to X based on the threat of a small fine may be publicly justified, while a law instructing all to X based on a threat of years of imprisonment may not be. Draco (who codified the first set of laws for Athens) is said to have insisted that even the smallest infractions, such as stealing an apple, should be punished by death: Draconian laws are objectionable not necessarily because their aims are unjustifiable, but because the degree of coercion employed cannot be justified. To say, however, that a law that coerces to a higher degree requires a higher level of justification must be to say that coercion is a moral cost that triggers justification, and the higher that cost, the greater must be the law's benefits if it is to be justified.

Coercion limits liberty, and greater coercion limits liberty more. As Feinberg observes:

> There is a standing presumption against all proposals to criminalize conduct ... but the strength of this presumption varies ... with the degree to which [the] interest in liberty is actually invaded by the proposed legislation. Invasions of the interest in liberty are as much a matter of degree as invasions of the interest in money, though we lack clear-cut conventional units for measuring them. The interest in liberty as such ... is an interest in having as many open options as possible with respect to various kinds of action, omission, and possession.[65]

---

[64] Robert Audi further explicates this idea of degrees of coercion in his *Religious Commitment and Secular Reason* (Cambridge: Cambridge University Press, 2000), 87–88.

[65] Joel Feinberg, "The Interest of Liberty in the Scales," in his *Rights, Justice, and the Bounds of Liberty* (Princeton, NJ: Princeton University Press, 1980), 36.

A coercive law that closes off only one or two options is, other things equal, less coercive than a law that makes the same threats but closes off many options. F. A. Hayek stresses this perhaps more than any recent liberal theorist: "coercion occurs when one man's actions are made to serve another man's will."[66] For Hayek, the more one's options are restricted to one or a few options – the more the coercer succeeds in getting you to do the thing she seeks – the more you are serving another's will, and so are coerced. In contrast, if the coercion forecloses few options – say, it attaches to a law that simply forbids you to take up one of your many options – you are only minimally subject to the will of another.[67] As Benn points out, coercive laws seek to render some options ineligible by "threatening penalties for a prescribed action, attaching to it costs which make it significantly less attractive an option than alternative ones."[68] Coercive laws restrict freedom by rendering options considerably less eligible as choices; as the law renders a larger set of actions less eligible in this way, it is more coercive and its cost to liberty increases.

B.   The Redistributive State and Coercion

Classical liberals have long maintained that the redistributive state is more coercive than the classical liberal state. The debate between classical and egalitarian liberals on this matter has been extensive, protracted, and often confusing. Some of the familiar claims made are the following:

- Classical liberals such as Jan Narveson insist that we cannot distinguish liberty and property: "Liberty is Property."[69] For Narveson, "[it] is plausible to construe all rights as property rights."[70] Others insist that property rights simply are a type of liberty rights.[71] Thus, any redistribution of property is ipso facto an interference with personal liberty, and so needs to be justified. I believe that it can be readily shown that the conception of property rights underlying this view is, at best, dubious.[72]

---

[66] F. A. Hayek, *The Constitution of Liberty* (London: Routledge, 1960), 133.

[67] Hayek actually seems to go so far as to say that you are not coerced at all in this case. Ibid., 141.

[68] Benn, *A Theory of Freedom*, 144.

[69] Jan Narveson, *The Libertarian Idea* (Philadelphia, PA: Temple University Press, 1988), 66.

[70] Ibid.

[71] See, for example, Loren E. Lomasky, *Persons, Rights, and the Moral Community* (New York: Oxford University Press, 1987), 132.

[72] As I have tried to show in "Property, Rights, and Freedom," *Social Philosophy and Policy* 11, no. 2 (1994): 209–40.

- Libertarians such as Eric Mack hold that basic to a person's claim to live her own life in her own chosen way is both a natural right of self-ownership and a natural right to acquire property.[73] Actions that deprive, or threaten to deprive, a person of property that she has acquired through the exercise of this latter right infringe her basic right to lead her own life in her own way. This, however, is the crux of the ambitious case for classical liberalism, which we have rejected (see Section IV).

- Advocates of more redistributive forms of liberalism argue that, since property rights are purely conventional, the state may determine their shape as it sees fit, and this includes determining the level of taxation. We have seen that this argument too should be rejected (Section IV.D).

It is often wondered how increasing a marginal tax rate increases coercion. Will Wilkinson, a philosopher specializing in public policy matters, poses a challenge:

> [L]ibertarians and many conservatives often talk about lower taxes as a matter of liberty. But a higher tax isn't more coercive than a lower one. You're either being coerced or you're not. A guy who mugs five people with thin wallets is no less guilty of coercion than a guy who mugs five people with thick wallets. The harm from coercion might be greater if more is taken, but there is no more or less coercion.[74]

Once we get beyond paradigmatic instances of coercion, claims about what constitutes coercion are, notoriously, open to dispute. Let me explore one reasonable understanding of coercion. I do not claim that it is philosophically incontrovertible; it is, though, clearly a plausible and in many ways a compelling view. Begin with a simple contrast between two states with a flat-rate income tax: a low-rate and a high-rate state. To make the distinction stark, suppose that the low-rate state has a flat rate of 20 percent, the high-rate state of 80 percent. Otherwise, the tax codes are identical, including both monetary penalties and prison terms. For at least two reasons, the high-rate state will, other things equal, seem more coercive.

(i) As tax rates rise, noncompliance will also rise; it is hopelessly utopian not to expect increased noncompliance as tax rates increase. As tax

---

[73] Eric Mack, "The Natural Right of Property," *Social Philosophy and Policy* 27, no. 1 (2010): 53–78.
[74] Will Wilkinson, 'The Fly Bottle' (this webpage, accessed July 28, 2008, no longer exists). Wilkinson is suggesting a topic for discussion, and the claim is based on theories of freedom commonly held by classical liberals.

rates rise, so does the opportunity cost of voluntarily complying; self-interested citizens have increasingly strong incentives to become noncompliers, and we must assume that in the real world a significant number of citizens will be so motivated. As noncompliance increases, the state will increasingly turn its attention to identifying and coercing noncompliers. The amount of money involved will be enormous, and we can expect states to turn increasingly to the criminal law. Something along these lines has occurred in the United States. In the last twenty years, the United States Internal Revenue Service developed the concept of a "tax gap" – "the difference between the amount of tax owed and the amount paid."[75] In 2001, the Internal Revenue Service estimated that the total tax gap in the U.S. was approximately $312 to $353 billion, resulting from a very significant noncompliance rate of roughly 16 percent.[76] As the tax gap has grown, the Internal Revenue Service has undertaken a "zealous fight" to close the gap, implementing a "Tax Gap Strategy" that involves increased efforts to detect violations and criminal law enforcement.[77] Tax enforcement thus increasingly comes to stress criminal penalties. The problem clearly is that taxpayers do not at present sufficiently fear detection.[78]

(ii) The criminal law seeks to make options ineligible – no longer choice-worthy – because of the threatened costs to one's person. In our 80 percent rate state, tax policies have the effect of making a large number of options basically ineligible. To be sure, the threat is conditional: if you engage in a range of activities that generate detectable income, you must either pay 80 percent to the state or be punished. The state essentially demands that one pay 80 percent to take up an option, and threatens one's person if one does not. And indeed a wide range of options are made less eligible. Market transactions involving traceable monetary transfers become far less eligible than alternatives such as informal bartering, leisure activities, writing philosophy, artistic pursuits, and political activities. As the state radically increases the costs of a wide range of market activities, these activities are made far less eligible as a result of the state's power to

---

[75] Ted F. Brown (Assistant for the Criminal Division of the IRS, 1998), quoted in Liezl Walker, "The Deterrent Value of Imposing Prison Sentences for Tax Crimes," *New England Journal of Criminal and Civil Confinement* 26 (Winter 2000): 1 n. 4.

[76] "Understanding the Tax Gap" (FS-2005-14, March 2005), Internal Revenue Service, www.irs.gov/pub/irs-news/fs-05-14.pdf.

[77] Walker, "The Deterrent Value of Imposing Prison Sentences for Tax Crimes," 6.   [78] Ibid., 7.

coerce. If we adopt a metaphor of Feinberg's, and think of one's options as a series of railroad tracks that one might follow, high tax rates make it very difficult to follow a great many routes; given the costs involved in taking those routes, they are effectively closed.[79] Of course, one still can engage in these activities if one is willing to pay the 80 percent, but it is equally true that one still can engage in criminal activities if one is willing to pay the penalties.[80]

As a rule, we should expect that increases in taxation (and, generally, the redistributive activities of the state) will be strongly positively correlated with increases in coercion.[81] Both the variables I have noted – increasing noncompliance and decreasing eligibility of options – are continuous, and we should expect that throughout most of their range, the effects noted here will be monotonically related to tax rates. This is not to say that the relation between taxation and coercion is linear: coercion may be insignificant at very low levels of taxation and become really oppressive at very high levels. And, of course, the overall relation between the degree of coercion and tax rates may differ depending on historical circumstances. In the Great Depression, for example, an attempt by the state to enforce basic

---

[79] Feinberg, "The Interest of Liberty in the Scales," 36.

[80] It might be objected that this must be wrong: whereas the criminal law seeks to render options less eligible in order to deter, an effective tax law (putting aside sin taxes) must hope that citizens continue with the activity in order for revenue to be generated. The will of the state is not for citizens to refrain, but to persist, so they are not being coerced in Hayek's sense. Coercion thus may seem to require an intention to deter people from the act, but that is exactly what the state does not seek to do with taxation – and that is why the state does not close off options, but only makes them more difficult to pursue. One who threatens, however, need not wish to deter, for often enough those making the threat hope that the target will not give in to the threat. In 1918, for example, Germany issued an ultimatum to the neutral Dutch, demanding the right to ship materials across their territory, and threatening the Netherlands and Dutch ships in its colonies if the demand was not met. At the time, this threat was seen by many observers as a pretext; they believed that Germany hoped the Netherlands would not give in to the threat but would instead enter the war. What Germany's intentions were did not nullify the coercive threat. See *The New York Times*, April 23 and 28, 1918.

[81] By comparing only flat-tax states, I have greatly simplified the analysis. With variable-rate taxation, what constitutes a high-tax country depends on the combined score on several dimensions. Consider a study of fifteen OECD countries from the period of 1974 to 1997 (Australia, Belgium, Canada, Denmark, Finland, France, Germany, Italy, Japan, the Netherlands, Norway, Spain, Sweden, the United Kingdom, and the United States). We might define a high-tax country as one that has highly progressive rates and high marginal tax rates. On that definition, the high-tax states are Sweden, the United States, Finland, the United Kingdom, the Netherlands, and Belgium; the low-tax states are Spain, Australia, Norway, Germany, Japan, and Italy. If we define a high-tax state as one that has a high average personal tax rate and a high degree of progressivity, the high-tax states are Belgium, Canada, and France; Germany, Norway, and Denmark are low on both dimensions. Sonedda, "Wealth Inequality, Income Redistribution, and Growth in Fifteen OECD Countries," 19–20.

property rights with no significant redistribution against, say, a general population in great economic distress might have required a great amount of coercion, while a state that engaged in modest redistribution may well have secured social peace with much less need for threats. We must not succumb to the simple idea that tax rates and the degree of coercion are perfectly correlated in all circumstances. Nevertheless, based on the plausible analysis we have been examining, classical liberals have strongly favored property regimes that typically employ less coercion, while the heavy reliance on the expansive state favored by Rawls and his followers would seem to rely on relatively high levels of taxation, and thus favor more coercive states. Let me stress that I do not contend that this is the only plausible view of the relation of coercion to taxation; as we are about to see, even though it is simply one plausible view, it has important consequences for justificatory liberalism.

C. A Formal Analysis of Justification Given the Costs of Coercion

Recall the deliberative model (Section III.C). Members of the public rank all proposals; this would yield for each an ordinal utility function. It is absolutely crucial to keep in mind that the idea of a "utility function" is simply a mathematical representation of a member of P's views about the choice-worthiness of a proposal based solely on her reasonable evaluative standards (Section III.B). This point is of the first importance; utility is not an independent goal, much less self-interest, but a mathematical representation of an ordering of the choice-worthiness of outcomes.[82] It will help to translate each person's ordinal ranking of the alternatives (based on her set of evaluative standards) into a cardinal function.[83] Because our interest is in the way that the costs of degrees of coercion figure into the deliberations of members of P, let us take the costs in terms of the coercion imposed by a law and separate them out from each member of P's utility function. For each person, we then have (α) her evaluation of all the costs and benefits of the law (based, as always, on her evaluative standards) except for the element we have separated out: namely, (β) her evaluation of the coercive costs of the proposal. Members of P, I assume, will disagree about the level of costs. For now (but see Section V.D), I suppose they agree that the costs increase as coercion increases. Call (β) the member of the public's pro tanto evaluation of the law (1 = best law; 0 = a law that is

---

[82] See also my *On Politics, Philosophy, and Economics* (Belmont, CA: Wadsworth, 2007), chap. 2.
[83] This is merely for purposes of exposition; a cardinal analysis is not required.

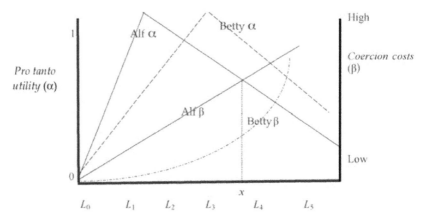

Figure 5.3.   Two utility functions, each split into two parts (α and β)

not better than no law at all), and call (β) her estimate of the coercion costs
of the law. It is important that (β) concerns simply the coercion costs imposed
by the law: we do not count as part of the coercion costs of a law nonstate
coercion that might occur under a law. A law that itself imposes low coercion
may fail to stop nonstate coercion; a law that imposes greater coercion may do
a better job at halting nonstate coercion. But nonstate coercion that is reduced
by a law falls under the benefits of that law; if nonstate coercion is rampant
under a law, that will reduce its pro tanto utility.

In Figure 5.3, Alf and Betty are members of the public deliberating
about five systems of law concerning property rights/redistribution. (Recall
that we have accepted the argument that ownership cannot be justified
prior to distributive justice.) L1 involves the least state coercion; L5 the
most. If we consider only their pro tanto evaluations, each of the five laws
is better than no law at all (L0). But the costs of increasing coercion have
been omitted from the pro tanto utility. Once we factor in these costs, as
long as the pro tanto evaluation stays above the costs-of-coercion curve, the
member of the public holds that the overall benefits of the law exceed
the costs; once the pro tanto curve dips below the coercion-costs curve, the
costs of coercion outweigh the other net benefits of the proposal. We can
see that point x defines the boundary of the eligible set: at point x, the total
coercion costs of the law just equal the total net benefits for Alf; after that
point, the costs of the law (measured as always in terms of the satisfaction
of Alf's evaluative standards) exceed the benefits, and so he has no reason
to endorse the law.

In Figure 5.3, Alf's ordering is $L_1 > L_2 > L_3 > L_0 > L_4 > L_5$; Betty's is $L_2 > L_3 > L_1 > L_4 > L_0 > L_5$. The additional coercion required for L_4 or L_5 is such that now the total costs exceed the total benefits. Alf does not see as justified the additional coercion required for L_4 or L_5. Given his evaluation of the coercion costs involved, and the benefits that the coercion yields, for Alf the costs of coercion outweigh the pro tanto utility of L_4 or L_5, and so they are not in the eligible set.[84] What we see here is that, as proposals involve higher degrees of coercion, they tend to be dropped from the eligible set because of the evaluations of those such as Alf, who evaluate the proposals' coercion costs as high and are more skeptical about the benefits. Thus, in this version of the model, we witness a tilt toward the least coercive options. Note that this version of the model (1) assumes members of the public agree on the ordering of proposals from least to most coercive but (2) incorporates disagreement about the costs of coercion: some may see coercion as a less serious matter than others.

D. *Formal Analysis II: Disagreement about Rising Coercion*

The first assumption – that members of the public agree on the ordering of the proposals from least to most coercive – is too strong.[85] As I have stressed, the thesis that coercion rises as redistribution increases is subject to reasonable disagreement. Some have advanced analyses of coercion according to which redistributive states with high tax rates are not necessarily more coercive than states that tax much less.[86] Let us accept this as a reasonable view. We now need to build reasonable disagreement about the relation of coercion and the extent of the state into the formal analysis. Figure 5.4 models the revised situation.

In Figure 5.4, Alf's utility function remains as it was before; the laws are arranged in his order of increasing coerciveness (so his utility function is single-peaked). Betty holds that the net benefits are highest at L_3, and the costs of coercion are also lowest around L_3. In Betty's judgment, the redistributive effects of L_3 are, overall, coercion-minimizing.

---

[84] All this was implicit in our original ordinalist idea of an eligible set. A law is only in the eligible set if each member of the public believes its benefits outweigh its costs compared to a condition of liberty. If a member of the public holds that a law has negative net costs, he has no reason to accept it. And one of the costs to be considered is the cost of coercion: if the law is really in the eligible set, the costs of coercion have been conclusively justified to all.

[85] I am grateful to Paul Gomberg for this point.

[86] See Andrew Lister, "Public Justification and the Limits of State Action," *Politics, Philosophy, and Economics*, forthcoming. I respond to Lister's arguments in the same issue of the journal.

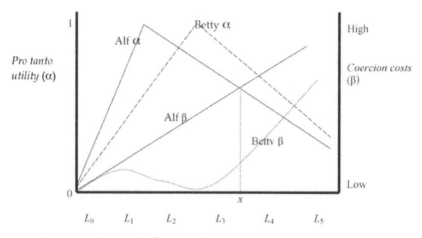

Figure 5.4.   Two utility functions, disagreeing about the nature of coercion

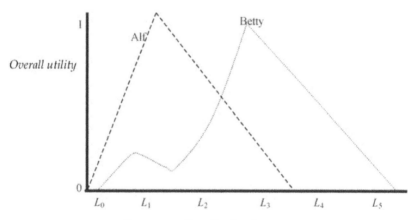

Figure 5.5.   Overall utility functions

Note that this weakening of the model's assumptions does not change
the result: Alf's judgments of the range of the laws in which the benefits of
coercion outweigh the costs are still decisive. This is so because the limits
of the eligible set (x) are defined by those reasonable members of the public
whose evaluative standards are such that they see the least benefits and the
most costs of coercion: that is, classical liberals. This is clearer if we
recombine each person's utility function to reflect all costs and benefits –
that is, if we no longer separate out the costs of coercion (see Figure 5.5).

Ultimately, the important point is that, given Alf's views about the rising costs of coercion and his modest evaluation of coercion's benefits, the eligible set still shrinks to {L1, L2, L3}.

VI.   Justificatory Classical Liberalism

A.   *The Influence of Classical Liberal Standards in Public Justification*

One interesting result thus far is that for a justificatory liberalism, the presence of members of the public whose evaluative standards lead them to assign higher costs to coercion will push the eligible set toward less coercive laws. Classical liberals such as John Stuart Mill have stressed that a central element of their evaluation of laws is the laws' coercive character. This is basic to the argument of Mill's *On Liberty* but, importantly, also to Mill's defense of laissez-faire in *The Principles of Political Economy*:

> To be prevented from doing what one is inclined to, or from acting according to one's own judgment of what is desirable, is not only always irksome, but always tends, pro tanto, to starve the development of some portion of the bodily or mental faculties, either sensitive or active; and unless the conscience of the individual goes freely with the legal restraint, it partakes, either in a great or in a small degree, of the degradation of slavery. Scarcely any degree of utility, short of absolute necessity, will justify a prohibitory regulation, unless it can also be made to recommend itself to the general conscience; unless persons of ordinary good intentions either believe already, or can be induced to believe, that the thing prohibited is a thing which they ought not to wish to do.[87]

Because coercion has such high costs, Mill repeatedly stresses that it should be used sparingly, and only where there is great social benefit to be obtained.[88] To justify legal coercion, we must show real necessity, "and there are large departments of life from which it must be unreservedly and imperiously excluded."[89]

The presence in the public of those with this sort of Millian view pushes the eligible set toward less coercive laws: they will be the first to come to the conclusion that the benefits of increased coercion are less than the additional costs of coercion. They will not be dictators: the optimal eligible set may well contain proposed laws far from their ideal proposal. As long as

[87] Mill, *The Principles of Political Economy*, 7th ed., 938 (Book x, chap. xi, sec. 2).
[88] See for example Mill's discussion of the proper bounds of moral sanctions in *Auguste Comte and Positivism*, in Mill, *Collected Works*, vol. 5, 337ff.
[89] Mill, *The Principles of Political Economy*, 937 (Book x, chap. xi, sec. 2).

for everyone the benefits of endorsing the law as authoritative exceed the costs, the law is in the eligible set. It will be important that some matters be regulated by an authoritative law, and thus the conclusion that some proposed law is worse than no authoritative law at all on a particular matter will not be quickly reached.[90] Indeed, on many basic matters even Millians may place outside their eligible set only extremely coercive proposals. (It is also important to keep in mind that we are not concerned with strategic and other bargaining behavior, but with people's sincere evaluations of whether the reasons for legal regulation out-weigh the reasons against.) Nevertheless, insofar as laws can be arranged from least to most coercive, Millian members of the population will move the eligible set in a classical liberal direction.

Some are apt to insist that this is unfair. Why should Millians, whose evaluative systems strongly disvalue coercion, have so much influence in public reasoning? Shouldn't they have to compromise with those who think that coercion is relatively benign? As Rawls might say, shouldn't Millians be concerned that their views on coercion be acceptable to others, and shouldn't they exercise the virtue of meeting others halfway?[91] Rawls is undoubtedly correct that in public justification we must only appeal to evaluative standards that are not outrageous or absurd. More than that: we have seen (in Section III.B) that when I am justifying myself to another, I must understand his deliberation to be based on intelligible and reasonable values. However, Mill's view of the dangers of coercion is manifestly an intelligible and reasonable basis for deliberating about laws; it connects up with a wide range of basic and intelligible human values.[92] To reason in a way that is intelligible to others and relevant to the problem of the justification of laws need not mean that others agree with your reasoning: that is the very point of evaluative pluralism. There is no good reason, then, to think that Millian anticoercion values would have been excluded by a plausible specification of the extent of reasonable pluralism in the deliberative model. Once the standards of some member of P are acknowledged as a reasonable basis for the evaluation of laws, it is objectionable to

---

[90] We must keep in mind that the members of the public deliberate about whether to accept the law as the basis for justified claims on each other. To say that there is "no law" is not to say that there is no social practice that allows us to coordinate our actions, but that there is no law that grounds justified claims on each other. Consequently, to say that there is "no law" is not to say that there will be chaos.

[91] Rawls, *Political Liberalism*, 253.

[92] I try to show just how broad this range is in my essay "Controversial Values and State Neutrality in *On Liberty*," in C. L. Ten, ed., *Mill's "On Liberty": A Critical Guide* (Cambridge: Cambridge University Press, 2009).

add a further requirement that she must seek to meet others halfway or compromise with them in order to reach an agreement. This is to turn justification and self-legislation into a bargain. Because our members of the public are committed to adopting only publicly justified laws, they already are taking account of each other's evaluations, and refuse to impose any law not validated by everyone's reasons. Respect for the reasons of others is built into the public justification requirement.

B. A Critique of the Small State

Because the classical liberal suspicion of coercion is entirely reasonable, and thus is a part of the evaluative standards of some members of the public, classical liberals exercise an important influence on the range of the eligible set. However, there may seem to be the possibility that their influence could be countered by critics of the "small state" whose evaluative standards are such that they conclude that laws characterized by low levels of coercion do more harm than good. Consider, for example, Jack's utility function in Figure 5.6 (for simplicity, I assume agreement about the costs of a law's coercion). For Jack, the costs of coercion exceed the pro tanto net benefits until L2; when he is included in the public, the eligible set contracts to {L2, L3}; importantly, L1 is now excluded. Suppose that we are justifying a property rights regime: Jack might hold that a classical liberal state that enforces property rights with a modest provision for the poor imposes coercion costs on the poor that exceed the benefits, and thus

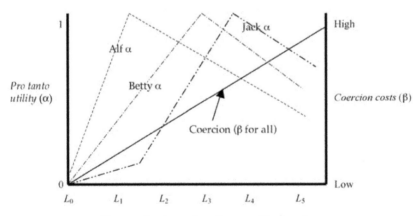

Figure 5.6. An anti-small-state utility function

that such a state is not justified. We can easily imagine more radical versions of Jack's position, contending that in no state short of total egalitarianism would the positive values brought about by inegalitarian states compensate for the costs of coercion. What is important about Jack is that he accepts Alf's "Millian" evaluation of the costs of coercion, but nevertheless rejects the least coercive option.

Classical liberals need not, and should not, insist that utility functions such as Jack's are intrinsically unreasonable. Some regimes might employ coercion so selectively and unfairly that, even though they employ it sparingly, their laws may be ranked as worse than no law at all by some members of P. The eligible set need not include the least coercive laws for just this reason. However, we have seen (in Section IV) that the evidence strongly indicates that private ownership is a necessary foundation for core liberal values. As a general rule, positions such as Jack's will not undermine justificatory liberalism's classical tilt, since all reasonable persons devoted to the basic liberal rights of the person, bodily integrity, speech, and so on accept that the benefits of private ownership exceed the costs across a wide range of private ownership systems. Given the canonical liberal order of justification, the basic liberties of the person and civil rights themselves ground a social and economic order based on extensive rights of ownership. As I have stressed, political orders based on the protection of property rights and economic freedom provide the only known basis of a regime that effectively protects the basic rights of persons. This is a great political value, and all reasonable members of the public must acknowledge it. Consequently, while some may reasonably believe that a larger (more coercive) state would better satisfy their evaluative standards, liberal critics will not generally be in a position to reasonably claim that a small state does more harm than good.

VII. Conclusion: The Odd Turns of the Dominant View

Justificatory liberalism tilts toward classical positions. Widespread private ownership will be endorsed by all reasonable members of the public as necessary for a liberal regime. Property institutions that include significant redistributive elements certainly may be justified, but as they become increasingly coercive, they are almost sure to be deemed ineligible by those whose evaluative standards deem coercion to be a great cost, which can only be justified if it brings great benefits. Justificatory liberalism leads not to socialism, or a thoroughgoing egalitarian liberalism, or to libertarianism, but to the more nuanced approach to legislation we find in the fifth book of Mill's *Principles of Political Economy*, allowing that there are a number of tasks that government justifiably performs, but having a strong overall inclination toward less rather than more "authoritative" (i.e., coercive) government.

I have deployed both empirical evidence and formal arguments to show why this is so. The basic idea, though, is intuitively clear and compelling. What I have called justificatory liberalism rests on five main claims: (1) in a fundamental sense, individuals are free and equal; (2) there is a presumption against coercing free and equal individuals to induce them to do what we want – coercion must be justified; (3) the greater the coercion, the stronger must be the justification; (4) free and equal persons reasonably disagree on many matters involving degrees of coercion, but many reasonable people believe that states with high rates of taxation and redistributive institutions are more coercive; and (5) only laws that can be justified to all can reconcile coercion and respect for everyone's freedom and equality. Given these commitments, justificatory liberalism must "tilt" against more coercive states, and it must at least be a crucial concern of justificatory liberals that they show that their favored proposals deploy coercion efficiently: that its benefits clearly outweigh its costs in the evaluation of all reasonable citizens. In my view, it is remarkable that this line of reasoning is barely even acknowledged within contemporary justificatory liberalism. Let me close by suggesting two reasons for this odd state of affairs.

First, at least since Rawls's 1967 essay "Distributive Justice," and certainly in his 1971 book *A Theory of Justice*, the main aim of appealing to principles which all free and equal persons can accept has been to justify a certain egalitarian account of distributive justice. Rawls saw that his early formulations of his model led to the indeterminate results I have analyzed here: the parties would endorse (what I have called) an eligible set of economic arrangements, all of which would work in some way to everyone's advantage.[93] Rawls, though, explicitly sought a determinate solution to the deliberative problem; in order to generate a determinate egalitarian result, he constrained the reasoning of the parties and the basis of their deliberations so that each reasoned in an identical way.[94] What started out

---

[93] Rawls suggests that one way to avoid the resulting indeterminacy is "to choose some social position by reference to which the pattern of expectations as a whole is to be judged." From this point on, the focus becomes the representative person of the least advantaged social position. Rawls, "Distributive Justice," in Freeman, ed., *John Rawls: Collected Papers*, 137.

[94] "The restrictions on particular information in the original position are, then, of fundamental importance. Without them we would not be able to work out any definite theory of justice at all." Rawls, *A Theory of Justice*, rev. ed., 121.

as a collective legislation problem under conditions of disagreement became an account in which everyone cares about the same things, and reasons about them in the same way. Even though Rawls continued to describe his account as requiring "unanimous choice,"[95] the essence of a unanimity requirement has been lost: the outcome of the agreement is no longer in any way limited by deliberators whose reasonable evaluations of the costs are highest and whose evaluations of the benefits are lowest. We simply stipulate the correct single motivation in order to get the result we want, so that the unanimity requirement becomes a complete fiction. The theorist can generate a "unanimity result" justifying any state, even though we know that many reasonable people do not think this is the optimal result. Given this, the main contemporary versions of justificatory liberalism see no connection at all between a unanimity requirement and a more limited government. Think how odd this is: we start out with a deep respect for freedom, add a unanimity requirement, and we do not get a theory of limited government. Those who advocate such versions of justificatory liberalism proclaim that they respect the reasonable concerns of all, and then proceed to specify what these are in ways that allow them to justify precisely the range of government activities they privately endorse. At best, this is remarkably fortuitous.

Second, those engaged in the contemporary project of showing what systems of property holding can be justified to all have seldom even worried about the use of coercion, or have seldom thought hard about the relation of private property and the protection of basic liberal rights. Indeed, some of Rawls's followers have explicitly denied that there is anything presumptively wrong with coercion,[96] thus rejecting a fundamental liberal idea that runs from Locke through Kant and Mill to contemporaries such as Feinberg and Benn. We confront another odd turn: an account of liberalism that tells us how important it is to treat persons as free and equal, but sees no presumption against forcing them to do things. Or else, under the guise of doing "ideal theory" according to which we assume perfect compliance with our preferred distributive principles, we are licensed to ignore the fact that, say, market socialist regimes would almost surely employ a great deal of coercion to prevent people from starting and expanding businesses, or that the governments of such

---

[95] Ibid.

[96] See, for example, Jonathan Quong, "Three Disputes about Public Reason" (this webpage no longer exists). See also Lister, "Public Justification and the Limits of State Action," and my response to Lister's essay.

states, controlling all sources of investment, would almost certainly have tremendous political power that would endanger the basic rights of their citizens. Thus, Rawls can say, without evoking stunned disbelief, that market socialism, which has only been institutionalized by General Tito's repressive Yugoslav state, is within the class of acceptable regimes partly because it protects political liberties, whereas a welfare state such as the United Kingdom, which probably protects political rights as well as any regime in history, is unjust because it fails to protect the fair value of political rights. Given this cavalier disregard for political reality, contemporary justificatory liberalism has been remarkably hostile to private property regimes, including even the contemporary welfare state.

A dominant view that has accumulated so many odd positions must be questioned. The time has come to free ourselves of the straitjacket of the Rawlsian formulation and rethink the justificatory liberal project afresh. In doing so, we should follow all of Kant's maxims of human understanding: to think from the standpoint of the public, to think consistently, and to think for oneself.[97]

---

[97] Immanuel Kant, *Critique of Judgment*, trans. Werner S. Pluhar (Indianapolis, IN: Hackett, 1987), 160 (sec. 40). See also Kant, "What Is Enlightenment?" in Hans Reiss, ed., *Kant's Political Writings*, trans. H. B. Nisbett (Cambridge: Cambridge University Press, 1977), 54–60.

PART II

Diverse Public Reason

CHAPTER 6

A Tale of Two Sets
Public Reason in Equilibrium

I. On Solving Two Problems of Public Reason Liberalism

Public reason liberalism is a family of theories according to which liberal political institutions, social structures, and/or basic social rules are politically or morally justified if and only if they can be endorsed from the perspective of each and every free and equal "reasonable and rational" person.[1] Let us call these persons "the members of the justificatory public."[2] Public reason liberalism idealizes the members of the justificatory public in three senses. First, the members of the justificatory public are assumed to be free from at least some of the cognitive distortions and biases that often characterize actual people; we suppose that they generally reason in a sound way on the basis of relevant information. Different versions of public reason liberalism press this idealization quite far, while others insist on a "moderate idealization."[3] Secondly, the members of the justificatory public are idealized insofar as it is assumed that each is a good-willed person, concerned with living with others on terms that are mutually acceptable. In Rawls's language, we suppose that they are not simply rational, but "reasonable": they have a form of "moral sensibility" according to which they are ready to propose fair terms of cooperation, and are willing to abide by them "provided others can be relied on to do likewise."[4]

I have greatly benefitted from conversations with John Thrasher and Kevin Vallier. My thanks to them for these, as well as for allowing me to read their insightful work-in-progress, which deals with some of these matters.

[1] These terms, of course, derive from John Rawls. See his *Political Liberalism*, paperback ed. (New York: Columbia University Press, 1996), pp. 48–54.

[2] I intend this as a general concept, which is filled out differently by various public reason liberalisms. Thus what I have called the "Members of the Public" in *The Order of Public Reason* (Cambridge: Cambridge University Press, 2011), esp. chap. 5, is a particular specification of the members of the justificatory public.

[3] This dispute is central to Kevin Vallier's "Liberal Politics and Public Faith: A Philosophical Reconciliation"(PhD dissertation, University of Arizona, 2011), esp. chaps. 8–10.

[4] Rawls, *Political Liberalism*, p. 81. Rawls identifies three other aspects of this moral sensibility.

The members of the justificatory public are thus idealized insofar as they are assumed to be moved by their sense of justice, or their aim to respect others as free and equal persons. This leads to a third idealization: by assuming that the members of the justificatory public are moved by this moral sensibility, it is supposed that they do not pay attention to their reasons to ignore their sense of justice (or, we might say, defect on moral arrangements when doing so better advances their cherished ends, aims, and projects). More generally, any specific version of public reason liberalism will hold that some reasons of actual people are not relevant to the justificatory question: the members of the justificatory public "bracket" (i.e., set aside) these reasons in their deliberations.

As Paul Weithman has shown in his recent study *Why Political Liberalism?*, these latter two idealizations raise a pair of problems for a public reason liberalism such as Rawls's.[5] First, we must consider whether once these last two idealizations are relaxed, actual well-reasoning citizens are apt to affirm that, all things considered, they have reasons to act on what was endorsed by members of the justificatory public. In the Rawlsian version of the problem, we have to inquire whether a person will continue to affirm that she has reasons to act on the conclusions of the justificatory public once she takes up the "viewpoint of full deliberative rationality" in which she knows her full set of reasons, such as her conception of the good.[6] If not, a society regulated by the principles endorsed by the idealized justificatory public is likely to evince an instability: when people consider their full set of reasons, they find the principles are not "fully" justified.[7] Let us call this the problem of justificatory instability. The second problem arises from the conditional nature of our moral sensibility. Assuming our first problem can be solved, we are prepared to act on just institutions only if "others can be relied on to do likewise." This, as Weithman points out, gives rise to an assurance problem.[8] Our sense of justice directs us to act on justified principles only if we can be assured that others will do so as well.

Weithman demonstrates that to solve these problems is to show how a society can reach a "just equilibrium."[9] The question I wish to explore here is whether achieving just equilibria is facilitated or hampered by requiring that citizens share the same set of reasons, or the same way of reasoning.[10]

---

[5] Paul Weithman, *Why Political Liberalism? On John Rawls's Political Turn* (New York: Oxford University Press, 2010).
[6] Ibid., p. 59.   [7] Rawls, *Political Liberalism*, p. 392.
[8] Weithman, *Why Political Liberalism?*, p. 54.   [9] Ibid., p. 49.
[10] This, of course, is a deeply ambiguous idea; I hope to clarify it as we proceed.

Rawls, we will see, originally thought that the problem of justificatory instability could be solved by showing that, from the perspective of "deliberative rationality," moral persons would endorse a common set of considerations that would lead them to affirm the dictates of their sense of justice. Weithman shows that Rawls's turn to political liberalism was based on the conviction that appealing to such shared reasons in our world of reasonable pluralism was unsustainable. Rawls thus developed a convergence equilibrium model of justificatory stability. I shall argue that not only was Rawls correct to do this, but once the convergence equilibrium model is in place, it largely supersedes the deep role of the argument based on shared reasons in the original position (although, of course, Rawls did not think so). I then turn to the second equilibrium problem, that of assurance. Weithman, and here he has recently been joined by Gillian K. Hadfield and Stephen Macedo,[11] holds that solving this problem requires, or at least is greatly facilitated by, citizens appealing to common public reasons. I shall argue that this is not so. Just as Rawls saw that the problem of justificatory instability in a world of reasonable pluralism can be solved by convergence reasoning, so too can the assurance problem be solved through each acting on those concerns that are relevant to her, but often not to others.

2.   The Problem of Justificatory Instability

2.1   *Justificatory Instability and the Gap between the Idealized and the Actual*

When deliberating whether to endorse some principle or rule P, the members of the justificatory public reason only on the basis of a subset of the reasons that an actual person or citizen might draw upon. Picking up on a suggestion of Rawls, let us divide a person's evaluative considerations into two sets.[12] Call the set of restricted admissible evaluative considerations R, and the larger, essentially unrestricted set of relevant reasons,

---

[11] Gillian K. Hadfield and Stephen Macedo, "Rational Reasonableness: Toward a Positive Theory of Public Reason," *Law and Ethics of Human Rights* (Israel), vol. 6, no. 1 (2012), pp. 7–46.

[12] Rawls, *Political Liberalism*, p. 38; Weithman, *Why Political Liberalism?*, p. 333. This distinction should not be confused with that between the thin and the full theory of the good in *A Theory of Justice*. The set R concerns those shared reasons that are necessary to the derivation of the principles of justice, and certainly relies on the thin theory's account of primary goods. Applied to Rawls's account in *A Theory of Justice*, U includes the general idea of a person's good, and aspects of the thin theory concerning the values of acting as a free and equal person, of friendship, and of social life, although it does not suppose that the person's good is structured by the principles of the right, as

U. Let us suppose for the moment that U contains R. The justificatory public, we assume, endorses principle P (and is conditionally willing to comply) on the basis of R, while actual people reason on the basis of U. The problem then arises that a person deliberating on the basis of U may no longer have reason to endorse and/or comply with principle P. This is a greater problem the greater is the gap between the restricted set R and the unrestricted U. If R and U are not markedly different, then it would not be surprising if, especially on fundamental matters, a person is willing to endorse and act on the same principle given R and given U. We might say in this case that because the restricted set is not radically different from the unrestricted one, we expect people to generally confirm the conclusions of the justificatory public once the idealization is removed. However, when R and U are very different sets – if R is a very restricted set of reasons – then we may well encounter justificatory instability. The idealized justification does not, as it were, stand up in the full light of day, and people might be expected not to comply.

This problem clearly confronts Rawls's version of public reason liberalism as the set of considerations available to the members of his justificatory public behind the veil of ignorance is radically restricted, leaving a very large gap between R and U. Weithman draws our attention to a neglected discussion toward the end of *A Theory of Justice* in which Rawls considers the "hazards of the generalized prisoner's dilemma."[13] Since the principles of justice secure the basis of fair and efficient social cooperation, we prefer (even reasoning on U alone) that everyone acts on them rather than no one (remember, we always have reason to endorse them on the basis of R). This much Hobbes taught us: "just institutions are collectively rational and to everyone's advantage from a suitably generalized perspective."[14] But supposing everyone else acts on them, one may have reason (given U) to ignore one's sense of justice and free ride on the cooperative efforts of others.[15] Or, as Weithman points out, if actual individuals often conclude that acting on their sense of justice (being guided by P) consistently clashes with the advice of U, they "may resent their own sense of justice because of its costs. Even if they do not try to extirpate their sense of justice, they may

---

does the full theory. See John Rawls, *A Theory of Justice*, revised ed. (Cambridge, MA: Harvard University Press, 1999), secs. 64, 66, 68.

[13] Ibid., p. 505. See Weithman, *Why Political Liberalism?*, pp. 47–51.

[14] Rawls, *A Theory of Justice*, p. 497, also p. 435.   [15] Ibid., pp. 504–05.

well wonder what place it is rational for them to give that disposition in their plans of life."[16] Call this the problem of ineffective endorsement.

Even more worrisome is that, should the gap between R and U be large, once a person is aware of all her reasons in U – her conception of the good, her religious beliefs, her commitment to a comprehensive value theory, and so on– she may no longer endorse principle P. She may say "yes, if I reason only on the basis of R, I endorse P, but once I tally up all the relevant reasons in U, the justification of P is 'overridden.'" [17] Here the person is saying that the set of reasons U-minus-R (the elements of U not in R) contains a defeater of the justification for P from R.[18] In this case the person's reasons, all things considered, are to not endorse P. Call this the problem of defeated endorsement. So our first problem of justificatory instability takes two forms: the (sub-)problems of ineffective and defeated endorsement.

These two forms of justificatory instability raise different issues. We may be tempted to say that the problem of ineffective endorsement is "merely" an empirical issue: it does not affect what is justified (in the sense of rationally endorsed) but "only" whether people will act on what is justified. This, though, draws far too sharp a contrast between the justificatory and the empirical. One of the important lessons to be learned from Hobbes is that justified political principles plagued by widespread ineffective endorsement fail as normative principles, since they are unable to help us solve the basic problems of social and political life. If a system of justice regularly confronts "generalized prisoner's dilemmas" that it cannot solve, it cannot serve as an effective basis of fair social cooperation for a society of free and equal persons. In this case, Rawls tells us, "the parties must reconsider the principles agreed to."[19] We see here a complex interplay between the "justificatory" and the "empirical." Yet it is clear that this

---

[16] Weithman, *Why Political Liberalism?*, p. 53. It may be thought that this simply cannot be the correct analysis of Rawls's public reason liberalism since it is an "ideal" theory that pre-supposes strict compliance with the principles of justice. However, the facts that members of the justificatory public endorse principles under the supposition of strict compliance, and that Rawls's proposed institutions are generally supposed to operate under full compliance, do not imply that he believes that actual compliance can simply be postulated, and so the temptation to non-compliance is assumed away. Principle P may well be the principle that members of the justificatory public would choose, supposing full compliance, and qua members of the justificatory public, on the basis of R they may be prepared to act on P. But if their less restricted set of reasons U generally endorses non-compliance, the just society will be unstable.

[17] I am paraphrasing Rawls here. See *Political Liberalism*, p. 386.

[18] On justificatory defeaters, see my *Justificatory Liberalism: An Essay on Epistemology and Political Theory* (New York: Oxford University Press, 1996), pp. 66–70.

[19] Rawls, *Justice as Fairness: A Restatement*, ed. Erin Kelly (Cambridge, MA: Harvard University Press, 2001), p. 89.

problem, while of justificatory relevance, is less deep than the problem of defeated endorsement. With defeated endorsement the justified principles are not ultimately to be rejected because they cannot perform a necessary function; rather, we see that in a broader context, they simply are not justified at all.

2.2   The Congruence of R and U (The Double Shared Strategy)

To overcome these two (sub-)problems of justificatory instability, public reason liberalism needs to show that once a person reasons on the basis of the unrestricted set U, she will continue to affirm P (and so the problem of defeated endorsement is resolved) and she will have reason to act on P provided enough others do so as well (and so the problem of ineffective endorsement is overcome).[20] Weithman shows us that in *A Theory of Justice*, Rawls focused on the problem of ineffective endorsement. The overriding aim in the third part of *A Theory of Justice* was to show the feasibility of justice as fairness in the sense that the choice of principles in the original position can be "carried through."[21] The key to doing this, Rawls tells us, is to appreciate the congruence of the right and the good.[22] When we consider the good in terms of plans of life validated by deliberative rationality, we will see that our sense of justice is part of our good (and so we will not be alienated from it), and that because humans have "shared final ends," we see our participation in a just society as an expression of our nature.[23] This solution thus proposes two shared sets of reasons: the members of the justificatory public share R, which yields principle P, but stability is ensured by them also sharing, as it were, a core chunk of U, their unrestricted sets of reasons. This is what is meant by saying that shared ends are central to their notion of the good life. Reasoning on the basis of R leads to P, and reasoning on the basis of U affirms the justification of P, underwriting both our sense of justice and

---

[20] We might note here that the problem of ineffective endorsement could be overcome if the typical member of society endorses P on the basis of U; as Weithman says of Rawls's account in *A Theory of Justice*, "congruence need not obtain 'person-by-person.'" *Why Political Liberalism?*, p. 59. The crucial thing is that a sufficient body of the citizens affirms P on the basis of U such that, in general, endorsement is effective. In contrast, avoiding defeated endorsement looks to require universal endorsement of P on the basis of U, at least for the idealized deliberative group. I return to these matters below in Section 2.

[21] Rawls, *Theory of Justice*, p. 508.   [22] Ibid.

[23] This, I'm afraid, is an absurdly condensed version of the complex argument from chapter 9 of *A Theory of Justice*, but it will have to suffice for our purposes.

our tendency to act on P. "The hazards of the generalized prisoner's dilemma are removed by the match between the right and the good."[24]

2.3 Overlapping Consensus (on Dropping One Requirement of Shared Reasons)

As is well known, Rawls became convinced that this reply to the problems of justificatory instability was, for a variety of reasons, untenable.[25] The first solution contends that liberal institutions guided by P will be stable because members of the liberal society living under P will share core parts of U. However, Rawls concludes this ignores that "a plurality of reasonable yet comprehensive doctrines is the *normal result of human reason within the free institutions of a constitutional democratic regime.*"[26] In short, life under a liberal P results in diversity of reasoning on the basis of U; even if members of a liberal society did share large chunks of U at some point, as they lived under liberal institutions, this agreement would dissolve. Failing to share the unrestricted set of reasons U is endogenous to life under P; thus P cannot be stabilized by sharing a great deal of U (more specifically, sharing a great deal of the part of U that does not contain R).

Rawls thus comes to insist that "a democratic political society has no such shared values and ends apart from those falling under or connected with the political conception of justice itself."[27] This is to deny that significant sharing of the unrestricted set of reasons can be the source of stability. In his later work, then, Rawls replaces the consensus account of stability advanced in *A Theory of Justice* with a convergence account, according to which each person, on the basis of her own unrestricted set of reasons, affirms the justification of P on the basis of R. Certainly by the time Rawls writes the "Reply to Habermas," the problem of defeated endorsement has joined that of ineffective endorsement: Rawls is explicit that reasoning on the basis of U may override the justification of P on the basis of the "freestanding" argument from R, the restricted set of justificatory reasons. Indeed Rawls tells us that the argument from R to P is simply a "pro tanto" justification, which is only a "full" justification once a person confirms it on the basis of her unrestricted set.[28] Note that in *A Theory of Justice*, Rawls spends a third of the book explaining why the shared part of U endorses the "freestanding" argument; in his revised

---

[24] Rawls, *Theory of Justice*, p. 505.   [25] Weithman's book masterly analyzes these considerations.
[26] Rawls, *Political Liberalism*, p. xviii (p. xvi of the 1993 edition). [Emphasis added.]
[27] Rawls, *Justice as Fairness*, p. 20.   [28] Rawls, *Political Liberalism*, pp. 385–96.

account this must be worked out by each citizen, since there are innumerable unrestricted sets that provide, hopefully, a variety of routes to endorsing the freestanding argument.

It is, I believe, a great mistake to maintain that Rawls in particular, or a revised account of public reason liberalism, can do without full justification based on U. Jonathan Quong, in his recent revision of Rawlsian public reason liberalism, explicitly denies that any further justification is required once the argument for the principles of justice (P) on the basis of the reasoning of R is completed. He writes:

> The objection [to the role of overlapping consensus, i.e., justification based on U] can be put in the form of a dilemma: (a) either the overlapping consensus is superfluous within political liberalism, since reasonable persons will *by definition* endorse the (correct) political conception of justice, or (b) ... the overlapping consensus is not superfluous and people could (in the second justificatory stage) reject the political conception without being unreasonable. But if we embrace the second horn of the dilemma, this leads ... to the ... worry that people could veto the liberal conception of justice by claiming that it is not congruent with their illiberal views. If we want to preserve the liberal content of our theory, it is essential that such people are excluded from the constituency of the overlapping consensus. But can they be excluded in a way that does not also make the overlapping consensus superfluous to the justification of the political conception?[29]

We must be wary of justificatory victory by definition. Quong defines the reasonable in such a way that a person is reasonable only if she accepts that the argument from R to P is conclusive, and hence only unreasonable people would reject it. So by definition, any reconsideration of the justification in a wider context of reasons holds liberalism hostage to unreasonable people. Now the case for P based on R is an inference on a limited set of reasons. As liberals we need to know whether we have justified P by tailoring the set of justificatory reasons so as to ensure the justification of P, or whether this case stands up when the public – as real rational practical and epistemic agents must – considers their endorsement of the principles in the light of their various wider commitments. Suppose that a wide section of the citizens rejects P when they consider U; to say that P is still upheld by all reasonable citizens is to ignore the fact that the liberal principle P simply fails to be justified to most citizens. The idealization (Section I) is thus doing all the work; remove the idealization, and the case

[29] Jonathan Quong, *Liberalism without Perfection* (Oxford: Oxford University Press, 2011), p. 167. [Emphasis added.]

collapses. What good can come of dismissing this as simply the objections of the unreasonable? It looks rather too much like dismissing as unreasonable anyone who fails to agree with us. At most (but see, Section 2.5), we might say that a citizen is reasonable only if she endorses the case from R to P; if a person does not have reasons R (say, reasons based on conceiving of others as free and equal and being disposed to be fair to them), then we might say that she is not reasonable. ("Why should I enter the original position?" such a person might ask. "I'm only concerned with number 1!"). So we might, without begging too many questions, say that a reasonable comprehensive doctrine is one that endorses the freestanding argument as a pro tanto justification. So it would still be an open question whether all reasonable comprehensive doctrines endorse P once citizens consider their wider sets of reasons. (This, I think, is something like what Rawls had in mind.) Note that doing this would not, as Quong fears, hold justification "hostage" to illiberal views, if we mean by illiberal views those that reject the freestanding argument.

Leaving aside the stipulative nature of the argument, Quong's defense of liberalism is consistent with the liberal state requiring great coercion to maintain itself. Many citizens may simply have insufficient reasons to endorse the liberal state or act on the endorsement they would give on the basis of R alone. Because liberal principles would not appeal to the reason of many, it is likely that they could only be upheld by the oppressive use of coercion, "with all its official crimes and the inevitable brutality and cruelties."[30] To the extent liberalism fails to resolve the problem of ineffective endorsement, widespread state coercion will be required to stabilize liberal practices; to the extent that the problem of defeated endorsement cannot be solved, in the name of reasonableness, the liberal state will force its citizens to act against their consciences. Such a regime will not be enduring or secure.[31] It constitutes a liberal authoritarianism.

2.4 *A Free Justificatory Equilibrium*

In a social world characterized by deep pluralism, Rawls came to realize that justificatory stability could only be achieved by a justificatory equilibrium in which citizens reasoning on their unrestricted set of reasons affirm, and tend to comply with, basic principles and institutions. Such an equilibrium can be contrasted to justificatory stability via a shared social

---

[30] Rawls, *Justice as Fairness*, p. 34.   [31] Ibid.

ideal. In a society stabilized by a shared social ideal, we affirm and act on our core moral and political rules, principles, and institutions for the same reasons: we share a common outlook or public way of life that stabilizes the social order. Such an order partakes of a community or an association: our shared social ideals and their shared basis unite us, and as participants in the social and political order, what separates us is simply not relevant. We are, one might say, first and foremost citizens. To use Durkheim's famous term, stability is achieved by a "mechanical unity" based on commonality.[32] As social thinkers from Durkheim to Rawls realized, modern pluralism undermines stability based on such unity. In a deeply pluralistic world, justificatory stability can only be achieved if endorsing and conditionally complying with the basic principles are each person's "best response" (determined by her U) to the endorsement and conditional compliance by others. We act the same way for different reasons. Justificatory stability is achieved by a sort of Nash equilibrium.[33] In such an equilibrium there is no need to bracket our differences and so base our social life on shared ends; we draw comprehensively on our reasons and determine whether our unrestricted set of reasons instructs us that just action is the best response to the just action of others. As I have argued elsewhere, such a Nash equilibrium is a genuine expression of our freedom as agents in a social world.[34] It is the freedom of a social agent, in a world of other agents, to act as he thinks best, given the legitimate actions of others.

A great benefit of stability through such an equilibrium is that, in stark contrast to stability via shared reasons, it can cope with the indeterminacy of our reasoning based on R. As is well known, while in *A Theory of Justice*, Rawls believed there was an unequivocally best liberal theory of justice ("justice as fairness"), he came to believe that there is a set of reasonable liberal views.[35] Suppose then that, employing their reasoning the best they can, members of the justificatory public arrive at the conclusion that principles P1 and P2 are better than all alternatives, but they cannot agree on a ranking. Without having shared reasons for either alternative, the shared reasons view appears to provide no clue as to how we could arrive at a stable equilibrium on either.[36] Appealing to U is supposed to allow us to equilibrate on the freestanding argument from R to P, but here we have

---

[32] Emile Durkheim, *The Division of Labor in Society*, trans. George Simpson (New York: Glencoe, 1964), Book I.

[33] See Weithman, *Why Political Liberalism?*, chap. 10.   [34] Gaus, *Order of Public Reason*, chap. 7.

[35] See Rawls, *Political Liberalism*, pp. xlvii–1, 223–27; Rawls, *Justice as Fairness*, pp. 133–34.

[36] Weithman does not see this as a deep problem. *Why Political Liberalism?*, pp. 333–35.

Table 6.1. *Impure coordination game*

		Betty	
		P_1	P_2
Alf	P_1	2 1	0 0
	P_2	0 0	1 2

arguments from R to P, and from R to Pr. Inference on the basis of R cannot help.

What can help is the idea of a best response on the basis of U to other people's actions. We are confronted with an impure coordination game as in Table 6.1 (higher numbers indicate more preferred outcomes). Here the differing results of the freestanding argument are ordered by each on the basis of their unrestricted set U. In Table 6.1, Alf and Betty disagree on which is best supported, but concur that that the best response to the other adopting a principle is to also adopt it.

A one-shot two-person game can give us some insight, but it is clearly an inadequate way to model the selection of a particular member of the set of principles justified by R. The relevant coordination problem is not a single-play game, but an iterated game. We have a number of encounters with others, and each can be understood as a play in a series of impure coordination games over many options. Now in an iterated game, a person's utility is a combination of her utility in this play, plus her expectations for utility in future games. Thus a person might sacrifice utility in one play to induce play in future moves that will yield her a more favored result. Now in large iterated games, a bandwagon effect manifests itself. As I have argued elsewhere, such large-person iterated coordination games exhibit a strong increasing returns effect: the more people come to embrace a particular option, the more reason others have to also embrace it.[37] In a wide range of circumstances, a society can come to coordinate on a stable outcome even given the indeterminacy of the freestanding argument if people can draw on U. Note here that U plays a crucial justificatory role in completing the justification of the principles of justice.

[37] See Gaus, *Order of Public Reason*, §19.3.

2.5   On Dropping All Requirements of Shared Reasons

Of course, to say that a free justificatory equilibrium is the only plausible device of justificatory stability in a deeply pluralistic world (in which we do not privilege a common thick set of shared values in our social and political relations) does not show that such an equilibrium can be achieved. If it cannot, the project of public reason liberalism fails: no stable political order among free and diverse people is possible (at least not one without a great use of coercion). It is thus a fundamental desideratum for public reason liberalism to facilitate the rise of a free justificatory equilibrium.

Consequently, the most plausible version of public reason liberalism must seek to maximize the prospects of a free justificatory equilibrium. Given this, we must inquire whether we should reconsider the requirement that all accept the freestanding argument based on the restricted set of reasons, R. The view we have thus far been considering advances two requirements for a justificatory stability:

(1)   P is justified only if it is endorsed on the basis of the shared restricted set R ("freestanding justification").
(2)   The freestanding justification of P must be affirmed by citizens when appealing to their unrestricted set U ("full justification").[38]

Let us consider four groups of citizens in relation to these two requirements:

A.   Those for whom both (1) and (2) apply
B.   Those for whom only (1) applies
C.   Those for whom only (2) applies[39]
D.   Those for whom neither applies

Quong, we have seen, holds that P is adequately justified for groups A and B; we might say that Quong's strategy is to maximize the population that endorses the principles by restricting all justification to the restricted set, R. But, as we have seen, this invites justificatory instability. Rawls seeks to avoid justificatory instability by holding that only for group A is P fully justified. Note that both Rawls and Quong hold that P is not justified to group C, even though when group C considers their unrestricted set of reasons U, they affirm it. So even though this group sees principle P as justified, given their all-things-considered judgments, they are excluded by

---

[38] I am focusing here only on the problem of defeated endorsement.
[39] Here we relax the assumption that U contains R.

both Rawls and revisionists such as Quong from the population to whom it is justified. Given the importance of solving the problem of justificatory instability, excluding these citizens simply because they have not accepted the canonical R-based argument looks myopic. Such public reason liberals are making it harder to achieve a free stable order.

We are led to the suggestion that the necessity of the shared freestanding argument from R to P be dropped. To be sure, we may still employ it in our exposition of the case for liberalism; to the extent we share reasons, that is all well and good, and the R to P argument may give us insights into the liberal justificatory project. But we do not require that a person accept the case from R to P in order for P to be justified to her. Note that by basing justification on U (or some subset, U* that is rather close to U), we pretty much eliminate the problem of justificatory instability, since the justificatory set of reasons approaches the all-things-considered set.[40]

The Rawlsian might advance two worries about this expansion of the set of reasons to be considered by the justificatory public. First, they are apt to worry that their favored principle P (say, the difference principle) will fail to be justified, given this wider set. This is manifestly Quong's concern: he is deeply concerned that "illiberals" will veto P, which is why he insists that the support of group B alone would be sufficient. Rawls – and here I have concurred – cannot take heart at this victory, for whatever justification is achieved by only requiring B as the relevant public is apt to incur a high cost in justificatory stability. Once we see that justificatory stability requires (2), why also insist on (1)? Again, I suspect that the Rawlsians' worry is that we will get the "wrong" results: once we abandon the two-staged account, we may achieve a more comprehensive equilibrium on some alternative principle P*. The two-stage account, like any elimination process, is path-dependent: an alternative P* that may be more favored by citizens' unrestricted sets (U) can be eliminated at the first stage based on R alone.[41] Surely, though, we do not wish a moral and/or political order among free and equal persons to settle on a certain principle because we have devised a path-dependent justificatory process that eliminates non-liberal (or at least non-Rawlsian) competitors at an early stage, although they would be endorsed in a wider setting. As liberals, we wish to confirm our conviction that liberal principles can be freely endorsed by all free and

---

[40] This is my strategy in chapter 5 of *The Order of Public Reason*.

[41] On path-dependence, see my *On Philosophy, Politics, and Economics* (Belmont, CA: Thomson-Wadsworth, 2008), pp. 164–71.

equal persons (or citizens), not show that we can devise a path-dependent procedure whereby they are selected. If a wider body of citizens freely endorses P* once they consider all that is relevant, what case remains for insisting that P is really the principle that is justified to all?

2.6 Interpretive Equilibria

To say that public reason liberalism should jettison the requirement that justificatory reasons be shared does not mean that nothing must be shared among actual citizens. We must share interpretations of the justified rules, principles, and institutions. If the rules, principles, and/or institutions are to structure a common cooperative social life, we clearly must entertain similar understandings of the rules, or look to the same procedures (such as the courts) to resolve any disagreements that arise. As Cristina Bicchieri stresses, for effective coordination via norms, rules, etc., participants must share "scripts": shared expectations about what is called for in various circumstances.[42] Norms, rules, and institutions can be understood as constituting "correlated equilibria" in which individuals focus on a common signal (the norm, rule, law) to "choreograph" their actions. Thus, for example, to "share" a property rule is to share a complex interplay of expectations about what a property owner will do when another trespasses on her land, or what signs one can post on one's buildings, and what will happen if one posts unacceptable signs.[43] We can explain the development of such correlated norms without supposing that the individuals share ends or reasons to endorse the norm. (Fred Astaire and Ginger Rogers need not have had common reasons for dancing together.) It is essential not to conflate this choreography inherent in all norms – our dance of first-order expectations – with shared public justificatory reasons.[44]

---

[42] Cristina Bicchieri, *The Grammar of Society: The Nature and Dynamics of Social Norms* (Cambridge: Cambridge University Press, 2006), p. 92.

[43] I develop this idea in "The Property Equilibrium in Our Liberal Social Order (Or How to Correct Our Moral Vision)," *Social Philosophy & Policy*, vol. 28 (Summer 2011), pp. 74–101. My account draws on Herbert Gintis, *The Bounds of Reason: Game Theory and the Unification of the Behavioral Sciences* (Princeton: Princeton University Press, 2009), esp. chap. 11.

[44] I believe that Gillian K. Hadfield and Stephen Macedo make this error in their "Rational Reasonableness." Drawing on a model developed by Hadfield and Barry Weingast ("What Is Law? A Coordination Model of the Characteristics of Legal Order," University of Southern California Law School, Law and Economics Working Paper Series, 2010, paper 123), they argue that successful legal coordination requires public "common logics" that allow us to anticipate each other's reaction to violations (especially punishments). I cannot consider the complexities of the model here, but I note (i) the common logics employed in the Hadfield and Weingast model are critical because they yield shared expectations of the behaviors required by the rule and its

Table 6.2. *Assurance problem*

		Betty	
		Act on P	Do not
Alf	Act on P	3 3	2 0
	Do not	0 2	1 1

3. Conditional Compliance and the "Assurance Problem"

3.1 The Assurance Problem and Rawlsian Public Justification

Suppose we succeed in fully justifying principle (or rule, or institution) P to all free and equal persons on the basis of convergence reasoning alone (that is, we drop all shared reasons requirements for full justification). Suppose further – as I have been arguing – that this best solves the problems of ineffective and defeated endorsements. Now Rawls seems quite right that the justification for P is still conditional: our citizens are willing to comply with P on the assumption that others do so as well. Thus, as Weithman points out, citizens face an assurance problem, a very simple version of which he models in a 2 × 2 game, as in Table 6.2 (again, higher numbers indicate more preferred outcomes).

In this assurance game, Alf and Betty both receive his/her highest payoff if they both act on P. However, Alf gets his second highest payoff if Betty acts on P while he does not (Betty acts fairly while he acts to advance his concerns in an unrestricted manner). Betty's reasoning is symmetric. Each ranks being the unilateral follower of P as the worst outcome. Thus, universal defection (no one acting on P) is preferred by Alf to unilaterally acting on P (and Betty prefers it to her unilaterally acting on P). This game has two Nash equilibria: both acting on P and the Pareto-inferior neither acting on P. We call this the "assurance game" because, unless Alf and

enforcement, and (ii) their model explicitly disallows that one could ever come to infer the "personal" scripts ("logics") used by others, and so by stipulation, only common knowledge of a "common logic" can provide the basis of coordination. Given the severe limits of the model's very simple account of coordinated behavior via norms and laws, it is surprising that Hadfield and Macedo (in their "Rational Reasonableness"), and Macedo, in "Why Public Reason? Citizens' Reasons and the Constitution in the Public Sphere" (August 23, 2010, http://ssm.com/abstract=1664085), appear to believe the model provides significant support for the necessity of "shared public reasoning." I consider some of the problems with the common knowledge assumption in Section 3.3.

Betty can be assured that the other will play cooperatively, they are apt to end up in the Pareto-inferior equilibrium.

Weithman writes that this threat of instability

> arises on the assumption that each person wants to act justly, but needs the assurance that he will not be taken advantage of. Since a WOS [well-ordered society] is a just society, everyone is already behaving justly, so what each person needs to be assured of is that others will continue to act justly rather than defect. Suppose that each person knows everyone else's balance of reasons tilts in favor of acting justly when others do. Then each knows that no one else has sufficient reason to take advantage of him and the mutual assurance problem is solved.[45]

Thus, Weithman argues that "public knowledge of an overlapping consensus is therefore sufficient to solve the mutual assurance problem."[46] This knowledge, Weithman and others hold, is conveyed through what Rawls identifies as the third stage of justification – public justification. After the pro tanto justification of the freestanding argument and the overlapping consensus of full justification, comes public justification, which

> happens when all reasonable members of political society carry out a justification of the shared political conception by embedding it in their several reasonable comprehensive views . . . A crucial point here is that while the public justification of the political conception depends on reasonable comprehensive doctrines, it does so only in an indirect way. That is, the express contents of these doctrines have no normative role in public justification; citizens do not look into an account of others' doctrines, and so remain within the bounds of the political.[47]

Public justification so understood appears to be a public knowledge that overlapping consensus has been achieved. For Rawls and his followers such as Weithman and Macedo, this is achieved by a public political culture that restricts itself to some ideal of public reasoning as shared reasoning on the basis of the justified political conception.[48] By constraining their public reasoning to the shared political conception (let us call this "a display of shared public reasoning"), it is supposed, citizens assure each

---

[45] Weithman, *Why Political Liberalism?*, p. 49.   [46] Ibid., p. 328.
[47] Rawls, *Political Liberalism*, p. 387.
[48] For Macedo, see his "Why Public Reason?"; Hadfield and Macedo, "Rational Reasonableness." Rawls revised his view to the extent to which this disallows appeal to comprehensive doctrines in political discourse concerning matters of basic justice. See Weithman, *Why Political Liberalism?*, pp. 329–35; Rawls, "Public Reason Revisited" in his *The Law of Peoples* (Cambridge, MA: Harvard University Press, 1999), pp. 131–80.

other that they have embedded this political conception in their comprehensive doctrine, and so they assure each other that it is justified in the unrestricted set U. Note that, if this is so, it demonstrates why we cannot do without the two-staged argument I criticized in Section 2.5. Once we have solved the problem of justificatory instability by embedding the argument from R to P in our unrestricted sets, we solve the assurance problem by, essentially, only appealing to the R to P argument (and the ways of reasoning it licenses) in certain fundamental political discussions.[49] Thus those who endorse P on the basis of U but not on the basis of R cannot help solve the assurance problem.

3.2   Why a Display of Shared Public Reasoning Will Not Solve the Assurance Game

There is an insight at the heart of the Rawlsian argument: overt communication within a group that indicates allegiance to group norms can indeed increase a tendency to trust each other. We can understand Rawlsian displays of shared public reasoning as what economists call "cheap talk" – and that can positively influence cooperative behavior.[50] We certainly should accept the insight that a display of shared public reasoning might be one way to convince others that one is a trustworthy citizen, but there is no reason to suppose that it is a unique, or indeed especially effective, way to do so. Displays of allegiance to the political system, affirmations of the importance of upholding the law, all may serve the function of assuring others of our propensity to cooperate. Whether conducting arguments – and so disagreeing – in a certain constrained language is an effective way to display trustworthiness is controversial. In these contexts, we are disagreeing with others, and so the display of shared public reasoning will also be a display of disagreement. We are sending a mixed message of agreement and disagreement; sending such messages may not be the most effective way to establish trust. If the main claim is a psychological one about what types of communications and displays are apt to induce trust in very large groups, then the matter depends on the psychological evidence. For now, let us grant that some sorts of public displays are of use in engendering mutual trust. However, I will argue in Section 3.3 that they are of secondary importance in our political context.

---

[49] See Rawls, *Justice as Fairness*, p. 89.   [50] See Bicchieri, *Grammar of Society*, pp. 153–57.

If we move from general psychological claims about inducing trust to the more technical problem of the assurance game, displays of shared public reasoning will not suffice to solve the problem, and this is for two reasons. (i) In the assurance game in Table 6.2, Alf's communication that he intends to cooperate will not help Betty form beliefs about what Alf will do, because regardless of what Alf intends, he would have a reason to send an "I will cooperate" message.[51] If Alf plans to cooperate, he would tell Betty so (since he will get his best payoff if she also cooperates), but if he plans to defect, he still has reason to give a display of trustworthiness, since he prefers his unilateral defection to mutual defection, and so has an incentive to induce Betty to cooperate. So in Table 6.2, communication of one's readiness to comply does not help the other form beliefs about one's intentions.[52]

(ii) It is not enough to solve the assurance problem that "each person knows everyone else's balance of reason tilts in favor of acting justly when others do." We need something considerably stronger: we need common knowledge of this fact.[53] Suppose that I know that everyone else's balance of reason tilts in favor of acting justly when others do, but I am not sure that others know that I know this. That we each know X does not imply that we each know that we each know X. I not only have to be sending the signal that I endorse the "R to P" reasoning, but I also have to know that the others are properly receiving my message and, so, for example, do not infer from the fact that I am disagreeing with them on the basis of shared public reasons that I am simply trying to manipulate them and will defect if I do not win the debate. And, in turn, should they know that I am not a defector simply using shared public reasoning, they must know that I know that they know I am not a defector. Common knowledge is a very strong assumption; as Hadfield and Macedo recognize, it implies a common knowledge of each other's logicality as well as information. But we are seldom in a world of such knowledge; a solution to the problems of large-scale assurance and coordination that depends on it cannot be convincing.[54]

[51]   See Ken Binmore, *Natural Justice* (Oxford: Oxford University Press, 2005), p. 68.
[52]   In a slightly different game, sometimes called "the Stag Hunt," where one is indifferent between one's unilateral defection and mutual defection, communication that one intended to cooperate would have an unequivocal message.
[53]   Weithman, as well as Hadfield and Macedo, endorse the common knowledge assumption. See Weithman, *Why Political Liberalism?*, for example, p. 328; Hadfield and Macedo, "Rational Reasonableness."
[54]   See Gintis, *Bounds of Reason*, chap. 5.

3.3 Thinking about Stability under Conditional Compliance

Even though thinking through the issue in terms of a simple one-play assurance game is not helpful, the problem of conditional compliance is real. In a plausible account of norm following, we have to suppose that (i) even if a person has overall reason to follow P, (ii) she only has reason to act on P if enough others follow P.[55] It is important to stress that, while there is a role for the normative expectations of others in explaining why we comply, a critical factor is our first-order empirical expectations about what others will do. There is sound evidence that a person's first-order empirical expectations about how others actually act ("Do people comply with the norm?") is a powerful explanatory factor in explaining whether a person will comply. Indeed, the evidence indicates first-order empirical expectations are a much more powerful factor than normative talk ("This is our norm, which I affirm").[56] I stress that these are first-order expectations: they are one's beliefs about what others will do, not my beliefs about their beliefs about my beliefs, and so on, which are required for common knowledge solutions to assurance problems.

To begin to see how we might explain the evolution of conditional cooperation, let us consider some very simple dynamic models. Call β_i person i's threshold level as to what is "enough" compliance: suppose that β varies between O (in which case the person is a unilateral complier) and N-1, in which case the person will only comply once everyone else is complying. There is no reason to think that all have the same β values. Some may have a β of 0, being essentially unconditional compliers.[57] Let us assume a roughly continuous range of β values, perhaps with some normal-like distribution around mid-range values. Important in modeling the evolution of compliance would be information about what others are doing. Let us consider two cases: evolution under perfect/near-perfect information about the actions of all others, and only local knowledge about what others are doing.

3.3.1 Perfect Information

If we assume that each and every person has full knowledge of the compliance of others, and continuous range of β values, we can see how iterated interactions can lead to full compliance. Starting with the

---

[55] See Bicchieri, *Grammar of Society*, p. 11; Gaus, *Order of Public Reason*, p. 167.
[56] See Gaus, *Order of Public Reason*, pp. 168–72.
[57] See Weithman, *Why Political Liberalism?*, p. 338.

unconditional compliers in the first round, those with greater than but near O would then have their threshold met, and so on, ending with compliance by the person for whom p = N-1. As we leave the tail ends of the distribution and approach the middle, the process would speed up, and again slow down as we near the further tail. Call this the compliance cascade.

While the compliance cascade is easy to envisage under these conditions, it is subject to two possible problems under less-than-perfect information: a reverse cascade and "stalled" cascades. Suppose that we have reached full compliance: as does Rawls, we assume a well-ordered society with full compliance. Suppose now that the person for whom β = N-1 mistakenly comes to believe that another has failed to comply; if so (mutatis mutandis by the reasoning above), that error will lead to a reverse cascade to zero compliance (assuming that there are no countervailing errors along the way that block the reverse cascade).[58] However, this reverse cascade depends on a number of assumptions. It will be thwarted if the highest β values are well short of N-1. That is, if we suppose that the top β values are, say, 0.9, then even a number of mistaken judgments of non-compliance will not unravel the well-ordered society. Especially if we begin with the assumption of full compliance (rather than having to explain how it comes about), plausible distributions of β allow for the stability of first-order expectations, and so fulfilling the conditions required for conditional compliance.

Allowing for mistaken judgments about the compliance of others can also stall the cascade: the person who, as it were, should now be ready to comply mistakenly thinks that her threshold has not been met, and so refuses to comply, perhaps halting the cascade. Interestingly, this would be a problem early and late in the process; when we are at the tail end of the distributions, the mistakes of a few people could either stop the process from getting going, or halt it short of full compliance (assuming again that there are some for whom approximately β = N-1). In the middle of the distribution, where many people have the same threshold, we would not expect small mistakes to have such consequences. And this seems correct: intuitively it is easy to see how the cascade may have a hard time getting going or completing itself.

---

[58] Compare Bicchieri, *Grammar of Society*, pp. 196ff.

3.3.2 Local Knowledge

Usually we only know what those around us – those with whom we have opportunity to interact – are doing. Under these conditions, the dynamics of assurance and compliance, not surprisingly, are much more complicated.[59] Let us start with the Rawlsian problem: will a society of full compliance be stable? Again we need to suppose that compliance is a first-order expectation about what people will do: we have knowledge of the norm, and so can detect who is cheating (or, at least, not complying).[60] In this case, breakdown of compliance may be caused either (1) by some citizens withdrawing their support of the rule such that for the mass of citizens, actual compliance falls below their value and/or (2) by mistaken judgments that (1) is occurring, which cause such a breakdown. Suppose then that person i only can form judgments about what is going on in some group of neighbors H. A Rawlsian would say that stability can be achieved within H by people advocating the public conception of justice and stressing their devotion to the R to P freestanding argument as well as the principles of public reasoning it establishes. It is not clear how helpful this will be. The worry about the stability of the equilibrium only arises once a citizen observes (1), or makes the mistake of (2), in her H. If observed violators continue to give the public message affirming the public conception, citizen Betty is confronted with, as it were, talk ("I, Alf, affirm P on the basis of R given my U") that clashes with observed behavior (Alf just violated P). Given Alf's incentive to affirm his endorsement of P regardless of whether he has conformed or intends to conform (Section 3.1), Betty cannot much rely on such talk for evidence about Alf's compliance. Surely it will be Alf's behavior that will be crucial in making her judgment.

On the convergence account, there is no canonical argument for P; whether P is justified is a matter of whether citizens' unrestricted sets endorse it. As a convergence reasoner, in observing her neighborhood (H), Betty will be concerned with observed rates of defection. Supposing that P is in equilibrium with citizens' unrestricted set of reasons, rates of defection should be low. Mistakes about the rule, and mistakes about whether others have conformed to the rule, will lead to some baseline rate of perceived defection in H. So long as within the neighborhood H this baseline rate of perceived defections does not drop Betty below her

[59] See Brian Skyrms, *The Stag Hunt and the Evolution of Social Structure* (Cambridge: Cambridge University Press, 2004), chap. 3.
[60] The ability to detect cheaters on rules is a basic human proficiency. See Gaus, *Order of Public Reason*, section 8.

Table 6.3.
Neighborhood interaction

H_1	H_2	H_3
H_4	H	H_5
H_6	H_7	H_8

threshold of compliance (β), she will continue to conform to P. It is thus crucial for stability that few citizens have β values approaching 1; such values render the justificatory equilibrium susceptible to "trembling hands" – mistakes and errors about compliance.

However, there are bound to be outlier neighborhoods: those in which noncompliance is high (perhaps because of unusually high p values). A resident of this neighborhood will form pessimistic estimates of overall compliance. She (and others like her in H) may be driven below her threshold, and so also cease to comply with P. Suppose, then, that everyone in neighborhood H ceases compliance; note that H borders other neighborhoods (say H1 ... H8) as in Table 6.3.

We suppose that those at the edge of a neighborhood interact with, and so know about, those on edges of adjacent neighborhoods. Now that H is a non-compliant neighborhood, the adjacent neighborhoods all will have significantly increased their interactions with non-compliers. This raises the troubling possibility that their interactions with H may push some or all of them below their compliance thresholds, spreading out non-compliance.[61] Whether this occurs will, of course, depend on the values of the members of the other neighborhoods, as well as the initial perceived rates of defection in them; but we do know that interaction with H will tend to push down perceived compliance in these adjacent neighborhoods.

Perhaps the most effective way to check the danger of such a non-compliance epidemic is through punishment.[62] We have been assuming that Betty is merely reactive: she establishes her estimate of compliance and

---

[61] Of course the epidemiological dynamic can go the other way, inducing compliance. I assume that we do not wish stability to depend on a hope for a countervailing tendency.

[62] For evidence, see Gaus, *Order of Public Reason*, §7. It should not be thought that punishment has no place in Rawlsian stability arguments; see Rawls, *Theory of Justice*, p. 504.

checks to see whether it meets her threshold level. Should non-compliance increase, Betty may find that her neighborhood is now below her value, and so she herself ceases compliance. However if Betty is a "Rule-Following Punisher,"[63] she not only has a conditional tendency to follow rules (or norms, etc.), but she is willing to forgo some resources to punish those who do not comply, thus stopping an epidemic of non-compliance. This sort of decentralized enforcement helps to counteract non-compliance, thus stabilizing norms in the face of temptation to defect.[64] It is very hard to see how stability can be secured in the face of imperfect information without willingness of many to punish perceived violators.

4. Conclusion

The move from *A Theory of Justice* to *Political Liberalism* was characterized by a conviction that a stable equilibrium on justice could be achieved without citizens sharing a great part of their unrestricted set of reasons. What I have called the "double shared" strategy of *A Theory of Justice* (Section 2.2) was abandoned by Rawls in favor of (to, of course, simplify an exceedingly complex corpus) a single shared view (Section 2.3), in which we share the freestanding argument, but fill out the full justification of the principles in different ways. I have argued that the best prospect for a stable equilibrium on justified rules and principles is to drop all requirements of shared justificatory reasons (Section 2.5). Such an approach has the best prospects of solving the problems of ineffective and defeated endorsements, and, pace Rawls and some of his followers, there is no good reason to think that a public display of a shared conception of justice is needed to show (or even is particularly helpful in showing) why conditional compliers will become, and remain, actual compliers (Section 3). Rawls's followers may well be worried that if we drop the canonical shared reasons requirement (underlying the freestanding argument), we can no longer be guaranteed that liberal principles will be the core of a justified equilibrium. However, the fundamental commitment of those devoted to a free social order is that our social rules, norms, and principles must be a justified and stable equilibrium. I have faith that those will be the fundamental liberal principles – but that, hopefully, is the outcome of our justificatory investigations, not their premise.

---

[63] Gaus, *Order of Public Reason*, §7. See also my "Retributive Justice and Social Cooperation" in *Retributivism: Essays on Theory and Practice*, ed. Mark D. White (Oxford: Oxford University Press, 2011), chap. 4.

[64] Rawlsians have begun to perceive the importance of decentralized punishment for norm maintenance. See Hadfield and Macedo, "Rational Reasonableness."

CHAPTER 7

Self-Organizing Moral Systems
Beyond Social Contract Theory

> But what if morality is created in day-to-day social interaction, not at
> some abstract mental level?
>
> Frans de Waal

1 Integrity and Reconciliation in Moral Thinking

Contemporary moral and political philosophy is torn between two modes
of moral reasoning. A common view of moral thinking – perhaps most
characteristic of moral philosophy – understands reasoning about moral
claims to be, in a fundamental sense, akin to reasoning about ordinary
factual claims. On this commonsense approach, when Alf deliberates
about a moral claim or demand (say, that people ought to respect property), he considers the best reasons as he understands them for and against
the claim, including what he takes to be the correct normative principles,
perhaps checks his conclusions with others to see if he has made any errors,
and then comes to the conclusion, 'we all ought to respect property'. His
moral reasoning may refer to facts about other people (say, their welfare),
but it is not a general requirement on the moral reasoning of any competent agent that he always takes as one of his inputs the moral deliberations
of others.

As far back as Hobbes (and probably a good deal further), many political
philosophers have been deeply impressed how this first, individualistic,
mode of moral reasoning leads to disagreement. When we employ our
'private reason', there is, says Hobbes, great dispute about the application
of the laws of nature, and so we require some common reason – a public
reason – to reconcile our judgments and provide a common interpretation
of what the law requires.[1] More recently, public reason moral and political

---

[1] Hobbes (1994: 98, Ch. 15, para. 30). See also Gauthier (1998: 43–66, 50 ff). This same point was
made earlier, and in more detail, by Ewin (1991: Ch. 2). See also Gaus (2015).

theory has focused on how reasonable disputes about the good and the right can be reconciled via common conceptions of justice or shared moral rules.[2] This mode of moral reasoning aims to cope with – often by seeking to rise above – the moral disagreements engendered by the individual mode.

Yet many resist this second, reconciliation, mode. Why, they ask, must I give up my own conclusions about justice for the sake of agreement? Isn't the search for reconciliation a violation of my moral integrity? To this, the theorist of public reason reasonably responds by saying that one's own understanding of morality – that arrived at by the individual mode of reasoning – itself drives one to seek moral reconciliation with others, for on many matters one seeks to live a shared moral life with them. After all, one cannot institute a just system of property rights on one's own; one needs others, and this very moral need drives one to reconcile with others about the demands of justice. I shall argue that this response, as far as it goes, is correct: Even when we consult only our own, individual, moral reasoning, almost all of us come to the conclusion that a moral life is to a very large extent a social achievement, and so we have moral reasons to seek out others who can share it with us. This, we shall see, is the great insight of the social contract. However, I shall argue, the contractual project flounders on the very supposition of moral disagreement on which it builds. It insists that because we disagree about the demands of morality and justice, we need to reconcile with others, yet this very disagreement in individual moral reasoning leads us to disagree on a further matter: To what extent should we reconcile with others? Having reasonably seen that we disagree in our first-level moral judgments, the contractualist seeks to resolve this problem by assuming we agree on the required degree of reconciliation and then constructs a device to secure it. The reflective contractualist may admit that this is a strong assumption but, she insists, one that must be made if we are to secure a social existence based on justice.

Having analyzed this problem in Sections 2 and 3, Sections 4 and 5 develop models of moral self-organization that show how it might be overcome. Each person, we shall assume, is committed solely to her own integrity – understood as her own judgments about first-level moral matters and the degree of reconciliation that her moral perspective

---

[2] This was the aim of my *Order of Public Reason* (2011). Although Rawls began by focusing on disputes arising from the good, by the introduction to the paperback edition of *Political Liberalism*, he was explicit that individual reasoning about morality and justice also leads to disagreement (Rawls, 2005: xxxv–lx).

endorses. I shall assume that free, reasonable, and competent moral agents will disagree about both of these. Nevertheless, we shall see that under a surprising array of circumstances, they can secure a shared moral life endorsed by all. The social contract's aim of full reconciliation can be secured without any contract device. And, perhaps most surprisingly, moral agents can arrive at this full reconciliation just because they disagree about the importance of reconciliation.

2 The Two Modes Analyzed

2.1 The Individual Mode

To be a bit more precise, we can identify the individual mode of reasoning as:

> The 'I conclude we ought' implies 'I ought' View: As a competent moral agent, if (i) Alf conscientiously deliberates and concludes that, given what he takes to be the correct normative premises and relevant empirical information, one ought to f (ought not f, or may f)[3] under conditions C, where this does not require taking account of the conclusions of the deliberations of others, and (ii) he reasonably concludes that morality instructs that we all ought to f under conditions C, then (iii) he ought to f in circumstances C, even if others fail to do as they ought.

It is important that on the 'I conclude we ought' implies 'I ought' View (henceforth simply the 'I conclude we ought' View), Alf does not typically assert that we all ought to f in C because he has concluded that we ought to f: Alf may believe that 'we ought to f' in C because it is a moral truth that we ought to f, or that an impartial spectator would approve of our f-ing. The important point is that once Alf conscientiously comes to the belief that one ought to f in C – it is, we might say, his best judgment about the morally best thing to do – then, as a competent moral agent, he will justifiably f in circumstances C, and indeed insist that we all do so, for that is what we ought to do.[4] And, as I have stressed, none of this necessitates

---

[3] Henceforth, I shall not state these alternatives, assuming that they are implicit.

[4] I assume here that conditions C are so defined that typical justifications for not f-ing (duress, and so on) would show that C was not met. Recall that C cannot include the deliberations of others about what is moral in this circumstance. It can, though, take account of what Alf expects others to do. Given this, it is possible to construct a statement of conditions C that partially mimics the reconciliation view, where Alf reconciles his understanding of morality with what others do, but he will still not reconcile with what others hold to be moral or just. I consider this possibility in §2.3.

(though it may be epistemically recommended) that Alf factors into his moral deliberation the moral conclusions of others.

2.2 The Reconciliation Mode

On one reading the social contract offers another view of justice and morality. Hobbes, Locke, Rousseau, and Kant all hold that individuals' 'private judgments' about morality or justice radically diverge, and because of this individual private judgment is an inappropriate ground – or at least, I shall argue, an inappropriate sole ground – for the demands of justice. Kant famously insists that even if we imagine individuals 'to be ever so good natured and righteous', when each does what 'seems just and good to him, entirely independently of the opinion of others', they live without justice.[5] This apparently paradoxical conclusion – that a world of people who acted only on their own sincere convictions about justice would live without justice[6] – derives from two commitments of social contract theory. (i) It is taken as given that reasoned private judgments of justice inevitably conflict. This is partially because of self-bias, but only partially: innate differences in emotional natures; differences in beliefs that form the basis of current deliberations; and differences in education, socialization, and religious belief – all lead to pervasive disagreement. (ii) Secondly, it is assumed that a critical role of justice in our social lives is to adjudicate disputes about our claims and coordinate normative and empirical expectations. For Kant, the problem of universal private judgment was that 'when there is a controversy concerning rights (*jus controversum*), no competent judge can be found'.[7] Each, thrown back on her own reasoning, ends up in conflict, and ultimately unjust relations, with others. Understood thus, a necessary role of justice (or morality) is to provide an interpersonally endorsed adjudication of conflicting claims.[8] Securing justice, on this second view, is inherently something we do together.[9] If no other good-willed and conscientious moral agent accepts that in circumstances C justice demands f, Alf's demand will not secure just social relations. Given points (i) and (ii), social contract theorists have endorsed a reconciliation requirement: Individuals must seek out some device of

---

[5] Kant (1999: 116, §43). Emphasis added.
[6] I have defended this paradox in some depth in 'The Commonwealth of Bees: On the Impossibility of Justice-through-Ethos' (2016b: 96–121).
[7] Kant (1999: 116, §43). Emphasis added.   [8] See Rawls (1999b: 1–19).
[9] It is not only contract theorists who think this. See Cohen (2008: 175) and Brandt (1979: Ch. 9).

		Betty R_1	Betty R_2
Alf	R_1	4th / 1st	2nd / 2nd
Alf	R_2	3rd / 3rd	1st / 4th

Figure 7.1. 'I believe we ought f' implies 'I ought to f' (go your own way game)

agreement that reconciles their differences so that they can share convictions about what justice demands we do.

2.3 *Justice as a Social Good*

The worry about relying exclusively on 'I believe we ought' reasoning is that my conclusion is about the justice of a joint action – what we do – but as a competent moral agent, my deliberations control only what I do, not what others do, so I alone cannot produce the joint action. Consequently, my 'I believe we ought' judgment is very often ineffective in securing what I believe we both ought to do.[10] Rather than focusing on individual actions, I shall henceforth consider disputes about the rules of justice that should be followed in some circumstances, supposing that rules are specific enough to provide people with guidance about how to act both now and in the future.[11] Alf, then, has concluded that, say, 'we ought to both act on rule R1', but the question remains whether he ought to do so if Betty refuses to. In this case, whether or not Alf's 'I believe we ought' judgment is action guiding even for Alf depends on how he ranks the alternative joint rule-based outcomes in terms of justice. Contrast, for example, the interactions modeled in Figures 7.1 and 7.2.

In the interaction of Figure 7.1, each orders the outcomes: (1) we act on (my view of) the just rule, (2) I act on the correct rule of justice and the other acts on the inferior rule, (3) I act on the inferior rule and the other acts on the correct rule (at least someone does!), and (4) we both act on the

[10] If, as do some, we suppose that judgments of justice are not intended to be action guiding, this is not a problem. I consider the extent to which judgments of justice are inherently practical in *The Tyranny of the Ideal* (2016a: 11–18). Here it is simply assumed that our concern is action-guiding judgments; if there are other notions of justice, they raise different issues.

[11] See my *Order of Public Reason* (2011: Ch. 3) for a defense of these assumptions.

Betty

Figure 7.2. 'I believe we ought f' does not imply 'I ought to f' (reconciliation game)

inferior rule. In this game, the sole equilibrium is that Alf acts on his view (R1), and Betty acts on her view (R2), of justice. At either of the coordination solutions (when both play R1 or both play R2), one of the parties would do morally better by changing his or her move, and acting on his or her favored interpretation of justice. So here, even if the other does not do as you have concluded 'we' ought, you still ought to do it. In this game, each goes their own way.

Figure 7.2 does not support this conclusion. There are two equilibria in this impure coordination game: both act on R1 and both act on R2. Here, both parties agree that from the perspective of securing just social relations, it is best that they do not necessarily act on their understanding of the best rule of justice, for if they do so, they may secure social relations that are inferior from the perspective of justice. Thus, based solely on what they each believe justice requires, they are playing a reconciliation game. Now insofar as the aim of justice is securing social relations of a certain moral quality, we would expect Figure 7.2 would be a typical interaction. We need each other's cooperation to produce just social relations. It might be thought, though, that it would be enough for Alf and Betty to coordinate their actions, not the endorsement of the same rule of justice. So long as, say, in Figure 7.2, Alf and Betty both act in the way R1 requires, or R2 requires, it does not matter what rule they endorse as just (enough). Justice, it might be thought, demands only coordinated action, not judgments. But while mere coordinated action would secure them some social goods, as Kant insisted, they remain in conflict about justice. If, say, Betty acts on R1 only because she is being coerced or simply to secure some nonmoral social good, she will fail to see their joint action as just. Indeed, while Alf thinks they are acting justly, Betty may well conclude that she is a victim of injustice and will respond to the R1 action as a wrong. Thus, Alf is unable to appeal to the justice of R1 to regulate their interactions, for she sees it as an unjust way of relating. Such an appeal would only aggravate conflict, not help resolve it. In such situations, relations of moral account-ability are undermined: Betty will not see herself as accountable for failing to abide by R1, as she does not understand it to be a rule of justice.[12] They thus will have failed to secure an interpersonal relation informed by justice.

I suppose in this essay, then, that judgments of justice are typically about interactions along the lines of Figure 7.2 rather than Figure 7.1. Judgments of justice seek to secure a certain type of moral relation and, especially among large groups of people, an individual's unilateral action seldom can secure this relation. It is this sense in which, I suppose, justice is a social moral good. As Plato stressed in the *Republic*, it is about relations among individuals rather than unilateral action; that is why the theory of justice has been a part of social and political philosophy right from the beginning. Much moral thinking can be described as simply 'I believe I ought' reasoning, where my only concern is what I ought to do, come what may. One can be chaste, honorable, and honest alone; one cannot make promises, keep contracts, or determine mutual expectations about what is proper and improper on one's own. Here, the moral theorist switches from 'I believe I ought' to 'I believe we ought' judgments, but once that move has been made, there is still a problem: I have concluded what we ought to do, but I cannot secure this without your cooperation. That is why with justice we often play the reconciliation game in Figure 7.2 rather than the go your own way game of Figure 7.1. This is the great insight of the social contract tradition.

3   Reconciliation via the Social Contract

We thus come to appreciate that determining the rules and institutions of justice is – at least to some extent – a social problem. A natural interpre-tation of this, which we might see as definitive of the social contract tradition, is to understand it as a collective problem. My concern here is not to present a thorough criticism of this idea – which, I think, has offered, and continues to offer, fundamental insights[13] – but to clearly contrast it to the alternative I shall develop.

---

[12] See Gaus (2016a: 180 ff) and Gaus (2011: Ch. 4).
[13] For important recent contributions, see Moehler (2017); Vanderschraaf (2018).

3.1 Substantive Contracts: 'We Believe We Ought' Views

Consider first a substantive version of the social contract, presenting a theory that suitably characterized individuals would agree to common principles of justice to structure their social and political lives. Rawls' contractualist theory is, of course, the quintessential case. Such substantive theories seek a 'we believe we ought' judgment. The theory constructs an account of what reasonable and rational persons with certain motivations would agree that we should all do. The theorist, then, actually presents something like an 'I believe that [we believe we all ought to]' view of justice. That is, the theorist provides an analysis of what she thinks we would collectively agree to as common, shared, principles of justice to regulate our relations. Rawls suggests an even more complicated view. As he presents his theory of justice, 'you and I' develop a theory of what all reasonable people would agree to.[14] We thus seem to have something like an 'I [Rawls] believe that [<you and I believe that> we believe we all ought to]' view.[15]

Now, from the perspective of reconciliation, a theory that acknowledges that we disagree about justice, yet need to coordinate, is certainly a great improvement upon simple 'I believe we ought to' reasoning, as it seeks to confront at a basic level the fundamental moral insight that unless you and I concur about the demands of justice, our social relations will be deeply flawed from the perspective of justice itself. Yet, at the end of the day, it is a theory of what the theorist believes that we all believe that we all ought to do. That is, at the end of the day, it is one person's conviction about what we all believe we ought to do; and for the same reasons we disagree in our simple 'I believe we ought' judgments, we disagree in our 'I believe we believe we ought' judgments.[16] Rawls, indeed, came to recognize that reasonable people do disagree about the most reasonable conception of justice – about the conception of justice that we would agree to.[17] Rawls acknowledges that his own theory of 'justice as fairness' – a theory about what we will agree on – is controversial. And even if two philosophers, Alf and Betty, accept Rawls' principles of justice, they are almost certain to disagree on their interpretation, leading them to interactions along the lines of Figure 7.2.

---

[14] Rawls (2005: 28 ff). See also Rawls (1999a: 44).
[15] It is for this reason that Habermas is correct to characterize Rawls' theory as 'monological' at the highest level. Habermas (1995: 109–131, at 117).
[16] Or 'I believe that [<you and I believe that> we believe we all ought to]' judgments.
[17] Rawls (2005: xlvii).

3.2   Bargaining about Reconciliation

The substantive social contract, then, seeks a path to reconciliation by articulating a collective judgment about justice – what we believe we ought to do – but it is ultimately a theorist's judgment about what is the collective judgment. Implicit in this is the theorist's judgment about how much reconciliation among diverse views is called for – but that is one of our deep disagreements, and thus the substantive view struggles with the problem of disagreement of private judgments about justice.[18] If the problem is that each individual has a different estimate of the moral costs and benefits of reconciliation, a second version of the social contract seems promising. Combining substantive and procedural elements, the bargaining contract takes this problem seriously, seeking a reasonable balance between the two modes of reasoning. Abstracting from important technical details, the heart of this approach is to identify two points for each individual, say Alf and Betty: The justice-based 'payoff' that one would receive from unilateral action based on one's 'I believe we ought' reasoning (the so-called no-agreement point) and the best 'payoff' that one could receive from coordinated (reconciliation) action. Note, then, that the outcome depends on the relation between these two concerns for each agent. We suppose both would gain 'moral utility' (better moral out-comes)[19] through some form of coordination; if this was not the case, they would not be playing the reconciliation game, but the go your own way game. Consider, then, Figure 7.3, which is an asymmetric version of the reconciliation game (Figure 7.2) in cardinal utility.

In Figure 7.3, the no-agreement point (R1, R2) is each person's third option (1, 1); it is the best outcome that each could receive if, as it were, they walked away from an agreement to coordinate. Both would gain by moving to (R1, R1) [(4, 2)] or to (R2, R2) [(3, 4)]: the question is which is to be chosen. Drawing on bargaining theories that focus on the division of a distributable good such as, say, money or time, some social contract theorists suggest we might see Alf and Betty's problem as deciding how

---

[18] See further Gaus (2015).

[19] It is critical to keep in mind that 'utility' is simply a mathematical representation of a person's ordering of states of affairs, not itself a good which is sought. To say that an agent maximizes utility is simply to see her as one whose actions are directed to obtaining the state of affairs that she ranks as best. If her rankings are based solely on moral criteria, then, assuming that common formal consistency conditions are met (for example, if a is better than b, then b is not better than a), her choices can be represented in terms of maximizing (moral) utility: she has a moral utility function.

Betty

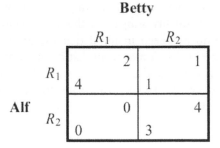

Figure 7.3.   An asymmetric reconciliation game

much utility it would be rational for each to give up to secure a bargain. On the most common approach, axioms are defended that identify a unique division of the utility gains.[20] If we employ, for example, David Gauthier's principle of minimax relative concession, at (R1, R1), Alf makes no concession and Betty concedes 2/3; at (R2, R2), Betty makes no concession and Alf concedes 1/3.[21] Thus of the two, (R2, R2) minimizes the maximum relative concession. On Gauthier's account, (R2, R2) is a more rational bargain: The relative concession of the party who gives the largest relative concession is less than in the (R1, R1) bargain.[22]

Formalizing decision problems in terms of utility representations can make many issues clearer, as I hope to show in the following sections. As Rawls recognized, even deontological theories such as W.D. Ross' can be faithfully represented in terms of standard cardinal utility measures.[23] But this important insight by no means licenses forgetting about what the

---

[20] See, for example, Nash (1950: 155–162); Gauthier (1986: Ch. 5); Kalai and Smorodinsky (1975: 513–518); and Kalai (1977: 1623–1630). For a noncooperative formulation, see Rubinstein (1982: 97–109).

[21] According to minimax relative concession, we compute relative concession according to the formula:

$$\frac{u(fp) - u(fc)}{u(fp) - u(ip)}$$

where $u(fp)$ is one's 'first proposal' (the most which one could claim from the bargain without driving the other party away [for both this is 4]; $u(fc)$ is what one actually receives from a bargain (at (R1, R1), this is (4, 2); at (R2, R2), this is (3, 4)) and so represents one's 'final concession'; I suppose that $u(ip)$ is the utility of one's initial position – the utility one comes into the agreement assured of, in this case (1, 1).

[22] There is a better solution I shall not explore: if they employ a correlated equilibrium and play (R1, R1) one-third of the time, and (R2, R2) two-thirds of the time, each concedes only 2/9. On correlated equilibrium, see my *On Philosophy, Politics, and Economics* (2008: 140–141).

[23] Rawls (2005: 332n).

numbers are representing, and so treating all 'utility' as essentially a homogenous abstract quality subject to the same types of disputes and resolutions. If we do not keep in mind that the utility scores represent disagreements about justice, it may seem that Alf and Betty have a resource division or interest compromise problem, with the numbers indicating unequal splits of the 'gains'. Clearly, this is not the case. Neither party has approved of the other's understanding of justice and may in fact have severe doubts about it. Suppose Betty complains to Alf that at (R1, R1) she must concede 2/3, but at (R2, R2) he would only concede 1/3. Fair's fair, after all; and the maximum concession should be minimized.[24] But Alf might reply thus:

> 'A basic reason why you concede relatively more when we both act on rule R1 than when we both act on R2 is that you place too much value on living according to your preferred rule of justice and too little on reconciliation; I "concede relatively less" at R2 because I place so much more value on reconciliation than do you, even on those rules I consider to be inferior, while you more highly evaluate living according to your "I believe we ought" judgments. You are free to do so, but I fail to see why that decision gives you a claim to additional consideration in our reconciliation – because you undervalue reconciliation!'

Alf disagrees with Betty about justice, including on the importance of reconciliation. Both the importance of acting on his 'I believe we ought' judgments and of sharing a rule are factored into his utility. Note that all this is about justice from his own perspective, which includes a commitment to his own insights about perfect justice and the importance of living according to shared rules. That his own conception of justice leads him to take account of what rules he can share with others in no way commits him to treating his and other people's views of justice as somehow 'on par' and each having a symmetric claim to the 'moral gains' produced by shared rules. On reflection, the very idea of a fair distribution of moral gains between those who disagree about morality seems rather bizarre.[25]

---

[24] Some have argued that common bargaining axioms are only about rationality and have no implications concerning fairness. I believe this is wrong; motivations for the critical symmetry axiom invoke a general notion of equality. See Thrasher (2014: 683–699). Interestingly, in his final statement of his view, Gauthier sees minimax relative concession not as a solution specifying a rational bargain, but as a standard of justice. See Gauthier (2013: 601–624).

[25] Some argue that bargaining solutions simply predict what splits agents will agree to and are not in any way normative. The evidence for this claim is uncertain: in empirical studies, people easily play one of the pure Nash equilibria in impure coordination games and, indeed, teach this to the next generation. See Schotter and Sopher (2003: 498–529).

4 Self-Organization in Morality

4.1 *From Constructivism to Spontaneous Orders*

I have tried to stress the importance of the two modes of reasoning about justice. When employing 'I believe we ought' reasoning, a moral agent inquires, given her standards of justice, about the extent to which the rules of justice R_1 and R_2 are appropriate standards for just relations among moral agents. Given her understanding of justice, suppose that she can score every rule from 0 to 10, where 10 indicates perfect agreement with her standards and 0 indicates a rule that is entirely unacceptable as a rule of justice. A critical assumption in the model to be developed is that a moral agent acknowledges acceptable approximations to her understanding of justice, as her own individual mode of deliberation judges it (scores of 1–9).[26] The reason that she would accept living according to an imperfect rule is supplied by recognition of the social character of justice: Justice cannot be fully secured by unilateral action. Just social relations require participation of others, and so one's complete understanding of justice will ultimately weigh the relative importance of 'I believe we ought' judgments and reconciliation.

We have seen that the social contract tradition takes seriously the social nature of justice, providing accounts of how we might collectively reason about the shared rules of justice to live by. In an important sense, however, these accounts are what Hayek would call forms of 'constructivism'.[27] They remain versions of 'I believe that [<the set of reasonable deliberators believe that> we all ought to]' judgments, in which the theorist constructs his version of the reasonable compromise among our moral views. It is not, I think, going too far to say that social contract views are 'top-down' (from the philosopher to us) theories of what a 'bottom-up' (what we collectively would choose) morality might look like. Once we recognize this, the question looms: What would a genuine 'bottom-up' social morality look like? Such a morality, I shall argue, would be the result of each person acting on what might be called, more than a little inelegantly, her 'I believe what, taking account of the justice-based choices of others, we ought to do – and that's what I ought to do' view of justice. Here, there is no collective choice: The theorist seeks to inquire what would occur if each

---

[26] See further Gaus (2016a: 45–49) and Gaus (2016b). We could formalize these into von Neumann–Morgenstern utility functions, but nothing critical turns on this point.

[27] Hayek (1973: Ch. 2); Rawls (2005: lecture III).

agent genuinely followed her own view of justice, taking into account her commitment to reconciliation.[28] Would agents who disagree in their (i) 'I believe we ought' judgments of justice and (ii) judgments of the relative importance of reconciliation converge on common rules, or would they each go their own way? Under what conditions might free individual moral reasoning replace the collectivist constructivism of the social contract? These are the questions I shall now begin, in an admittedly simplified and tentative way, to pursue.

4.2   Justice-Based Utility Functions

The following analysis is purely formal and does not presuppose any specific substantive theory of justice or social morality. Each person is assumed to be solely interested in acting justly, as she sees it. Each is thus characterized by a justice-based utility function that represents her judgments as to the justice of states of affairs, defined in terms of what rules of justice are acted upon. Recall that – at least as I have characterized it – the aim of the social contract theory is to see how free and equal moral persons who do not agree in their individual mode of reasoning about justice can share a common system of moral rules or principles. Substantive-contract attempts to secure this, we have seen (Section 3.1), valorize a specific conception of justice that the theorist claims 'we all [could] share', but this claim itself succumbs to the problem of reasonable pluralism. Some good-willed moral agents who wish to share a system of justice with others do not accept the theorist's conclusions about what 'we believe we ought to do'. Consequently, I seek here a theory of shared moral life that does not advance a correct answer about justice, but instead endeavors to model how individuals who disagree about the correct answer might nevertheless converge on a common moral life.

Given the analysis thus far, I assume that the justice-based utility of each person can be divided into two parts. What I shall call person A's (aka Alf's) inherent (justice) utility of rule R1 (denoted mA(R1)) represents Alf's scoring of R1 in terms of how well it satisfies his 'I believe we ought' reasoning about justice. I suppose that this ranges from 0 to 10 for all agents, with 0 representing any rule that the agent judges to be unacceptable from the perspective of justice. These utilities do not support interpersonal comparisons. Now, agents who recognize the social dimension of

---

[28] I have considered in some depth the relation of this theoretical perspective to the choices of individual moral agents in Gaus (2016c).

justice also place weight on whether others share a rule. A rule R1 where mA(R1) 10, but is shared by no one, will be seen by Alf as inferior to R2, where mA(R2) 9 but is shared by all. However, again reasonable disagreement asserts itself. Good-willed competent moral agents reasonably differ on the relative importance of the two modes of moral reasoning. Some place greater weight on their 'I believe we ought' reasoning (a rule's inherent utility), while others put more emphasis on the importance of reconciliation on a rule of justice. This is a critical difference that must be at the core of our analyses. To take account of moral disagreement (that is, about inherent justice-based utility) while imposing a uniform weighting of these two modes of reasoning misses a fundamental source of our moral differences.[29] We thus suppose that each person has a weighting function that takes account of how many others act on a rule – how widely it is shared – and the importance to her of that degree of sharing. This weighting function for person B (aka Betty) will be denoted as $wB(n)$ (R1), which is the weight that Betty gives to rule R1 when n others act on it. I suppose weights vary between 0 and 1.

There are an infinite number of weighting systems. Figure 7.4 presents the ones on which we shall focus, here with n 101.

All four types acknowledge that reconciliation is part of their view of justice, so appreciating the social dimension of justice. 'Quasi-Kantian' agents recognize some value of reconciliation: They give no weight to a rule that is not practiced by 10 percent of the population, but by 50 percent, they give a rule a maximal weighting of 1. Moderately conditional agents have similar shape to their weighting function but are more typical of Humean conditional cooperators: until a significant share of the population acts on a rule they are not willing to act, and so give it a 0 weight.[30] A rule must have 30 percent uptake before they give it any weight and reaches a maximal weight at 80 percent. Both Quasi-Kantians and Moderately conditional agents, we might say, seek a moral community but not a maximally large one. Linear agents have, unsurprisingly enough, a linear weighting function: The more who share the merrier, but as long as someone acts on their rule, they give it some positive weight. Lastly, Highly conditional cooperators are resolute in stressing the importance of reconciliation, and only weight rules highly when the large majority has

---

[29] In this sense, the present analysis presses beyond that in Gaus (2011).

[30] Cristina Bicchieri models conditional cooperators as having a certain threshold, often requiring that 'most' others share a rule before they will act on it. Our types do not have abrupt thresholds, but Moderately conditional cooperators have a significant threshold of about 30 percent. See Bicchieri (2006: 11 ff).

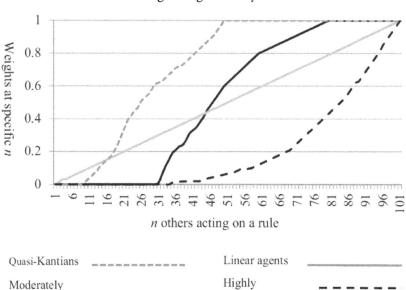

n others acting on a rule

Quasi-Kantians _ _ _ _ _ _ _ _ _ _   Linear agents _____

Moderately
conditional agents   ▬▬▬▬   Highly
                                    conditional   ▬ ▬ ▬ ▬ ▬ ▬
                                    cooperators

Figure 7.4.   Four weighting (reconciliation) types

already joined in. These Highly conditional cooperators are, as it were, willing to play the justice game only if most others do. Highly conditional cooperators give no weight to a rule unless about a third of the population follows it and give very little weight to any rule practiced by less than 60 percent. They do not give really high weights until approximately 90 percent practice it. They are thus highly conditional moral agents. Highly conditional cooperators are in some ways the mirror image of our Quasi-Kantians, perhaps died-in-the-wool Humeans.

In this analysis, then, an agent is concerned with both his own evaluations of the inherent justice of a rule (that is, his 'I believe we ought' conclusions) and reconciliation with the judgments of others ('we believe we ought') and will ultimately make his decision based on his own view of the inherent justice of the rule given his evaluative standards and the weighted number of others who are acting on the rule. Letting UA be Alf's total justice-based utility of acting on rule R_1, $mA(R_1)$ the inherent justice-based utility of R_1 given Alf's evaluative standards was his social weighting, and n the number of people acting on R_1, we get:

Equation 1

If Alf is confronted by two rules, he will act on that which maximizes UA. So, Alf acts on R1 rather than R2 only if UA(R1) 2: UA(R2).[31]

4.3   *Agent-Based Modeling and Parametric Rationality*

Gauthier usefully distinguishes two rational choice contexts. In:

> *parametric* choice . . . the actor takes his behavior to be the sole variable in a fixed environment. In parametric choice, the actor regards himself as the sole center of action. Interaction involves *strategic* choice, in which the actor takes his behavior to be but one variable among others, so that his choices must be responsive to his expectations of others' choices, while their choices are similarly responsive to their expectations.[32]

As with most theoretical distinctions, this one is perhaps not quite so crystal clear as it first seems, but it highlights an important difference in rational choice. In the go your own way (Figure 7.1) and reconciliation (Figures 7.2 and 7.3) games, Alf's action was dependent on what he thought Betty was going to do and what she chose to do depended on what she thought he was going to do. Indeed, ultimately Alf's choices depended on considerations such as what he thought she thought he thought she was going to do, and so on. Thus, the crucial importance of common knowledge assumptions in game theory, whereas in situations of parametric choice a person takes the actions of others as a given. She simply asks herself, 'What is my best course of action given the actions of others, over which I have no influence?' In contrast to strategic situations, she supposes that her choice will not affect the choices of others; their choices are taken as a parameter – a given or constraint – in her decision. Thus, as Gauthier recognizes, rational choice of a consumer in a large market is quintessentially parametric – she simply adjusts her action to the given prices, compared to a traditional shopping bazaar in which she is a price-taker and setter, and so is engaging in strategic interaction. In parametric contexts, an individual still may seek an equilibrium result: that is, one in which, given the context in which she finds herself, she cannot unilaterally increase her utility by changing her choice.

As I said, as with most distinctions, this one becomes less clear as we inspect it more closely. In a large market, at any given time, each consumer is a price taker, not a price setter, but over a series of periods in the market

---

[31] And he will act on R1 if UA(R1) > UA(R2).   [32] Gauthier (1986: 21). Emphasis in original.

each consumer's parametric choices affect the price and are minute influences in setting the price in subsequent periods. So, it is an exaggeration to say that one's choices have no effect on others' choices.[33] The critical point is that at each choice node, one takes the actions of others as an exogenous variable that is simply a parameter in one's maximizing decision. It is also something of an exaggeration to say that in parametric choice expectations about others do not matter, as such expectations may be a critical parameter. If one is on one's way to the airport and wishes to minimize travel time by choosing the fastest route, one confronts a parametric choice, but of course one's empirical beliefs about which road is presently congested (one's empirical expectations about how much traffic one will encounter on each route) are critical. Parametric choice requires empirical beliefs about what others are doing, so that one can efficiently respond.

Moral and political philosophers tend to underappreciate the insights of parametric analysis. Indeed, even Gauthier, who has a much deeper appreciation of it than most, holds that morality only enters when strategic choice arises.[34] Strategic choices are often small number interactions, and so 'PPE-inclined' philosophers, often wedded to the strategic outlook, have repeatedly analyzed morality in terms of small-number (very often dyadic) interactions. We know, though, that a social system of justice is typically a large numbers phenomenon, in which many individuals interact, each adjusting her action to what she sees as the current social parameters. As generations proceed, the aggregation of parametric choices changes the social parameters (as with prices in large markets), which in turn change what is parametrically rational. Here, parametric models can be most enlightening, which suppose that each person has a utility function (a representation of a preference ordering)[35] and beliefs about the state of the world at time t (which typically include what others are now doing) and each acts to maximize her utility. In some agent-based parametric models, the system will stabilize in the sense that, at some iteration i, further states

---

[33] This is a familiar point in agent-based models of adaptive system: '. . . as agents adjust to their experiences by revising their strategies, they are constantly changing the context in which other agents are trying to adapt' (Axelrod and Cohen, 2000: 8). In evolutionary game theory, replicator dynamics can make it look as if players are strategically responding to each other. In my view, they best model evolutionary adaptive systems.

[34] Gauthier (1986: 21, cf. 170–171).

[35] Again, it is important to always keep in mind that a preference is simply a binary relation according to which one state of affairs (action, etc.) is better than another; it is not a reason or explanation as to why one is better than another. To say that Alf holds that 'a is preferred to b' because that 'is his preference' is a tautology, not an explanation. A utility function is a mathematical representation of a consistent preference structure.

of the system confront all the members with exactly the same parameters such that no one henceforth changes their choices (leaving aside preference change, errors in beliefs, and factors exogenous to the system). In other systems, there can be endless adjustments; they will never reach system-wide equilibrium.

All the following analyses are agent-based models of the former sort. Each agent has a simple binary option set of acting on either R1 or R2, which are assumed to be alternative rules of justice over some areas of social life, say property rules, promising rules, privacy rules, and so on.[36] It is also assumed that whether a person has acted on R1 or R2 in the last period is reliable public information; in period i, each has a correct first-order belief about what rules of justice others endorsed and acted upon in period i-1. Our aim is to get some preliminary insights when free moral agents, each with her own distinctive justice-based utility function and fully committed to acting on it, are apt to converge on a shared rule of justice, and under what conditions they are less likely to.

5 Some Dynamics of Self-Organization

5.1 Model I: Fully Random

We start with a population of 101 agents, with m(R1) and m(R2) scores between 1 and 10 that were randomly assigned. Thus, all agents hold each rule is an acceptable approximation of justice, if only barely (a score of 1). Agents were randomly assigned to one of our four weighting types.[37] In the first period, each individual simply acts on her 'I believe we ought' judgment, maximizing her evaluative utility (m). In ties (that is, U(R1) U (R2)), an individual acts on R1; perhaps R1 is the simpler rule, and so individuals choose it in a tie. Our empirical updating rule is simple, if somewhat dumb: At each period, an agent calculates whether in the previous period she would have achieved more utility if she had acted on the alternative rule; if she would have, she switches in this period.[38]

---

[36] There are some difficulties in further formalizing this idea. See Gaus (2011: 267).

[37] For precise weightings, see the Appendix Table 1A.

[38] All the models discussed here are deterministic: once the distribution of inherent utilities and weighting types are assigned in a population, equation 1, along with our updating assumptions, generates a unique social outcome. Because of this simplicity, all simulations were done in Excel. This allowed easy tracking of the history of each agent's choices; we can see what agents join, and when they join, a cascade.

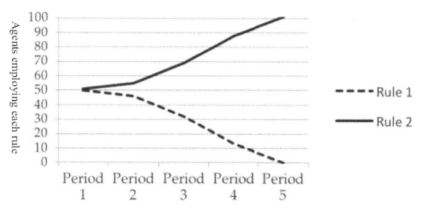

Figure 7.5.   Convergence in model I, all types

As Figure 7.5 shows, R2, randomly favored by 51 agents compared to R1's 50, went to fixation after five periods. The explanation is that valuing reconciliation with others generates an increasing-returns dynamic. W. Brian Arthur famously showed that when a good is characterized by increasing returns – when the more others use it the more valuable it is to any single user – the possibility of cascades arises.[39] For all four of our weighting functions, over some range of n, the more people act on R1, the greater weight the agent gives it – the more value she puts on it. Each of our agents is seeking to balance devotion to her 'I believe we ought' judgments with some valuing of reconciliation. Within some range, the larger the number of others who share a rule, the greater its reconciliation benefits. While Alf may not switch from R1, supported by his individual mode of moral judgment when 50 percent of the population are acting on it, as the number shrinks (that is, as others come to endorse R2), the reconciliation benefits of acting on R2 are apt to eventually be so great that he will abandon R1. Note that this is not because he had changed his relative evaluation of the importance of the two modes of reasoning, but because the justice value of reconciliation becomes so large as more and more others endorse R2.

A cascade occurred in model I. The first agents to switch from R1 to R2 were those that, while their inherent utility deems R1 slightly more just than R2, place a sufficiently high value on reconciliation with others such that the greater benefits of reconciliation on R2 outweighed the slight

[39] Arthur (1994). See also Gaus (2011: 389–400).

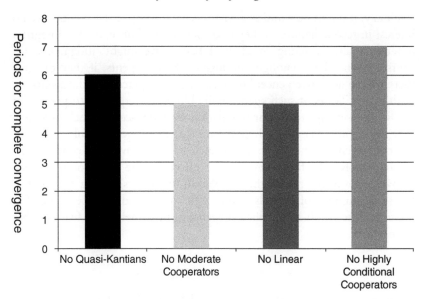

Figure 7.6.   Periods for convergence in model I, three types

inherent justice advantage of R1. Four agents made this reevaluation, but this was enough to get a cascade going. After they switched to R2, others, perhaps who thought the inherent justice advantage of R1 over R2 was slightly greater than our first group (and so did not switch in period 2), come to the conclusion that, given the slightly greater number of people following R2 in period 2, the reconciliation benefits of R2 now out-weighed R1's inherent justice advantage, and so they changed in period 3 (14 agents did this). And we can see that in period 4, many of those who thought R1 was considerably superior to R2 now came to the conclusion that an insufficient number was acting on R1, and so it provided insuffi-cient reconciliation (23 agents). By period 5, all R1 supporters decided to endorse R2.

It might be wondered whether any specific weighting type was crucial in producing convergence, but as Figure 7.6 shows, under this same popula-tion, any three of the weighting systems (again, randomly assigned) resulted in fixation on R2, giving some reason to believe that the conver-gence dynamic is not driven by specific types. However, we do see that combinations of types certainly have an effect; omitting the Highly con-ditional cooperators, for example, slowed down convergence.

Finally, it might be wondered what occurs if some of the agents have no interest in reconciliation: as they understand 'pure' or 'maximal' integrity, it requires always acting on their 'I believe we ought' judgments. Of course, given a large enough contingent of such agents, if they disagree there will be no convergence; but what if, say, 10 percent of the agents are of this sort? To see if such agents easily block convergence, 10 percent of the R_1 favoring agents in our population were replaced by such 'maximal integrity agents'. We might hypothesize that these agents would either tilt the convergence dynamic to R_1 or at least slow down the process converging on R_2. In fact, they had no effect on the behavior of others: Convergence of the rest of the population (96 agents) on R_2 occurred in the same number of periods (five), with the only difference being that these resolutely non-reconciliation agents formed their own, five-member R_1 network.

5.2   Model II: Moderate Polarity

I commenced with a fully random model to explore the core dynamics under conditions where the population was very closely divided and to better see some of the effects of the different weighting systems. It certainly is clear that the dynamic does not depend on one rule having an initial overwhelming advantage (51/50 was enough). Different weightings have different thresholds and values, which help induce convergence dynamics. However, fully random distributions of inherent utility and weighting functions are hospitable to cascades, since they tend to ensure that there will be continuity of degrees of $U(R_1) - U(R_2)$ differences, such that whenever some agents switch, this will decisively affect the choice of the next agents 'in line', who then switch in the next period, and so on. The question is the extent to which a convergence dynamic applies in nonrandom populations with discontinuities. An especially difficult case is a polarized population, divided into two mutually exclusive groups, one subgroup thinking highly of one option and scoring the other low, with the other subgroup doing the opposite.

To explore this possibility, our group of 101 agents was divided into two 'Hi–Lo' groups, one of which scored R_1 between 10 and 6 and R_2 between 4 and 1 (thus $m(R_1)$ are all 'high', while $m(R_2)$ are all 'low'); the other group was assigned the opposite 'Hi– Lo' inherent utilities. Each polarized group had approximately an equal division of all four types of agents. The suspicion that polarization makes convergence more difficult was confirmed; very closely split (52 agents $m(R_1)$ high; 49 agents $m(R_2)$

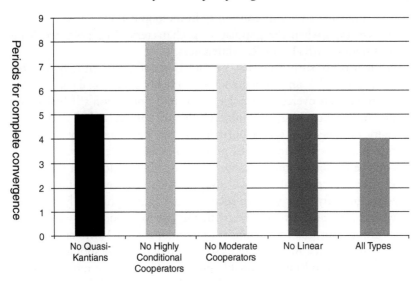

Figure 7.7. Periods for complete convergence in model II

high) polarized populations did not converge. Somewhat surprisingly, perhaps convergence on R1 did occur within four periods at the close but not finely balanced (56 agents m(R1) high; 45 agents m(R2) high). As Figure 7.7 shows, it was found at this 56/45 division complete convergence occurred with any three types; again, the omission of Highly conditional cooperators slowed down the process (taking eight periods), while omitting the Moderately conditional cooperators slowed convergence to seven periods. Conditional cooperators, of course, generally put greater weight on reconciliation, and so assist in overcoming polarity. Indeed, a Hi–Lo polarized population of all Highly conditional cooperators with an initial 53/48 advantage for R1 – a pretty evenly split polarized population – secured complete convergence on R1 in four periods. Quasi-Kantians, on the other hand, tend to reinforce the split; they have their maximal weightings at around 50 percent of the population, and so tend to reinforce polarity when the groups are about the same size. Quasi-Kantians who find themselves in subgroups who agree with them do not easily switch rules. Perhaps the truly striking thing is that even they can be induced to leave their Hi–Lo groups and converge on a common rule, and do so when any two of the other weighting types are well represented. If Hi–Lo polarity is not too finely balanced, then it can be overcome in a diverse population: The diversity of weighting types typically speeds up the process, inducing sufficient continuity in the populations' $U(R_1)$– $U(R_2)$ differences even when the population is characterized by polarized (thus discontinuous) $m(R_1) - m(R_2)$ differences.

While it is not surprising that a population composed entirely of those who put great value on reconciliation (the Highly conditional cooperators, for example) can overcome a polarization in a population's 'I believe we ought' judgments, it is, I think, worthy of emphasis that as we add diversity of weighting types, polarization can be more easily overcome than in many more homogenous populations: In Figure 7.7, convergence was quickest when all four types were present. This could point the way to good news, for not only do we disagree about justice, but for the last hundred and fifty years western societies have been significantly polarized between 'right' and 'left' justice, with the last forty adding a number of other groups (for example, feminists, environmentalists) who also tend to 'Hi–Lo' judgments. Rather than reasonable pluralism, we should, perhaps, be thinking of moderate reasonable polarity. The polarity model gives us some reason to suppose that these sharp inherent justice differences can be significantly moderated by a diversity of weighting types. It is not necessary that we all highly value reconciliation to overcome polarization. An uptake of this idea would constitute a fundamental change in the orientation of the public reason project, which has thus far supposed that diversity is the problem, and commonality the sole route to sharing. Here, we see the possibility that one type of diversity can counteract the centrifugal tendencies of another. So far from heterogeneity always being an impediment to convergence on a shared rule of justice, some configurations of diversity can help secure agreement. The issue is not 'do we agree enough to live together?' but 'does the overall pattern of homogeneity and heterogeneity induce convergence on common ways of living together?'

5.3   Model III: Differential Reference Groups

A simplification in the models thus far discussed is that each person takes the entire group as her reference group: In each period, her decision about reconciliation is based on what the entire group has done. But often people are concerned with narrower reference groups.[40] Alf might seek to reconcile his view of justice with his traditional cultural group, while Betty reconciles with those in her urban and work environments. In previous

---

[40] Bicchieri extensively examines the role of reference groups in her *Norms in the Wild* (2016). I made some preliminary remarks on this point in *The Tyranny of the Ideal* (2016a: 184–187).

work, I have supposed that we seek a practice of moral accountability based on shared moral rules with the widest feasible set of other moral agents.[41] But in many contexts, people might be committed to a practice of accountability – and so the shared understanding of the rules of justice on which it depends – only with those with whom they regularly interact, while others may be interested in a practice of accountability based on shared rules with some other group. In this case, the different elements of the population would have different reference groups – different groups of people with whom they seek to reconcile. Can there be shared rules by moderately polarized groups under such circumstances?

To take some first steps in understanding the effects of different reference groups on convergence, let us analyze a somewhat challenging case: The population is not only split into different reference groups but some of the reference groups display opposite Hi–Lo polarity. In group B, $3/5$ of the population has Hi–Lo bias in 'I believe we ought' judgments in favor of R1 (the other $2/5$ of the group has Hi–Lo inherent justice utilities in favor of R2), while the C group has just the opposite Hi–Lo divisions. Here, we might think, convergence within each group will occur, but not between them: Our polarized population models in Section 5.2 indicate that with such splits we should expect convergence on the most popular rule in each group. And of course, that is what would normally happen if these are entirely unrelated reference groups, for then we simply have two independent populations. The interesting case concerns populations with overlapping reference groups. In the differential reference group model, a population of 150 agents is divided into three main groups, with two of the groups having subgroups. They are:

Group A (50 agents): split population, not Hi–Lo (an agent may have any combination of m(R1) and m(R2) between 1 and 10; inherent justice utilities are randomly assigned).

Group B2 (25 agents): approximately $3/5$ Hi–Lo favoring R1; $2/5$ Hi–Lo favoring R2.

Group B1 (25 agents): approximately $3/5$ Hi–Lo favoring R1; $2/5$ Hi–Lo favoring R2.

Group C1 (25 agents): approximately $3/5$ Hi–Lo favoring R2; $2/5$ Hi–Lo favoring R1.

Group C2 (25 agents): approximately $3/5$ Hi–Lo favoring R2; $2/5$ Hi–Lo favoring R1.

---

[41] See Gaus (2011: 279–283).

Group	Reference group
B2: R_1 Hi–Lo biased, parochial (25 agents)	**B1, B2**
B1: R_1 Hi–Lo biased, involved (25 agents)	**B1, B2, A**
A: Random Group (50 agents)	**B1, A, C1**
C1: R_2 Hi–Lo biased, involved (25 agents)	**C1, C2, A**
C2: R_2 Hi–Lo biased, parochial (25 agents)	**C1, C2**

Figure 7.8.   Differential reference groups

Note that both subgroups in B have the same evaluative utility distributions, as do both subgroups in C. The difference is their reference groups, as indicated by Figure 7.8.

Group B2, then is 'parochial R_1 Hi–Lo biased' insofar as they update only in relation to the choices of group B, the Hi–Lo R_1 biased group. This means that group B2 (i) has a reference group of 50 agents and (ii) their entire reference group has a 3/5 Hi–Lo bias toward R_1. B1's reference group has 100 agents, encompassing all of groups A and B. I call this an 'involved Hi–Lo biased' group as it is concerned with reconciliation both with its entire R_1 Hi–Lo biased group and the 'wider' world of A. Group A, the random group, has a reference group of 100 agents, including all of group A itself, as well as half of both Hi–Lo biased groups (B1, which is biased toward R_1, and C1, which is biased toward R_2). Group C is the mirror image of group B. Note that we have two parochial subgroups, B2 and C2, whose reference networks are restricted to those who share their inherent justice Hi–Lo distributions.[42]

As in other models, each agent simply acts on her judgment of the inherent justice of R_1 or R_2 in the first period. However, because we have multiple reference groups that employ different updating calculations, an order of updating was applied in all periods after 1; first group A updated and acted, then B1, B2, C1, and finally C2. Thus, each period has five mini-periods; when a group updates, it considers the last move made by others in its reference group. This is by no means an entirely innocent stipulation: As Arthur pointed out, in closely split populations, those who move earlier can have significant effects on the outcome of convergence.[43]

[42] In these two subgroups with reference groups of 50 (B2, C2), all weighting systems were normalized so that maximum n = 50.

[43] Arthur (1994: Ch. 5).

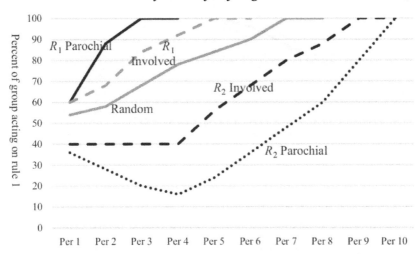

Figure 7.9.   Convergence: Five differential reference groups with Hi–Lo polarity in four groups

As some counterweight to the polarized groups B and C, the random group, A, was thus given the first move in each period, giving random factors some advantage over the effects of Hi–Lo polarity.

In the basic simulation, group A had a 54 percent to 46 percent tilt toward R1; group B was Hi–Lo polarized 60/40 percent toward R1, while group C was Hi–Lo polarized 62/38 percent toward R2 (group C2 had 64 percent having Hi-Lo bias toward R2). This resulted in the entire population group of 150 favoring R1 51 percent to 49 percent, a very closely split population with a good deal of polarity. Agent types were equally distributed among all five groups. As Figure 7.9 shows, convergence on R1 occurred in 10 periods.

Interestingly, the parochial R2 biased group (64 percent Hi–Lo bias toward R2) and those whose entire reference group also had a 60 percent bias toward R2 began, as we would expect from our analysis in the last section, by moving toward R2: at one point being 84 percent R2 followers. The involved R2 biased group (C1) was, as it were, initially pulled in two directions: some of their reference group (A) was moving toward convergence on R1, while C2 was moving toward R2. For several periods, then, the involved R2 biased group remained unchanged, until the movement in group A was strong enough to pull them toward R1. And, in turn, that eventually pulled C2, the parochial R2 biased group, in their wake, ending up with 100 percent R1 convergence. The last to switch to R1 were, as

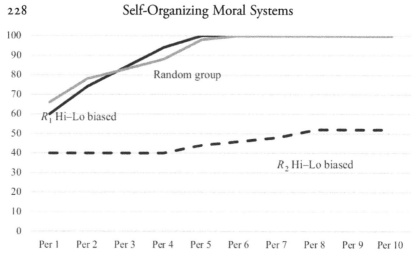

Figure 7.10.   Random distribution of types (linear agent and quasi-Kantians halt convergence)

would be expected, Quasi-Kantians favoring R2 in the parochial R2 biased group (and one Linear agent).

Diversity of types is important, though not always necessary – if we have the right sort of type. In a simulation with the same distribution of inherent utilities as above, a homogeneous population of Linear agents, for example, failed to converge on a rule in any of our five groups; the same occurred in a pure population of Quasi-Kantians. In a homogeneous population of Highly conditional cooperators, however, convergence was quickly achieved in five periods. This should not be surprising, since Highly conditional cooperators give great weight to convergence. As I said, they are died-in-the-wool Humeans. Nevertheless, the important and surprising lesson from our simpler models is confirmed: Sometimes adding more diversity makes agreement more likely.

In another model III simulation with all four types, the random group's (A's) inherent utilities were randomly reassigned, resulting in 66 percent of A favoring R1. Not surprisingly, given this strong initial tilt to R1, full convergence was achieved in the population of 101 agents very quickly – in four periods. More interesting is what occurred when not only inherent utilities, but agent types were randomly distributed in the population (Figure 7.10). Here, full convergence on R1 was not achieved: 24 (of the 50) members of group C (including all the Hi–Lo biased members of the parochial R2 biased group) maintained a small R2 network, while the rest of the population (126 agents) moved to R1. In group C1 (the involved R2 biased group), those with Hi–Lo evaluative utilities biased in favor of R2 were almost all Linear agents (with three Quasi-Kantians). As a result, those with Hi–Lo bias in favor of R2 in C1 were not very sensitive to movement in group A to R1, which in turn insulated C2 (the parochial R2 group) from the movement in the random group, A. Linear agents engage in such gradual updating that few could overcome their Hi–Lo bias (in inherent justice judgments) in favor of R2, even though there was some movement within the involved R2 biased group (C1) to R1. Recall that in a homogenous population of Linear agents, none of the five groups achieved convergence. Again, we see how a diversity of types can generate agreement: In the R2 biased group, there was not enough diversity of weighting types to overcome its Hi–Lo bias.

5.4 Modeling Moral Choice

All three of these models are rather basic analyses of perfectly moral and rational agents, providing an initial exploration of some dynamics of rational choice that lead a population with somewhat stark moral disagreements to reconcile on a shared moral rule. Like social contract theories such as Rawls', the point of these models is to understand rational moral persons and their choices, not to make predictions about actual systems of interactions.[44] The models seek to capture only motivations based on an agent's devotion to her 'I believe we ought' judgment and the weight she puts on reconciliation in her view of justice. I have tried to show here that under some conditions characterized by deep diversity, perfectly moral agents would be able to organize themselves into freely endorsed moral systems. At least from a purely normative point of view, central moral controllers (such as social contract theorists) are not necessary to secure a result that all would endorse, given their differing views of justice. A number of parameters are relevant to these models: agents' information about others, the depth and extent of their moral disputes, weighting functions, sizes of, and links among reference groups, and so on. These models investigated some of these in a preliminary way.

---

[44] Which is not to say that the self-organizing systems approach here is not relevant to the study of actual systems: it connects up with Bicchieri's project on the empirical study of actual normative self-organized networks. See Bicchieri (2016).

6 Moral Freedom and Unity in Diverse, Complex Societies

Contemporary moral theory and social philosophy divides into two opposing lines of thought or, we might say, research projects. The traditional,
still dominant, project carries on with articulations of the 'I believe we
ought' View. These accounts are often sophisticated and admirable exercises in philosophical reasoning, building on the fundamental intuition
that the best moral conclusion for one is the best for all. This research
project has great difficulty in even making sense of the idea of moral
diversity.[45] To be sure, there is moral disagreement and conflict – some
pig-headed and ill-informed and some, perhaps, more reasonable – but the
study of ethical life needs to be no more focused on diversity than
physics.[46] The second line of inquiry seeks, in disparate ways, to make
sense of the idea of fundamental moral difference. To Isaiah Berlin, the
romantic philosophers of the 17th and 18th centuries have 'permanently
shaken the faith in universal, objective truth, in matters of conduct' by
showing that 'ends recognized as fully human are at the same time ultimate
and mutually incompatible'.[47] Berlin repeatedly insisted that the romantics
taught us that there are many values, and that they are incommensurable;
'the whole notion of plurality, of inexhaustibility, of the imperfection of all
human answers and arrangements, the notion that there is no single
answer which claims to be perfect and true ... all this we owe to the
romantics'.[48] I have tried to show here that this second line of inquiry –
which somehow takes the diversity of moral conclusions as a basic datum
of ethical inquiry – is fundamental to the social contract tradition. Once
such diversity is understood not as moral reasoning gone awry, but as the
crux of free human moral reasoning, moral diversity in some guise
becomes the core of moral theory and social philosophy.

Yet the social contract – and this most definitely includes Rawls – never
really advanced beyond what we might call 'plans to manage difference'.[49]
Moral difference is seen as the fundamental problem for moral theory, but
the aim is to plan for mediation via a social contract that rises above
difference to show an underlying homogeneity. Certainly, mediation and
reconciliation are fundamental concerns of moral theory, for as soon as we

[45] I have greatly benefitted from discussing the issues raised in this section with Piper Bringhurst.
[46] This, of course, can be a two-edged comparison. See Kuhn (1977) and D'Agostino (2010).
[47] Berlin (1990: 207–237, at 237). See also Berlin (1999: 34 ff) and Williams (1981: 71–82).
[48] Berlin (1999: 146).
[49] An important exception to this broad claim is Muldoon's *Social Contract Theory for a Diverse World*
(2016) – though his is a rather unusual contract, sharing much with a self-organizing analysis.

cannot suppose that good moral reasoning alone shows us the path to a cooperative social life, we need to find new paths, which produce some unity in moral expectations and understandings out of diversity. Hayek stressed throughout his career that rational constructivism and planning is not usually a viable way to cope with heterogeneity. Central planners, be they economists or moral philosophers, do not have access to the necessary information about diversity: they can only cope with it by limiting admissible diversity, relying on 'normalizing' assumptions about agents.[50] I have tried to take some small steps here in theorizing how we might think of moral theory without that form of central planning practiced by social contract theorists. The guiding idea is to model morally autonomous diverse agents making choices in the context of each other's choices, seeing what dynamics lead to a shared rule that all endorse, and when different groups will go their own way. The motto of this project is that morality is best understood as a bottom-up affair. 'The moral law is not imposed from above or derived from well-reasoned principles' but arises from the values of individuals and their distinctive searches for justice and reconciliation in their social lives.[51]

Author's Note

Versions of this article were presented to the 2016 PPE Journal Conference, the 2017 PPE Society Conference, the Kadish Center Workshop in Law, Philosophy, and Political Theory at UC Berkeley and the University of Southern California. The author would like to thank all the participants for their helpful (and often spirited) comments and suggestions.

References

Arthur WB (1994) *Increasing Returns and Path Dependence in the Economy.* Ann Arbor: University of Michigan Press.

Axelrod R and Cohen MD (2000) *Harnessing Complexity.* New York: Basic Books.

Berlin I (1990) The apotheosis of the romantic will. In: Hardy Henry (ed.) *The Crooked Timber of Humanity: Chapters in the History of Ideas.* Princeton: Princeton University Press, pp. 207–37.

   (1999) *The Roots of Romanticism.* Princeton: Princeton University Press.

---

[50] See Gaus (2016a: especially Ch. 4).
[51] See de Waal (2013: 228). This essay's epigraph was from page 23.

Bicchieri C (2006) *The Grammar of Society*. Cambridge: Cambridge University Press.

(2016) *Norms in the Wild*. Oxford: Oxford University Press.

Brandt RB (1979) *A Theory of the Good and the Right*. Oxford: Clarendon Press.

Cohen GA (2008) *Rescuing Justice and Equality*. Cambridge: Harvard University Press.

D'Agostino F (2010) *Naturalizing Epistemology*. London: Palgrave.

de Waal F (2013) *The Bonobo and the Atheist*. New York: W.W. Norton.

Ewin EW (1991) *Virtues and Rights: The Moral Philosophy of Thomas Hobbes*. Boulder: Westview.

Gaus G (2007) *On Philosophy, Politics, and Economics*. Belmont, CA: Wadsworth.

(2011) *The Order of Public Reason*. Cambridge: Cambridge University Press.

(2015) Public reason liberalism. In: Wall Steven (ed.) *The Cambridge Companion to Liberalism*. Cambridge: Cambridge University Press, pp. 112–40.

(2016a) *The Tyranny of the Ideal: Justice in a Diverse Society*. Princeton: Princeton University Press.

(2016b) The Commonwealth of Bees: on the impossibility of justice-through-ethos. *Social Philosophy & Policy* 96–121.

(2016c) Social morality and the primacy of individual perspectives. *Review of Austrian Economics*. DOI 10.1007/s11138-016-0358-8.

Gauthier D (1986) *Morals by Agreement*. Oxford: Oxford University Press.

(1998) Public reason. In: D'Agostino F and Gaus GF (eds) *Public Reason*. Brookeville: Ashgate, pp. 43–66.

(2013) Twenty-five on. *Ethics* 123: 601–624.

Habermas J (1995) Reconciliation through the public use of reason: remarks on John Rawls's political liberalism. *The Journal of Philosophy* 92: 109–131.

Hayek FA (1973) *Rules and Order*. London: Routledge.

Hobbes T (1994 [1651]). *Leviathan*. Curley E (ed.). Indianapolis: Hackett.

Kalai E (1977) Proportional solutions to bargaining situations. *Econometrica* 45: 1623–1630.

Kalai E and Smorodinsky M (1975) Other solutions to Nash's bargaining problem. *Econometrica* 43: 513–518.

Kant I (1999 [1797]) *The Metaphysical Elements of Justice*. Ladd John (transl., 2nd ed.). Indianapolis: Hackett.

Kuhn T (1977) *The Essential Tension*. Chicago: University of Chicago Press.

Moehler M (2017) *Minimal Morality*. New York: Oxford University Press.

Muldoon R (2016) *Social Contract Theory for a Diverse World*. New York: Routledge.

Nash J (1950) The bargaining problem. *Econometrica* 18: 155–162.

Rawls J (1999a) *A Theory of Justice*, rev ed. Cambridge: Harvard University Press.

(1999b) An outline of a decision procedure for ethics. In: Freeman Samuel (ed.) *John Rawls: Collected Papers*. Cambridge: Harvard University Press, 1999, pp. 1–19.

(2005) *Political Liberalism.* expanded ed. New York: Columbia University Press.

Rubinstein A (1982) Perfect equilibrium in a bargaining model. *Econometrica* 50: 97–109.

Schotter A and Sopher B (2003) Social learning and coordination conventions in intergenerational games. *Journal of Political Economy* 111: 498–529.

Thrasher J (2014) Uniqueness and symmetry in bargaining theories of justice. *Philosophical Studies* 167: 683–699.

Vanderschraaf P (2018) *Strategic Justice.* New York: Oxford University Press.

Williams B (1981) Conflict of values. In: Williams B (ed.) *Moral Luck.* Cambridge: Cambridge University Press, pp. 71–82.

Appendix 1

Table 7.1A. *Agent types*

N	MC	LA	QK	HCC
1	0	0	0	0
2	0	0.01	0	0
3	0	0.03	0	0
4	0	0.03	0	0
5	0	0.04	0	0
6	0	0.05	0	0
7	0	0.06	0	0
8	0	0.07	0	0
9	0	0.08	0	0
10	0	0.09	0.02	0
11	0	0.1	0.04	0
12	0	0.11	0.06	0
13	0	0.12	0.08	0
14	0	0.13	0.11	0
15	0	0.14	0.13	0
16	0	0.15	0.15	0
17	0	0.16	0.17	0
18	0	0.17	0.2	0
19	0	0.18	0.24	0
20	0	0.19	0.29	0
21	0	0.2	0.34	0
22	0	0.21	0.39	0
23	0	0.22	0.42	0
24	0	0.23	0.45	0
25	0	0.24	0.47	0
26	0	0.25	0.51	0
27	0	0.26	0.53	0
28	0	0.27	0.55	0
29	0	0.28	0.58	0
30	0	0.29	0.61	0
31	0.01	0.3	0.62	0
32	0.06	0.31	0.63	0
33	0.11	0.32	0.65	0
34	0.15	0.33	0.67	0
35	0.19	0.34	0.69	0.01
36	0.21	0.35	0.71	0.015
37	0.23	0.36	0.72	0.017
38	0.24	0.37	0.73	0.0175
39	0.27	0.38	0.75	0.018

Table 7.1A. (*cont.*)

N	MC	LA	QK	HCC
40	0.31	0.39	0.77	0.0185
41	0.33	0.4	0.79	0.019
42	0.35	0.41	0.81	0.0195
43	0.38	0.42	0.83	0.02
44	0.41	0.43	0.85	0.03
45	0.45	0.44	0.87	0.035
46	0.48	0.45	0.89	0.04
47	0.51	0.46	0.91	0.045
48	0.54	0.47	0.94	0.05
49	0.57	0.48	0.97	0.055
50	0.6	0.49	1	0.06
51	0.62	0.5	1	0.065
52	0.64	0.51	1	0.07
53	0.66	0.52	1	0.075
54	0.68	0.53	1	0.085
55	0.7	0.54	1	0.095
56	0.72	0.55	1	0.09
57	0.74	0.56	1	0.095
58	0.76	0.57	1	0.1
59	0.78	0.58	1	0.11
60	0.8	0.59	1	0.12
61	0.81	0.6	1	0.13
62	0.82	0.61	1	0.14
63	0.83	0.62	1	0.15
64	0.84	0.63	1	0.16
65	0.85	0.64	1	0.17
66	0.86	0.65	1	0.18
67	0.87	0.66	1	0.19
68	0.88	0.67	1	0.2
69	0.89	0.68	1	0.21
70	0.9	0.69	1	0.23
71	0.91	0.7	1	0.25
72	0.92	0.71	1	0.27
73	0.93	0.72	1	0.29
74	0.94	0.73	1	0.31
75	0.95	0.74	1	0.33
76	0.96	0.75	1	0.35
77	0.97	0.76	1	0.37
78	0.98	0.77	1	0.39
79	0.99	0.78	1	0.41
80	1	0.79	1	0.43
81	1	0.8	1	0.45
82	1	0.81	1	0.47
83	1	0.82	1	0.49
84	1	0.83	1	0.51

Table 7.1A. (*cont.*)

N	MC	LA	QK	HCC
85	1	0.84	1	0.53
86	1	0.85	1	0.56
87	1	0.86	1	0.59
88	1	0.87	1	0.62
89	1	0.88	1	0.63
90	1	0.89	1	0.66
91	1	0.9	1	0.69
92	1	0.91	1	0.72
93	1	0.92	1	0.75
94	1	0.93	1	0.78
95	1	0.94	1	0.81
96	1	0.95	1	0.85
97	1	0.96	1	0.88
98	1	0.97	1	0.91
99	1	0.98	1	0.94
100	1	0.99	1	0.97
101	1	1	1	1

Note: MC: Moderately conditional; LA: Linear agents; QK: Quasi-Kantians; HCC: Highly conditional cooperators.

CHAPTER 8

Political Philosophy as the Study of Complex Normative Systems

It is an honor and a treat when innovative social theorists and philosophers take time out of their important work to think about one's own. The set of papers being published in *COSMOS + TAXIS* are especially flattering. Fred D'Agostino, Blain Neufeld, Scott E. Page, Kevin Vallier, Lori Watson and David Wiens all constructively engage *The Tyranny of the Ideal* and open up new issues to be explored. I am especially grateful to Ryan Muldoon for organizing this symposium (and, I should say, for all his work from which I have learned so much). I am also delighted that the symposium appears in *COSMOS + TAXIS* because the main theme of the book, which I hope to emphasize here (and which D'Agostino and Page bring out wonderfully in their essays) is that the subject matter of social philosophy is complex systems, something Hayek (1964 [2014], chap. 9) was one of the first to stress. Until, as Page puts it, "the imperative of complexity" is appreciated by political philosophers their work will remain what Hayek warned against – constructivist fantasies in which the critical problems of evaluative diversity, path-dependency, uncertainty, and inter-connectedness are assumed away.

My comments focus on three main themes. I begin (Sec I) by taking up some questions of method. To a large extent *Tyranny* (as I shall call it, hopefully sans unfortunate self-reference) is adamant that political philosophy greatly benefits from the rigor of more formal ways of thinking. This, unfortunately, is one of the features of the book which causes the most resistance, as political philosophers are generally deeply averse to abstract model thinking, and often dismissive of "metaphors." I then turn (Sec II) to discussing some aspects of the rugged landscape model I employ, and what I think it tells us about the nature of normative thinking. Section III turns to what D'Agostino calls my "constructive intention," the account of the Open Society. Many issues arise here, of which only a few can be addressed. In these remarks I make no effort to respond to all the ideas and, yes, criticisms, in these thoughtful essays, but I do believe that many

237

fundamental points will be addressed – hopefully in a way that enlightens readers who are not especially concerned whether *Tyranny* is bullet proof (it is not).

I. Models

Abstractness and Modeling

An explicit aim of *Tyranny* is to model a long-standing problem in political philosophy in a more rigorous and abstract way, which I believe alerts us to critical features of political theorizing that have hitherto gone unnoticed. When we model a phenomenon we always abstract from some of its features to better understand the working of others. All modeling is a selection process. We construct a simplified, abstracted, analysis to get insight into critical features that are obscured by more detailed descriptions. It does not follow that the features from which we abstract are unimportant; in another context we may construct a model to better understand them, perhaps putting aside the very features our first model highlighted. As Michael Weisberg (2013, p. 13) points out, philosophers generally prefer models that are rich in description, and this perhaps leads them to so often object to a model because it has left something out or is "blind" to it (as, for example, *Tyranny*'s model quite intentionally abstracts from the "logic" of justification advanced by a particular perspective – more on that anon). The aim of *Tyranny*'s modeling approach is to abstract from many features that have traditionally been in the foreground to discover those thus far overlooked. And the feature that I wished to stress – which I tried to show is implicit in the presuppositions of many "ideal theories" – is that seeking ideal justice involves optimization in a certain type of structured complex system. Once we understand that ideal theories are committed to analyzing the pursuit of justice as an optimization exercise in, strictly speaking, a mathematically complex system, we see them and their problems in an entirely different light. Indeed, we see political philosophy in a new light. I believe that this rather startling insight justifies abstracting from so many of the features and issues that have hitherto been the concerns of political philosophy. In a way my intention was to present political philosophers with an unfamiliar type of analysis, for it is through confrontation with the alien that we appreciate our presuppositions. That, indeed, is the theme of the entire book.

Tyranny advances an analytic result. If ideals are characterized by institutions, and institutions are "coupled" and so have "interactions" or "interdependencies" in their resulting justice, then as Page nicely summarizes in his essay, under the conditions I specify we are almost certainly confronted with "The Choice" between pursuit of local optima (local improvements in justice) and the global optimum (ideal justice). This is an inescapable conclusion. Of course, one can dispute the assumptions or the applicability of the model, but not the well-nigh inevitability of The Choice given them. To be sure, as Neufeld and Watson note, this makes the argument abstract (given the norm in political philosophy), but I believe that is a good thing, for it helps us to achieve distance from our ideological convictions and intuitions to see the relations between our commitments in ways that may surprise and enlighten us (Johnson 2014). And as we abstract from the details, we open up ourselves to what Page calls "transdisciplinary" insights – that the logic of the problem in, say, politics, is similar to problems in management or evolutionary theory (Lane 2017, chap. 1). Thus, *Tyranny* argues that Kauffman's NK and the Hong-Page models provide insights into what we might have thought was a distinctive feature of "ideal political theory." To be sure, we must proceed with care to ensure that our model captures the fundamental features we are interested in – thus my significant modifications of the Hong-Page model in understanding ideal political philosophy. Still, the aim is to abstract and see if we can distill the problem to its essentials, and so provide a general result. So like Rawls (2005, p. lx), I do not apologize for the abstract nature of the analysis.

Of Metaphors and Models

As Page explains in his essay (and in his path-breaking and, if I may say, often stunningly innovative work over the last two decades) different models can be employed to understand complex systems. I focused on what have been deemed "rugged landscape models." My idea was this. Some political philosophers have hit upon the metaphor of mountain climbing with two core dimensions: climbing up (achieving more justice) and moving laterally (getting closer to the arrangement that characterizes the most just social state, the ideal). The thought is that to move closer to the ideal on the lateral dimension may sometimes require first moving up (getting more just) but then, like an intrepid climber, going down for a while before forging up the next slope. Thus, at times we are decreasing justice (altitude) in order to make our society more like the ideal (a closer latitude). (We can make the model more complex by adding other dimensions (*Tyranny*, pp. 258–9) but two were enough for my purposes.)

Wiens's essay focuses on metaphors and models: what are we doing when we employ "metaphors," "models" (and "theories")? There is no canonical view; in her classic work Mary B. Hesse (1966) argued that models just are metaphors. I offer a somewhat different account here, according to which metaphors are typically basic or initial models. In scientific explanation we can distinguish primary and secondary systems; the primary system is the phenomenon (A) to be explained, the secondary system is the explanation of A in terms of the metaphor/model (B) (Hesse 1966, p. 158). "Sound (primary system) is propagated by wave motion (secondary system)" (Hesse 1966, pp. 158–9). Metaphors are critical in suggesting analogies, such that the primary system can be understood in terms of the working of some other system – which it patently is not. "For the conjunction of terms drawn from the primary and secondary systems to constitute a metaphor it is necessary that there should be patent falsehood or even absurdity in taking the conjunction literally. Man is not, literally, a wolf, gases are not in the usual sense collections of massive particles" (Hesse 1966, p. 160). To take, say, navigating a mountain range (B) as a metaphor for pursuit of the ideal social state is to suggest that we can begin to understand the primary system A (pursuing the ideal) as having similar relations to navigating a mountain range (B). It is important, as Hess notes, that metaphors are not mere similes: we do not know ahead of time in just what way A is like B, or the ways in which it functions analogously. When we think about A as a B, we begin to think about A as acting as we know B does, and we look for familiar features of B to see if they are in A as well. We can use B as the basis of analogies that help us understand some of the puzzling workings of A, and provide the basis of further investigations.

This already is a model; we focus on the features of the primary system that are revealed by our more thorough grasp of the metaphorical secondary system. At this stage B's dynamics and features are critical in picking out and understanding A's; still employing analogies we search for parts of A that seem a lot like B's, and use our knowledge of the way B works with those parts to model how A must work too. For example, early electricians sought to understand electrical phenomena (A) as a liquid (B); and since B could be bottled, so should we be able to bottle A – hence their successful effort to develop the Leyden jar (Kuhn 1970, p. 17). In my view this metaphor-analogy stage is often the first step in building a rigorous model of A that ultimately jettisons the metaphorical B as the base comparison and, so, no longer employs metaphors or analogies. The model is stated in axioms and equations, and variations in these, and anomalies encountered by our current model suggest further developments.

Perhaps even after a formal model is developed the original metaphor may be used as a basis for speculating what variations of the formal model are worth exploring, though often (and this is my point) at some juncture the original metaphorical base, B, may become a hindrance rather than a source of further discovery, even if we continue to keep some of the labels suggested by the now-discarded metaphor. Thinking of conflict as a game blossomed in Prussia in the nineteenth century in the fad of "Kriegspiel" (literally, "war game") – a board game of conflict, played both by the public and the general staff. Indeed, in 1825 the German chief of staff proclaimed "It is not a game at all. It's training for war!" (Poundstone 1992, chap. 3). Young John von Neumann and his brothers played their own version of Kriegspiel. Game theory built on this metaphor; and we still have terms like "players," "moves," "strategies," and so on. But von Neumann and others developed "game" theory such that now its categories and relations are strictly defined within it, and so reference back to the way board games function is not apropos. It has its own, well-defined, concepts and mechanisms – in Wiens' terms its own "mathematical objects" – and any lingering game terms are simply for ease of exposition or to help beginners by invoking in their minds the now-discarded metaphor, which can help them to begin to see their way around the fully formalized model. (On the other hand, the atavistic labels can be an impediment, as when neophytes are told that they are "playing a game" and so, going back to a "game frame," play iterated prisoner's dilemmas not to maximize their own outcomes but to ensure that they "beat" the other "player.") In my view, however, game theory is not a metaphor: it is a formal model. We explain the primary system (people in interdependent actions) in terms of a formalized secondary system.

Hence my basic idea. The mountain range metaphor recurring in the political philosophy of ideal justice is a basic model that gives us a clue to some important features, but this metaphor has been superseded by fully formalized and developed models employed in fields such as evolutionary biology and complexity theory. The development from model-as-metaphor to a fully axiomatized (which is not to say fully developed) model has already been made, and was awaiting exploitation by political philosophers. As Page explains in his essay, I relied extensively on Stuart Kauffman's NK model. In Kauffman's model, all the terms are fully specified and the relations mathematically determined. There are Boolean nodes (N) that may be linked to K other nodes each of which can be "turned on or off" by their connected nodes. If we are modelling genes, the state of each node (gene) affects the fitness of the organism. When K is greater than 0, some genes are interconnected, and so the overall fitness of the organism will not simply be an additive function of the fitness of each gene, but of their number and degree of interaction.[1] This implies that when K=0, an organism O' that is a one gene variant of O will have a fitness highly correlated with the fitness of O. When K=N-1, the fitness of O' will not be correlated with O. For ease of exposition we can label the former a "smooth optimization landscape" (when we graph the fitness of variants they will increase or decrease in smooth lines) and the latter "maximally rugged" (fitness values may jump all over the range from one variant to the next). On all but the smoothest such optimization "landscapes" there will be local optima (any one gene variant will be less fit), which are not the global optimum. Each optima can be called a "peak." For now, the critical point is that once the model is specified "landscape," "ruggedness," "peaks," "height" and so on are fully determined by the value function (e.g., adaptiveness, justice), the structure of the domain (the measure of genetic or world variations) and the NK dynamics. These terms are no more metaphorical than "player" and "strategy" are in game theory; they can be replaced by purely formal notation and nothing would change.

I have spent perhaps too much space on the relation of metaphors and models, but I have repeatedly encountered political philosophers who, confronting the rugged landscape model, conclude "well, that's a nice (or bad) metaphor, but let's get beyond metaphorical talk and do some real political philosophy" (e.g., contemplate our intuitions or the perennially-fascinating question of whether "ought" implies "can"). I hope it is clear that this is a basic misunderstanding of the place of both metaphors and formalized models in inquiry.

II. Complexity and Optimization

Pursuit of an Ideal and Ruggedness

Let us build on Page's {Market, Bureaucracy, Democracy} model to better see how the complex optimization model works. He writes:

---

[1] For useful summaries, see Page's essay and Mitchell 2009, pp. 281-6.

In the model, a society must allocate resources and opportunities across a set of domains. Within each domain, the society chooses among three pure institutional types: a market (M), a bureaucratic organization (B), or a democratic mechanism (D). For example, to select a construction firm to build roads, a society could hold an auction among qualified firms (M), it could construct a bureaucracy that develops criteria for selecting a firm (B), or it could hold a vote among elected representatives for the winner (D). If there exist ten such domains, then the set {X} consists of all vectors of length ten whose entries belong to the set {M, B, D}. Though a simplified characterization of the world, the model allows for a combinatorial explosion of social arrangements – 59,049 distinct possibilities to be precise.

We see how quickly the number of distinct possible social worlds expand. To simplify, suppose we have only a four-domain world, any of which can be organized on market, bureaucratic or democratic institutions. Suppose:

Domain 1: Decisions about supply of public goods
Domain 2: Decisions about the supply and distribution of private goods
Domain 3: Decisions about income distribution
Domain 4: Decisions about the distribution of employment

Suppose we have a certain market socialist ideal, {DMDD} (public goods, democratic; private goods, market; income distribution, democratic; employment allocation, democratic). We are now at {BMMM}. One thing we might do is simply list the justice of all 81 possibilities, but it is hard to know, say, how the {MBDM} world would function: what would a social world be like where public goods are determined by the market, private goods are distributed by a bureaucracy, income distribution is democratically voted upon, but allocation of employment is via the market? Hmm. The ways all these mechanisms would interact are, *Tyranny* claims, extraordinarily difficult for us to model and predict, as our social science is based on understanding market provision of private goods and market (and some bureaucratic) distribution of incomes.

On *Tyranny*'s analysis, ideal theory presents a perspective on justice that orients our quest for perfect justice by locating the ideal in relation to our current social state. A perspective (i) identifies what social states are similar to others (critical to orienting us in the quest for justice), and (ii) assigns a justice score to social states given their expected functioning. Considering just the first function, in our case we might have, say, the following perspective:

{BMBM} – **{BMMM}** – {DMMM} – {DMBM} – {DMDD}

(ideal)

On this perspective we are presently at {BMMM}; public goods are allocated by a bureaucracy, all others by the market. According to this democratic socialist perspective the ideal is a condition where public goods are allocated democratically, private goods by the market, while incomes and employment opportunities are decided democratically {DMDD}. Now on this perspective a world where public goods are decided by a democratic rather than a bureaucratic mechanism – {DMMM} – is pretty close to ours, and we can estimate how it would function and its justice. After all, for a democratic vote to replace a bureaucratic decision does not seem a huge jump in the social space. Bringing in now the second (value) function of a perspective, suppose this perspective judges that we are presently at 50, and the ideal is 100. What about {DMMM}? Here is a distinct possibility: while moving from {BMMM} to {DMMM} makes our society's structure closer to the ideal {DMDD}, it could decrease justice. In {DMMM} public goods are decided by vote but incomes by the market. Many social democrats such as Rawls believe that great wealth corrupts democracy, and so the provision of public goods in {DMMM} might produce a less just society, where the wealthy control their provision more than at present (so justice goes down to 40). On the other hand {BMBM}, instead of democratizing decisions about income distribution, puts them under bureaucratic decision-making. This, plausibly, leads us away from "bourgeois democracy" and its ideal of self-government by instituting an expert bureaucratic elite who end up exercising great control over the economy (Schumpeter 1950, 296ff; Levy and Peart 2017). Yet, it may lead to more distributive justice, and perhaps is superior in overall socialist justice to {DMMM}, say. Hence "The Choice" in Figure 8.1.

At our present {BMMM} we have a choice between moving to {BMBM} with a justice of 60, but at the cost of making our society's institutional structure less like the ideal (we move away from it). If we seek to make our society conform more closely to the institutional structure of the ideal, we will suffer a loss in justice. After that (as indicated by the multiple light grey lines), we are uncertain as to the justice of the next step, as we are modeling a world where the bureaucracy controls income distribution but not employment allocation. The ideal theorist need not always choose to move toward the ideal, but if the ideal theory is to provide significant guidance, she must often choose to pursue the ideal and forgo local improvements in justice. The Choice is really a choice.

It might be wondered, if we know so little about {DMBM}, how do we know so much about {DMDD}, the ideal? And, of course, that is the question: how can we be sure of the functioning, and so justice, of a set of

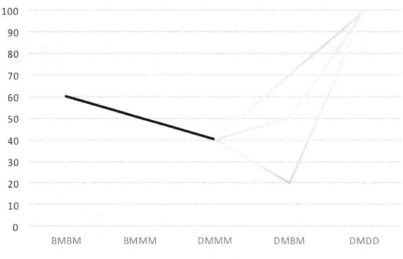

Figure 8.1 "The Choice"

social arrangements that are so different from our own? Should we ever get to {DMBM}, it is almost certain that we will drastically re-evaluate the ideal, {DMDD}. As we approach the ideal, it changes before our eyes, perhaps receding into the distance (or perhaps, alas, we spot it in our rear-view mirror).

As the number of domains, dimensions of evaluation, or distinct institutional structures involved in an ideally just society increases (N), and as the justice-relevant interdependencies among them increase (K), it becomes essentially certain that The Choice will arise. Neufeld and Watson are certainly right that institutions must be "mutually realizable" but that is not enough for their evaluation given the inevitable coupling in their functionings: some mutual realizations lead to excellent interactions (from the perspective of justice) while others interact in detrimental ways. This is the root of the complexity and uncertainty that confront all attempts to move us from one institutional scheme to a very different one.

I think it is important to stress that this is not a just-so modeling story. In their extensive fieldwork on real institutions Elinor and Vincent Ostrom stressed that institutions are composed of numerous rule configurations; the constituent rules have strong interdependencies, both with each other and with environmental conditions. "A change in any one of these variables produces a different action situation and may lead to very different outcomes" (E. Ostrom 1986 [2014], p. 111). When we talk about social states such as a "property-owning democracy" we are referring in a loose way to a myriad of interconnected rules and behavioral tendencies that constitute the working of the set of institutions that are summed up by this moniker. Building these institutions inevitably leads to problems of complex optimization and searching.

The Fundamental Diversity Insight

Vincent Ostrom (1972 [1999], p. 125) once remarked in respect to his empirical findings, "[t]he complexity of relationships ... is such that mortal human beings can never observe the 'whole picture.' Anyone who attempts to 'see' the 'whole picture' will 'see' only what is in the 'eyes' or 'mind' of the beholder." This insight is formalized in the Hong-Page model, where diverse perspectives, each seeing (coding) the problem in different ways, each see possibilities to which the other is "blind." For example, one might wonder about Figure 8.1: why is BMBM a move away from the ideal, rather than a step toward it? The Choice would not be confronted by the perspective:

{DMMM} – {BMMM} – {BMBM} – {DMBM} – {DMDD}

(ideal)

The Hong-Page model shows us how different perspectives on a problem can help each other in their searches for the best outcome. We can benefit from interactions with those who see the world differently: what is a tricky problem for me might, given your perspective, be an easy one. This is a fundamental insight, and *Tyranny* spends a good deal of time evaluating its applicability to the search for ideal justice. Page's essay nicely summarizes both the Hong-Page model's resources, and the reasons why I conclude that it has a restricted applicability to the problem of ideal theory. For now, I merely stress that I strongly endorse (stated approximately)

> *The Fundamental Diversity Insight*: Any given perspective Σ on ideal justice is apt to get stuck at poor local optima; other perspectives can help by reinterpreting the problem or applying different predictive models, showing better alternatives to be in Σ's present neighborhood.

Wiens believes the arguments for this and related diversity-relevant conclusions do not "rely much" on the rugged landscape (NK) analysis. I do not agree. It is just because we are navigating this sort of problem that our perspectives on justice are so apt to get stuck on poor local optima, from which we confront The Choice. Critically, as the Hong-Page model taught us, other perspectives can – sometimes – point the way forward.

A Tale of Two Models

Wiens's essay is, to a large extent, a contrast between his optimization model and the model we have been examining. Trying to be a little less formal, Wiens's (as I shall call it) "simple optimization model" seems characterized by:

1. A set of possibilities, X (options, states of affairs, social worlds, etc.). This is the domain of the value function on which it operates. In *Tyranny* they are alternative social worlds.
2. A binary value function (which I'll call V): the value relations among members of X are built up through binary comparisons. Letting (x, y, z) be elements of X (i.e., particular social worlds), xRy if and only if x is ranked by V at least as high as y. If xRy and yRx, x and y are ranked the same; if xRy and not yRx, x is ranked above y.
3. It also seems required that the binary relations generated by V be transitive among all triples in X; (xRy) & (yRz) implies xRz. Another requirement seems to be completeness, i.e., for all members of the domain X (x, y), either xRy and/or yRx. Other conditions on the ordering are allowed.
4. There is an additional set of constraints. These allow us to partition the domain, X, of possible social worlds, into those that meet these constraints and those that do not. Call XC the subset of X that meets some given constraints C.

As I understand Wiens (and I'm sure I have not grasped all the intricacies of his model, so apologies in advance), conditions 1–4 imply that the only structure among the elements of X that are not based on V (the binary value relation) is the partition of X into the subset XC and the rest of X. Consider, then, simply the XC partition. For all the social worlds in XC the only structure relating them is that yielded by V. Until the binary ordering is applied to the members of XC, they are an unordered set of social worlds that meet certain constraints.

Perhaps the most fundamental difference between simple optimization and NK-optimization is that the latter models a structure among the members of the domain (possible social worlds) that is not generated by the value function. As Page notes in his essay, we can make this point by saying that the simple optimization model's theory of justice T only has a measure of the range of T (the ordering produced by the value function) while *Tyranny*'s model has independent metrics for the range and domain of T. Without these two distinct metrics, as we have seen, The Choice does not arise. Rather than confronting an unordered set of possibilities to which we apply our value (justice) function, *Tyranny* assumes that all the members of X – "social worlds" – have certain justice-relevant features and these generate a structured domain, to which we apply our value function. (We should refrain from calling this domain metric simply "descriptive," as it is generated by the similarity of worlds' justice-relevant features, so they are, we might say, normatively loaded descriptions.) And in most of these landscape models – e.g., those in evolutionary biology – the structure of the option set is the similarity of the constituent features of the options, such as genotypes. If x is almost but not quite identical to y in the relevant respects (and, as always, "relevancy" is defined by the perspective or theory being employed, see below), then before any value function is applied, x is located close to y; if the defining features of z share very little with x, x and z will be located far apart. In a simple evolutionary biology model, y might be a one gene variation from x, and so we can entirely correctly say – before we know their adaptiveness (value), x and y are close (though it could turn out that in terms of adaptiveness they are not).

What Model Should We Use?

So which model should we use? A model that only looks at the range of value (i.e., the justice of the options) or one that includes a meaningful structure (i.e., the institutional similarity) of the elements of the domain? As soon as we phrase the question so bluntly, we see how misguided it is. The Fundamental Diversity Insight indicates that different models often provide different insights, so we are all apt to benefit when multiple models are pursued (Page 2016). The model we employ depends on our perspective on the primary system and our theoretical aims. As we know from economics, in many cases a simple optimization model, which only orders according to the value function (i.e., utility), elegantly analyzes the problem, say of most consumer choice. But as Harold Hotelling (1929) showed in his analysis of the location of shops, sometimes we get more insight by also including a structure of the option set – in Hotelling's case, the geographical location of shops along a street. Anthony Downs (1956) saw that this "spatial" model could be extended to include "ideological space" (as well as utility values defined by the value function) and so began spatial models of politics. Downs's model was not metaphorical, even though it was developed from a "geographical" model: ideological space was well-defined.

Hotelling's and Downs's models included a structured domain (as well as a value function), but were not NK models. I have tried to indicate why I believe the ideal of orienting our quest for justice by a fully just social state is well modeled by a rugged landscape in which our reliable knowledge is confined to our current neighborhood. Given the large number of institutions and background conditions that constitute an ideal social state, and the myriad of couplings between them that result in vastly different social states of different degrees of justice, setting out to pursue the ideal is an exercise in Knightian uncertainty (Knight, 1921 [1964], chaps. 7–8). For the most part, we only have useful assignments of probabilities within our neighborhood, so we simply do not have the information necessary for a fruitful simple optimization exercise.

Consider a mundane case: a manufacturer searching for innovations in product P. The advice to formulate an ordered list of possible variations of P, and then take the best choice is not of much help; the manufacturer cannot assign values to many of the options. Indeed, she doesn't yet even have the blueprints for many variations. So here is an entirely sensible approach to the development problem. Have most of the research teams work on near improvements (slight modifications of the technology underlying P); because there is so little fiddling with the structure of the present P we'll often find the new versions slightly better or slightly worse, and can further build on the slightly better ones, and then build on some of those, etc. This is a conservative "climb the gradient" heuristic, always seeking local improvements. But we may get stuck at a product for which no small improvements could be made (yet is not the ideal P). Think of Sony teams that were working on the best Betamax recorder.[2] So the manufacturer may also wish to invest in an R&D department that has some teams working on more radical innovations (say, laser discs), some of which could result in really high values, but it is almost impossible at this point to make sound judgments about whether they will pan out. Here we are dealing with hunches, hopes and dreams – not probability assignments. In the case just described, we are searching the value of options with a certain structure, and these structures are the very properties that yield valuable products. This structured space thus orients the product search. It is important that in this case one's optimization problem starts from a

---

[2] I write here as a great fan of Betamax, being among the last to abandon it.

location (a place in the structure), and we are thinking of how to best move given where we already are.

The claim of *Tyranny* is that an interesting class of ideal theories (I never say "all") have much in common with this case, except that these ideal theorists believe that they have already developed the blueprint for the perfect (or at least truly excellent) "product" but we can't build it right now (the blueprint may require components not yet developed, like public-spirited folk). Our job is, given our present location in the domain, to begin to develop structures that are more like those that generate this great result. That is what it means to build an ideally just society. To build is to assemble the components. Because the task of such ideal theories is to work from our given structure to the ideal one (and thereby achieve the perfect value score), an optimization model that includes structure (which is not simply generated by the value function) is necessary.[3] It is in this sense that, in a structured domain, the ideal "orients" improvements in justice in a much more complex sense than does the simple injunction "given some set of unordered social worlds, choose by maximizing the value function subject to constraints."

Does a Simple Optimization Model Capture Ideal Theory?

Although I favor an ecumenical approach to modeling, I am not a model nihilist who supposes that one modeling choice is as good as the next. *Tyranny* adopts a theoretical perspective on analyzing theories of ideal justice which, I think, is in many respects superior to a simple optimization model based on a binary value relation. Deriving "perfect" or even "good enough" from a value function that can only yield judgments about what is "better" is, I think, a job and a half. Theories based on a binary value function can only say that an option is the best in the sense that it is better than all the options in some set of options. So to say that a certain social state is ideally just is, essentially, to say that it is better than all other social states in the domain X, or more realistically in some XC partition. This makes it both too easy and too hard to find the ideal. It is too easy, because when a theory has some non-empty option set and can identify a best

---

[3] Sometimes simple optimization models seek to provide a non-V-based structure among the members of X through appeal to feasibility; it is offered as a way to say what options are "close" and "far" in a sense independent of the value function. *Tyranny* argues that while feasibility is an important and often critical idea, it does not have the characteristics to define coherent and well-behaved structural relations among the members of X. We cannot build a better coherent structure by asking, at each moment, what improvements on the current structure are the most feasible.

element, the theory then has apparently located an "ideal" – essentially every optimization exercise ends up as an ideal theory (which is why Wiens can see the Open Society as an ideal, since I think there is a set of "devices" that are maximal choices, even if no set is the best choice, to accommodate diversity). On the other hand, it is too hard to identify the ideal, as we need an exhaustive enumeration of all elements in the set XC of possible worlds to identify a "best" that is not simply dependent on the choice of the comparison set.[4] Thus we can only be confident that i is the ideal world if we are confident i is not merely the best in some subset of XC, but remains best when the set comprises all of XC: i is better than each and every element in XC. In formal terms, it must be the unique choice set from XC. Showing that is a daunting task, unless we very tightly specify the constraints that define XC. I don't think this is the usual way that ideal theorists have reasoned in the history of political thought. On my view, *The Republic*, More's *Utopia* and Bacon's *New Atlantis* are paradigmatic. Construct first an imaginary social world in which humans would relate to each other with full justice, etc., and that is the ideal. We score it as fully just, without a complete ordering of all worlds in XC. That then becomes our inspiration, even if we do not know of many of the other worlds in XC. Indeed, the common utopian theme that the ideal is a far-off land to which we have yet to find a path-to-construct-it implies that there are many unknown options between it and where we now are.

Of course, to inspire it does not have to be absolutely perfect – we might construct a world that is within the human horizon of workability and yet is essentially but not ideally just. For Rawls identifying such a "realistic utopia" was a critical task of political philosophy. At various times he agonizes over the question whether a reasonably just society is within the grasp of humans. "The wars of this century with their extreme violence and increasing destructiveness, culminating in the manic evil of the Holocaust, raise in an acute way the question whether political relations must be governed by power and coercion alone. If a reasonably just society that subordinates power to its aims is not possible and people are largely amoral, if not incurably cynical and self-centered, one might ask with Kant whether it is worthwhile for human beings to live on the earth" (Rawls 2005, p. lx). It is hard to see how showing some social world is "ranked first in our option set" could possibly assuage such worries. Rawls seeks to

---

[4] More formally, I think we would want our binary-based theory of the ideal to satisfy some version of expansion and contraction consistency. See Sen 2017, pp. 317–23.

find out whether the best among our options is truly just – and if there is one that is truly just it is to orient our long-term endeavors at reform.

Perspectives, Normalization and Generality

As we have seen following (though, as he points out, substantially modifying) Page's framework, I argue that a perspective provides an orienting structure to the complex optimization problem. A perspective on justice includes, as it were, all the elements needed to generate an ideal theory. It includes a set of evaluative criteria (perhaps liberty and reciprocity, perhaps sanctity and respect for authority), an identification of what parts of a social world are relevant when evaluating it in the light of these criteria and a model of the way these features interact to provide an overall social order, which then can be scored in terms of its justice. In addition, a perspective must have some view of how similar worlds are given their justice-relevant features; it must be able to say world x is almost identical to y in terms of the institutions, rules, motivations and so on that define the worlds. Now fundamental to *Tyranny* is that how all this is accomplished is internal to a perspective: in Wiens's language these must be "black boxes" the contents of which the model is "blind" to. Political philosophy is normally devoted to explicating the correct perspective, giving accounts of what the correct evaluative criteria are, how they should be combined and what institutions are relevant to justice. As D'Agostino puts it, this is part and parcel of the "legislative" stance in political theorizing. In addition, an ideal political philosophy seeks to show what the ideal is, and how far we are from it. Call this a fully normalized view of ideal justice. Sometimes, as with social contract theory, a set of perspectives is identified as "correct enough" because of their similarities in evaluative standards or their basic agreement on the relevant institutions; call this a partially normalized view of ideal justice. It was Rawls (2007, p. 226) who notes that all social contract theory supposes some normalization – all take a peek inside the box and seek to give us some idea how it ought to function.

Of course, we often do care about exploring evaluative criteria or, for Wiens, the logic of justification. When we do so we seek to develop a fully or partly normalized theory – one that commences by identifying a set of correct or minimally acceptable perspectives. However, the aim of *Tyranny* was to present a fully general model of ideal theory, one which analyzed ideal theory qua ideal theory, and not qua liberal ideal theory, or qua ideal theories that embrace a view of the logic of justification, or even ideal theories that accept a standard secular understanding of social reality. Two aims were regulating here. First, as I have been stressing, the aim was a fully general theory that uncovered the logic of ideal theorizing itself, as far as possible freed from familiar substantive commitments (a "pure theory of the ideal," we might say) and, secondly, to explore how a society with a truly radical diversity of perspectives, each committed to its own theory of justice, might not only live together, but learn from each other. It was thus important not to start out by imposing any normalization on perspectives.

Still, as Wiens perhaps suggests, isn't the model itself a form of normalization? It says that a perspective must have evaluative criteria, must identify features of the social world, must be able to score them and so on. Isn't this just another normalization? We might call this the "all theory implies normalization" objection. And this raises one of the most perplexing issues for what we might call ecumenical theories of a phenomenon (see Gaus, 2017b). Think of the difference between an objective theory of value (say, the labor theory) and a subjective one (such as Carl Menger's). On the one hand, a subjective theory seeks to allow that value is, in a basic sense, up to the agent, and she can place value where she wills. In that sense it is ecumenical about what can be "correctly valued." Yet, because it is a theory of value it must delimit its inquiry – valuing isn't the same thing as sleeping (even if sleeping is valuable). To give a theory of X, one must identify a class of X-phenomenon. Unless we characterize X in some way we can't even begin to talk about "it," and unless our characterization has enough structure we can't begin to analyze it. So, yes, categorizations and specifications cannot be avoided in theorizing. If all categorization implies normalization, so be it. The important point for *Tyranny* is that, having identified the basic elements of a perspective, the analysis does not proceed to employ additional criteria to distinguish "good" v. "bad" or "reasonable" v. "unreasonable" variants (though each perspective may make such judgments of the others, as we are about to see).

III. The Open Society

The Fundamental Diversity Dilemma

As I said above, *Tyranny* relies on Hong-Page reasoning to endorse The Fundamental Diversity Insight. A point of departure from their model is my analysis of, and emphasis on, the Fundamental Diversity Dilemma. A radically different perspective from Σ may provide important insights to Σ, but adherents of Σ will have great difficulty making sense of this radically different perspective. As Σ sees them, they categorize the social world in very odd ways, and employ strange evaluative standards. This should be familiar to everyone. Think of the radical atheist's claim that religious perspectives suffer from a cognitive dementia, or the religious view that the atheist is infected by evil. Under these conditions both see the other as saying barely intelligible things, and they certainly do not find each other's "searches" for the ideal of value. In a diverse society, sometimes we can learn a lot from other perspectives, sometimes we can use some of their discoveries, and sometimes we will dismiss them as lunatics.

As D'Agostino has argued in his marvelous *Naturalizing Epistemology* (2010), the trick is to "get it together," to assemble the insights of our different research programs in a way that leads to mutual enlightenment. Adapting D'Agostino's analysis of scientific communities, I employed his idea of a "republican community" to designate a community of moral inquiry, i.e., one that shares sufficient standards, problems and concerns such that the results of the searches of some in the community can be taken up by others. Of course, such "republican communities" come in all varieties, from the thick who share many deep commitments, to those who sometimes find some results of the others as somewhat enlightening. Employing a "small world model" *Tyranny* argues that a society composed of diverse groups, some of whom entirely dismiss each other's insights, might, nevertheless, be one in which everyone learns from everyone else. The basic idea is straightforward. Our Radical Atheist proposes committing the Evangelical Christian to an asylum, while the Evangelical Christian dismisses the Atheist as vigorously. They will never directly share insights. But, say, a Roman Catholic Scientist may engage the Evangelical and, in turn, what we might call the Broadminded Secular Scientist is willing to engage the Roman Catholic Scientist; so, there is a line of engagement from the Evangelical Christian to the Broadminded Secular Scientist. If the Radical Atheist engages the Broadminded Scientist, the network of mutual influence is complete. The Evangelical Christian and the Radical Atheist may end up enlightening each other. As we multiply the number of perspectives, diverse, crisscrossing networks of various "republican communities" of inquiry will arise. Such networks mitigate the Fundamental Diversity Dilemma. The Open Society, I argue, provides a framework that allows these networks to develop, and so a framework that allows each view of justice to better cope with its own internal challenges.

Communities of Moral Inquiry v. Moral Communities

Vallier's essay raises the important question of the relation of "republican" communities of inquiry to moral rule networks – people who share moral expectations and demands. Let us call a "moral community" a set of individuals who (i) share very similar perspectives on justice, (ii) interact on moral rules grounded on these perspectives and (iii) share very few moral rules with those outside of (ii). In the history of political philosophy, many have thought that an ideal way to cope with moral diversity would be for us to divide up into numerous like-minded moral communities (Nozick 1974, chap. 10). *Tyranny* tries to show why that is an error. In a network in which the moral rules reflect only similar perspectives, members are able to act on views of justice they take as superior, but at the same time they lose resources (interaction with other perspectives) that have the real potential to enlighten them about justice. What constitutes a "republican community of inquiry" is in constant flux; as Σ develops, perspectives that Σ previously saw as beyond the pale of sensible inquiry become intelligible, while some that it previously deemed sensible may now appear antiquated. *Tyranny*'s concern is with those who are devoted to knowing what real justice is, and that cannot be secured in like-minded moral communities. Thus, the crux of *Tyranny*: the subjects of my inquiry – those who are deeply devoted to knowing what a just society is – have powerful reasons to embrace the diversity of the Open Society.

One important difference between *The Order of Public Reason* (2011) and *Tyranny*, then, is that the latter is focused on those who are convinced there is a notion of perfect justice, and are committed to knowing what it is. Such folks would seem to be an especially hard case for a theory of public reason as given in *The Order of Public Reason*, as their primary concern is getting justice right. Why would they, of all people, want to share a moral order with people who are getting it wrong, much less accommodate them in some way? *Tyranny* (the book, that is), is an extended answer. Surprisingly (at least it was surprising to me), if you want to really get justice right, you must live with, and learn from, those who get it wrong – if knowing the perfectly just society is a complex problem.

Polycentrism and Accountability

A second difference concerns the model of moral relations. As Vallier points out, *The Order of Public Reason* analyzed morality in terms of the social rules endorsed in some group, G. It was supposed that the persons in G share a network of moral rules. As I noted, groups come in many different sizes, but my concern was typically with the largest interacting group, what Hayek called "the Great Society." *Tyranny* develops a more nuanced account – polycentric moral networks. What I have called "moral communities" are typically confused with what Elinor and Vincent Ostrom called "polycentrism." The Ostroms argued that a "highly frag-mented" system in which different groups were largely confined to their own "jurisdictions" (or communities) is apt to result in conflict and institutional failure (Ostrom and Ostrom 1977 [1999], p. 96). They thus modeled a successful polycentric order in terms of many crisscrossing and overlapping jurisdictions and norm networks. *Tyranny* relies on polycen-trism thus properly understood. In *Tyranny* "the group" dissolves into complex and overlapping moral rule networks. On some fundamental matters, the moral rule network is coextensive with the Great Society of strangers, the group that I had in mind in *The Order of Public Reason*; but on many other matters "the group" disaggregates into moral networks that are subsets of G. As the Ostroms stressed, whether moral rules and institutions are needed in the eyes of some individuals depends on what sort of problem they are facing; some problems can only be solved with the participation of almost everyone, others have much more restricted scope.

Within each moral network – i.e., people who have shared normative and empirical expectations about what is to be done in some circum-stances – each is accountable to others in his network for violating the rule.[5] This is not the case in relation to outsiders: one is not answerable to outsiders for one's failure to conform, nor can they hold one accountable. So, if, in a moral network of vegetarians, Alf defects and has foie gras, he is not answerable to me (a devoted carnivore), unless we begin to tell a story with more detail that draws me into the matter. But he is accountable to others who share the rule, and have well-grounded normative and empir-ical expectations about Alf's eating habits. In the Open Society, of course, Alf can withdraw from many such moral networks, as others can join them. This is an engine of moral change.

---

[5] Thus the idea on which Vallier focuses: that a violation of a moral rule in one's network is "everyone's business." To be sure, I used this as something of a motto rather than a strict necessity, as a network can develop moral rules in areas like marriage (e.g. fidelity), but interests in privacy may lead to the conclusion that violations are only the business of the family unit. Nevertheless, without further considerations the general statement holds within any given moral rule network. In economic terms, rule violation is a public bad, so all are concerned when violations occur. Except for the special case of human rights, I did not, however, hold that conformity is the business of those outside the network (in *The Order of Public Reason*, outside of G). As I stressed, other groups may have different moral rules, and in most cases (human rights aside) one cannot hold them accountable for failing to conform to our social morality. So, yes, within some given G, violations are almost always a concern to all.

This is a critical point. Philosophers usually see morality as homogenous – and each is accountable to everyone else for failing to act as morality requires. When we look around us, we see the moral world is not at all like this. A normal university professor participates in a wide array of moral networks. At the university as a scientist she participates in networks that have high expectations about evidence and impartiality; a student who flouts them will be the subject of intense moral criticism and, perhaps, severe punishment. But as a member of a church she does not hold others accountable to them: it would be inappropriate for her to start condemning her pastor for lax evidential standards in his Sunday sermon. She may be a vegetarian and hold her university circle of vegetarians to high standards, but she would display outrageous behavior if she walked into a Subway and commenced to berate customers' choices. This is not to deny that the professor might believe that her pastor really ought to pay much more attention to evidence, or that everyone ought to refrain from eating meat. Her judgments about morality may or may not be universal. But this is to say that the conditions to hold the pastor or the Subway customers accountable do not obtain, and so their actions are not her business – that is, they are not accountable to her for their violations. We navigate these various networks of accountability constantly – so unconsciously that we may be surprised that is what we are doing.

Trendsetter Networks

Although *Tyranny* is critical of the idea that republican communities of inquiry should form "moral communities" (as I have defined them), we must distinguish a moral community from a group of individuals, perhaps who are joined in a republican community of inquiry, who seek to establish a new rule on some matter (Bicchieri 2016, chap. 5). In a polycentric moral order this innovative activity will be restricted to a single moral rule or a small set. Those adopting this new rule will be enmeshed in many other moral rule networks, and so constantly confronting diverse perspectives. They will not form a moral rule community.

On some matters a polycentric order can contain competing moral rules. Given such competition a trendsetter group (say, university students in the '60s) begin experimenting with a new rule (say, concerning sexual morality), withdrawing (usually very publicly) their allegiance to the old. In the case of sexual morality the new networks expanded but did not go to fixation – in many towns and rural areas, and in much of the south of the United States, the old rules of sexual conduct held pretty firm. Moral

innovation on some rule of social morality certainly can, then, occur by
spreading out from a trendsetting network (that may also be a republican
community of inquiry). As Robert Boyd and Peter J. Richerson (2005)
have argued, under some conditions group beneficial rules can spread very
fast. Sometimes all of society will cascade to a new rule; at other times this
competitive process leads to a polycentric order in which different sub-
networks adopt different rules (Gaus, 2017c).

Vallier's essay is especially valuable in stressing how moral innovation
requires moral space – a protection from universal accountability – for
moral diversity and experimentation. So very often today those advocating
moral change take their role as requiring that they browbeat others to
conform to the moral rules they and their core network are convinced are
correct (Gaus 1996, 123ff). They hold the world accountable for not
living up to their convictions. An aggressive moral self-righteousness is
often seen as mandatory for anyone who seeks a more perfect justice.
Anything else is "relativism" or, to again harken back to the '60s, liberal
"repressive tolerance." That, however, is to ossify one's current understanding of justice and to undermine the social conditions for knowing a
more perfect justice. We are not at the end of history – and that includes
our knowledge of a perfectly just social state.

The Fundamental Rules of the Moral Constitution

Some rules, however, are so fundamental to cooperative social life that it is
very difficult to have sustained interactions with those who do not adhere
to the same ones we do. If some reject our rules about harm to bodily
integrity, property, truthfulness, etc. it will be immensely difficult to share
a social life with them. These fundamental rules require a different analysis
of moral reform than the competing networks account. When it comes to
the rules of sexual morality, university students could practice their own
rules freed of the hang-ups of the rest of the society (and eventually convert
a good deal of it). Sexual relations are certainly social, but even in the '60s
they weren't especially large-scale social phenomena.[6] Some can go their
own way. But, leaving aside retreating to a commune, it proved impossible
for the '60s trendsetters to informally change property rules. Given our
own deep commitments, we have strong reason to share a basic framework

---

[6] Although according to what my daughter calls "the source of champions," Wikipedia, up to 100,000
people participated in the summer of love.

of such moral rules, but given the diversity of our moral perspectives we disagree about what those rules should be.

The Order of Public Reason introduced the idea of a socially eligible set of rules, which *Tyranny* employs. The basic idea is straightforward. In a large diverse social network (the Great Society, for example), individuals have clashing views about the specific form these moral rules should take (what should be the rules about harm? what should be the rules about property?). However, these types of rules are so fundamental to an ongoing scheme of moral accountability – which itself is fundamental to effective social life – that almost all individuals are prepared to endorse and adhere to specific versions that fall a long ways short of their most favored formulation. The socially eligible set, for any specific matter to be governed by a moral rule in a particular social network, is the set of all the rule variations being advanced that everyone (or, as near as possible, everyone, a point to which I shall return) in the network has sufficient reason to conclude are at least minimally worthy of endorsement and adherence. Since for these fundamental rules we really need to coordinate on a single, shared, rule, the socially eligible set identifies the set of possible rule variations all can understand as grounding a shared practice of moral accountability. For every rule in the socially eligible set, each person would endorse and adhere to it should it be the rule that their society (network) has hit upon.

How, then, can an Open Society change such rules? As I argued in *The Order of Public Reason* democratic government reforms the fundamental rules of our society through legislation. When the law moves us within the socially eligible set, the result is still a rule that everyone holds is a basis of genuine moral accountability, but many believe is a better rule (given their moral perspectives) than the one it replaced. Democratic decision-making is, I think, indispensable in reforming our truly fundamental rules. In *Tyranny*, however, I explored informal, social mechanisms by which social movements can seek to move us to what proponents see as a superior basis for accountability. One interesting avenue I consider is to exploit rule ambiguity. All rules are ambiguous in many places, and typically in such situations others will accept several alternative actions as plausibly fitting the rule. In these circumstances we can nudge the rule in directions we morally favor (in the eligible set), without denying the validity of the normative expectations of others. For example, when I was growing up the basic rules about physical violence toward children allowed corporal punishment, but not too much violence. The ambiguity about what constituted unacceptable violence toward children allowed a change in the basic rules, as some began to employ increasingly stringent interpretations of what "violence" was and when it was unwarranted. This was extraordinarily effective in changing the moral rule. When I was a lad seeing a mother smack her child in the supermarket was not especially rare or noteworthy. Now it is clear violation of a basic rule.

The Limits of Moral Space

In an earlier paper D'Agostino (2013) worried that, instead of finding an "eligible set" of acceptable moral rules, the "null hypothesis" will hold – there will not be any rule all deem eligible – worthy of endorsement. His paper in this symposium develops this worry: there seems to be precious little chance of an eligible set in a society split into opposing perspectives that "are increasingly likely to treat those whose adopt different social ideals as pariahs, unworthy of moral regard." The obvious case here is the great animosity in the United States between so many Republicans and Democrats.

D'Agostino is surely correct that this dismissal of the moral status of others is one of today's most serious threats to the Open Society. However, while recognizing the danger this poses to the Open Society, I also think we should be aware that to a large extent this a political problem more than a generalized moral one (reflect on the obvious example). As Milton and Rose Friedman (1980, p. 66) long ago pointed out, political decisions require "conformity without unanimity" whereas self-organizing systems (like the market) produce "unanimity without conformity." In a highly morally diverse society, when political decision-making pushes beyond maintenance of core rights and liberties to the legal codification of deeply controversial conceptions of justice, hostility and contempt for the law are apt to be triggered (Gaus 2017a). Politics is ill-equipped to cope with deep moral disagreement (i.e., where the null hypothesis holds). Each party, hopeful that a majority win in the next election will allow it to institute true justice, simply sets the stage for the next iteration of mistrust. To argue that democratic societies need to develop more trust, while seeing them as a struggle about which controversial conception of justice will be imposed on the appalled minority, is ultimately incoherent. One cannot make politics a justice jihad and hope to induce trust (see Vallier, forthcoming).

The idea of a polycentric moral order helps to show how we can secure "conformity without unanimity."[7] Although we are currently understandably obsessed by the hatred underlying so much American politics, we

---

[7] Brian Kogelmann (2017) has rigorously analyzed the proposal that the political system draw on polycentrism to secure this.

should not forget that Democrats and Republicans share a myriad of rules about bodily integrity, property, gender equality (yes, though they disagree on the policies to pursue it). They cooperate in neighborhood organizations (my own neighborhood, for example, has about an equal distribution of hybrids and pickups, yet an active neighborhood organization). The more our moral rules track networks of individuals seeking to live together and solve their social problems, the less the null hypothesis will be a worry.

I do not want to seem Pollyannaish. The debate about the status of abortion rights is a deep moral disagreement that inevitably flows to political dispute. Even about this vexed issue, however, I think a more decentralized politico-legal system that is responsive to the differences of locality and region could at least mitigate the depth of hostility (Gaus 2017a; Kogelmann 2017, chap. 4). A morally diverse society is bound to have deeper political conflicts than one that gives the appearance of moral homogeneity (because some perspectives have been silenced or have been dismissed as unreasonable). Politics amplifies disputes, and these can obscure well-functioning informal networks on which an extended order of cooperation is built. Perhaps the main message of my last two books has been the importance of the social and informal, which contemporary political philosophy almost wholly ignores.

Still there are limits. I agree with Rawls in holding that the moral space of endorsed cooperation is always limited. Some will simply refuse to live with others on terms that ground mutual accountability and mutually endorsed expectations. Recall, though, that Rawls (2005, pp. 197–8) credits Isaiah Berlin with this thought. Whereas Neufeld and Watson see it as bound up with the Rawlsian ideas of reasonableness and reciprocity, I see it as simply following from the recognition of Berlin's core theme of deep diversity. Given a deep enough diversity of moral perspectives, it is inevitable that some won't be able to see their way to endorsing the rules of cooperation that almost all others employ to structure their social-moral lives. Neufeld and Watson, as Rawlsians, would tend to describe these folk as "unreasonable." Of all the Rawlsian categories, this is the most vexed. While I do not believe it is hopelessly vague or confused, I certainly do not wish to employ it in any formal way. As I see it, typically these "excluded perspectives" are those who value their own purity (or, perhaps we should say, less controversially, their integrity) over reconciliation and living with others. I have recently modeled them as "maximum integrity agents" (Gaus, 2017c). These may be devoutly religious folk, or Kantian moral philosophers. I am not prepared to say the maximum integrity stance renders one unreasonable, but it does tend to make one unfit to live with many others. One need not embrace reciprocity to find a path to recon-ciliation with the moral perspectives of others: that is one route, but there are many – yet some may fail to find any of them.

However, we must remember that, pace the social contract tale, living with others on moral terms is not a single decision, such that one is "either in or out." That social-moral life is so clearly not like that should lead us to question the entire social contract approach. No one except a sort of cartoon nihilist (more plausibly, a psychopath) is a "holdout" on social morality per se, but rather one "holds out" on this or that moral rule in this or that network. Some who insist that the very idea of living with diverse others is an insult to their integrity will find themselves with a shrunken and impoverished moral space, but they will participate in some networks. However, they will not be able to reap the benefits of the Open Society. And the rest of us will have to beware of them and probably guard against them, as they may seek to undermine the basis of our public moral world.

IV. The Imperative of Complexity and the New Program for Political Philosophy

In 1971 Rawls's *Theory of Justice* revolutionized political philosophy, taking as its subject principles for a society characterized by enduring rational, normative disagreement. Today, in a society in which basic facts are in dispute and perspectives face each other with mutual incomprehen-sion, the idea that all rational moral agents would agree on the difference principle[8] as regulating social and economic inequalities seems rather quaint. Rational moral agents disagree on the good life, but not about social justice! We can only try to remember when that seemed like deep disagreement. To his great credit, Rawls continually explored the basis of disagreement about the justice of our society, leading him deeper and deeper into the problems of social organization under diversity. Yes, I believe that at the end his political liberalism project was in disarray, in the sense that its unity and organization broke down (I would certainly not say, as Neufeld and Watson think I would, that it was a "jumbled mess"). As Chad Van Schoelandt and I (2017) argue, this disarray is a testimony to the protean nature of Rawls's project. He was constantly inventing new terms and advancing new analyses to capture evolving insights. I see no

---

[8] That is, social and economic inequalities should be arranged so that they maximally benefit the least well-off class.

point in freezing an ongoing project at a moment in time, and insisting that it was finished. It manifestly was not.

What Rawls entirely failed to appreciate, however, was that as we make a system of interaction increasingly diverse, not only does the basis for consensus become increasingly thin, the system becomes increasingly complex. Diversity and complexity are intimately related (Page 2011). To accept that the subject of political philosophy is a system characterized by the dense interaction of diverse moral agents leads to the conclusion that its subject is in the formal sense a complex phenomenon. It is this "imperative of complexity" that is at the heart of the new program in political philosophy that D'Agostino announces in his essay. As Hayek insisted throughout his career, constructivist blueprints for complex systems often look wonderful on the drawing board but simply cannot be built. The new program accepts the imperative of complexity, and so focuses elsewhere: on the perspectives of diverse moral agents and under what conditions they can organize themselves into a fruitful and cooperative social life that all endorse as moral – given their heterogeneous understandings of that contested concept. As I understand it, this new program switches focus from the moral convictions and plans of the philosopher to those of the agents who form the self-organizing and self-governing moral order. Once they abandon the legislative and planning tasks, political philosophers have much to contribute, especially if they are willing to engage in trans- and inter-disciplinary inquiry. In place of conceptions and plans for justice the new program – or at least my version of it – seeks to identify "devices" of public reason, to analyze how markets, democracy, polycentrism, liberty rules and jurisdictional rights provide the framework for diverse moral perspectives to form moral and political orders that not only accommodate, but improve, their disparate understandings of justice in an open society.

References

Bicchieri, C. (2016). *Norms in the Wild: How to Diagnose, Measure, and Change Social Norms*. New York: Oxford University Press.

Boyd, R. and Richerson, P. J. (2005). Group-Beneficial Norms Can Spread Rapidly in a Structured Population. In: *The Origin and Evolution of Cultures*. Oxford: Oxford University Press, pp. 227–40.

Colander, D. and Kupers, R. (2014). *Complexity and the Art of Public Policy: Solving Society's Problems from the Bottom Up*. Princeton: Princeton University Press.

D'Agostino, F. (2010). *Naturalizing Epistemology: Thomas Kuhn and the 'Essential Tension.'* London: Palgrave Macmillan.

(2013). The Orders of Public Reason. *Analytic Philosophy*, vol. 54 (March): 129–155.

Downs, A. (1956). *An Economic Theory of Democracy.* New York: Harper & Row.

Friedman, M. and Friedman, R. (1980). *Free to Choose.* London: Secker & Warburg.

Gaus, G. (1996). *Justificatory Liberalism.* Oxford: Oxford University Press.

(2011). *The Order of Public Reason.* Cambridge: Cambridge University Press.

(2016). *The Tyranny of the Ideal: Justice in a Diverse Society.* Princeton: Princeton University Press.

(2017a). The Open Society and Its Friends: With Friends Like These, Who Needs Enemies? *The Critique*, January 15, 2017, www.thecritique.com/articles/open-society-and-its-friends. Accessed May 23, 2017.

(2017b). Social Morality and the Primacy of Individual Perspectives. *Review of Austrian Economics*, vol. 30: 377–396.

(2017c). Self-Organizing Moral Systems: Beyond Social Contract Theory. *Politics, Philosophy and Economics*, vol. 17: 119–147, https://doi.org.10.1177/1470594X17719425.

(2018). The Priority of Social Morality. In *Morality, Governance, and Social Institutions: Reflections on Russell Hardin*, edited by Thomas Christiano, Ingrid Creppell and Jack Knight. New York: Palgrave Macmillan, 2018.

Gaus, G. and Van Schoelandt, C. (2017). Consensus on What? Convergence for What? Four Models of Political Liberalism. *Ethics*, vol. 128: 145–172.

Hayek, F. A. (1964 [2014]). The Theory of Complex Phenomena. In: *The Market and Other Orders*, edited by Bruce Caldwell. Chicago: University of Chicago Press, pp. 257–266.

Hesse, M. B. (1966). *Models and Analogies in Science.* Notre Dame: Notre Dame University Press.

Hotelling, H. (1929). Stability in Competition. *Economic Journal*, vol. 39: 41–57.

Johnson, James (2014). Models Among the Political Theorists. *American Journal of Political Science*, vol. 58 (July): 547–560.

Knight, F. (1921 [1964]). *Risk, Uncertainty, and Profit.* New York: Augustus M. Kelly.

Kogelmann, B. (2017). *Agreement, All the Way Up: An Essay on Public Reason and Theory Choice.* Doctoral dissertation, University of Arizona.

Kuhn, T. S. (1970). *The Structure of Scientific Revolutions*, second edn. Chicago: University of Chicago Press.

Lane, R. (2017). *The Complexity of Self Government: Politics from the Bottom Up.* New York: Cambridge University Press.

Levy, D. M. and Peart, S. J. (2017). *Escape from Democracy: The Role of Experts and the Public in Economic Policy.* Cambridge: Cambridge University Press.

Mitchell, M. (2009). *Complexity: A Guided Tour.* Oxford: Oxford University Press.

Nozick, R. (1974). *Anarchy, State and Utopia.* New York: Basic Books.

Ostrom, E. (1986 [2014]). An Agenda for the Study of Institutions. In: *Choice, Rules and Collective Action*. Ed. Fillippo Sabetti and Paul Dragos Aligica. Essex: ECPR Press, pp. 97–119.

Ostrom, V. (1972 [1999]). Polycentricity (Part 2). In: *Polycentricity and Local Public Economies*. Ed. Michael D. McGinnis. Ann Arbor: University of Michigan Press, pp. 119–38.

Ostrom, V. and Ostrom, E. (1977 [1999]). Public Goods and Public Choices. In: *Polycentricity and Local Public Economies*. Ed. Michael D. McGinnis. Ann Arbor: University of Michigan Press, pp. 75–103.

Page, S. E. (2011). *Diversity and Complexity*. Princeton: Princeton University Press.

(2016). Not Half Bad: A Modest Criterion for Inclusion. In: *Complexity and Evolution: Toward a New Synthesis for Economics*. E. David S. Wilson and Alan Kirman. Cambridge, MA: MIT Press, pp. 319–26.

Poundstone, W. (1992). *Prisoner's Dilemma: John von Neumann, Game Theory, and the Puzzle of the Bomb*. New York: Random House.

Rawls, J. (1971). *A Theory of Justice*. Cambridge, MA: Harvard University Press.

(2005). Political *Liberalism*. Expanded edn. New York: Columbia University Press.

(2007) *Lectures on the History of Political Philosophy*. Ed. Samuel Freeman. Cambridge, MA: Harvard University Press.

Schumpeter, J. A. (1950). *Capitalism, Socialism and Democracy*. Third edn. London: George Allen & Unwin.

Sen, A. (2017). *Collective Choice and Social Welfare*. Expanded edn. Harmondsworth: Penguin.

Vallier, K. (forthcoming). *Must Politics Be War? Restoring Our Trust in the Open Society*. Oxford: Oxford University Press.

Weisberg, M. (2013). *Simulation and Similarity: Using Models to Understand the World*. Oxford: Oxford University Press.

Index

abstraction, 55–59, 238–39
adaptive systems, 217
advertising, 130
agency, 58
agency freedom, 60–63, 65–67, 69
agent-based models
    general considerations, 214–19
    specific models, 219–30
aggregation procedures, 52–54, 69, 72
ambiguity, 259
American Civil Liberties Union, 121
anarchism, 125
arbitrators, 32–35, 108
"Are There Natural Rights?" (Hart), 3
Arrow, Kenneth, 52
Arrow's theorem, 52, 69
Arthur, W. Brian, 219
assurance problem, 180–81, 193–201
authoritarianism, 187
authority. *See* moral authority; political
    authority
autonomy, 44, 109–11

Baier, Kurt, 21, 64–65, 67
bandwagon effect, 95, 189
bargaining, 170, 210–13
basic structure of society, 55
beliefs. *See also* comprehensive views
    conclusively justified, 29–30
    good-faith, 23
    philosophical and religious, 13–16, 29
    reasonable, 20–22, 27–29
Benn, Stanley I., 45, 56, 111, 134–35,
    160
Berlin, Isaiah, 13, 83–84, 230, 261
Bicchieri, Cristina, 192–93, 215
Bosanquet, Bernard, 118
Boyd, Robert, 257
burdens
    of judgment, 19, 21
    of justification, 68, 88–89

capitalism
    justifiability of, 131, 169, 171
    socialism dominated by, 149–56, 172
cascade effects, 197–99, 220, 222, 257
central planners, 230
cheap talk, 195–96
choreographing actions, 192
citizens. *See* free and equal persons; members of
    public
civil rights, 148–53
civil society, 90
classical liberalism
    ambitious case for, 148–60
    condemnation of, 131
    Millian, 169–73
    modest case for, 160–69
    social justice liberalism versus, 38, 130,
        171–72
    state's role in, 130
coercion. *See also* justification of coercion; laws
    degrees and costs of, 122, 160–61, 165–67,
        169–72
    evaluative diversity and, 122–24
    and rights of person, 9
    by states, 9–11, 25
collective choice, 73–75, 90, 100
common human horizon, 83–84
common knowledge, 192, 196
common law, 60
common logics, 192
communication, 194–97
communities, 254–58
complexity
    of moral systems, 11–12
    of relationships, 13
    of value disputes, 14–15
compliance, 162, 182–83, 193–94,
    197–201
comprehensive views
    legitimacy of politics based on, 23–25
    oppressiveness of power based on, 2

266

members of public (cont.)
idealized, 54, 179–83
information available to, 148, 156, 197–201
proposals by and for, 81, 142, 145–48, 156, 165–69
rights schemes acceptable to, 100–4
toleration by, 91–95
metaphors, 239–42
Mill, John Stuart
authoritative interventions, 121
civil (social) liberty, 77
coercive laws, 169–70
liberalism of, 39
presumption of self-knowledge, 46, 112
rights, 78, 90
minimax relative concession, 211–12
models. *See also* agent-based models
general considerations, 238–42
Market, Bureaucracy, Democracy model, 242–46
rugged landscape models, 239, 241–47, 249–50
simple optimization model, 247–52
spatial, 248
modus vivendi, 93–98
moral accountability, 207, 224, 256–60
moral anarchy, 66
moral authority
claims to, 79–80
devolution of, 68, 73–75, 89–90, 98–100
moral autonomy, 44, 109–11
moral claims
to authority, 108
of governors, 114
modes of reasoning about, 202–6
moral persons' advancement of, 44–45, 109
neutrality in, 115–16
to property, 115
validation of, 46, 48, 51, 64–65, 76, 111–13
moral communities, 254–58
moral constitutions, 258–60
moral disagreement, 2, 202–3, 205, 260–62, *See also* diversity of beliefs; evaluative diversity; reasonable pluralism; reconciliation
moral equality, 43–46, 111–12, *See also* free and equal persons
moral judgments, 31–32, 46, 113, 117, *See also* moral claims; reconciliation
moral laws, 85–88
moral obligations, 44, 67, 115, 128
moral persons, 43–45, 54, 63–64, 109, *See also* free and equal persons; moral equality
moral realism, 49, 82, 114

moral reasoning, 202–8, 213, *See also* public reasoning
moral reasons, 113–14
moral reform, 65–66
moral relations, 2–4, 55, 79, 207–8, 213, 255
moral rules. *See* rules
moral sensibility, 179
moral space, 258, 260–62
moral systems
complexity of, 237–39, 242–50, 263
self-organizing, 219–29
moral validation
among free and equal persons, 118
problem for, 49–52
for public justification, 121
testing conception of, 64–67
moralities, 64–65, 67, 76
morality, 113–14
Murphy, Liam, 157–59
mutual accommodation, 31, 170

Nagel, Thomas, 157–59
Narveson, Jan, 161
Nash equilibria, 104, 187, 193–94
natural law, 44, 110
Netherlands, 164
Neufeld, Blain, 238
neutrality
liberal moral, 109–17
liberal political, derivation of, 117–22
liberal political, implications of, 122–27
meaning of, 105–9
New Diversity Theory, 5–6, *See also* diversity of perspectives
night-watchman state, 130
Nisbett, Richard, 28
NK models, 241, 245, 247, *See also* rugged landscape models
Non-coercion Principle, 117–18
normalization, 252–53
norms, 192, *See also* rules
Norton, Seth, 149–50
Nozick, Robert, 52, 122, 130

OECD countries, 153–56, 164
Open Society, 254, 256–62
opportunity costs, 51, 123, 142
oppression, 10, 25–26, 32, 75
optimization, 238–39, *See also* models
options, range of, 160–61, 163
Order of Public Reason, The (Gaus), 3, 255–56, 259–60
original position, 55–58, 86, 91, 128, 145, 186–87
Ostrom, Elinor, 245, 255–56

For EU product safety concerns, contact us at Calle de José Abascal, 56–1°,
28003 Madrid, Spain or eugpsr@cambridge.org.

www.ingramcontent.com/pod-product-compliance
Ingram Content Group UK Ltd.
Pitfield, Milton Keynes, MK11 3LW, UK
UKHW022314060425
457166UK00020B/250